THE SHETLAND SHEEPDOG

POPULAR DOGS' BREED SERIES

THE
SHETLAND SHEEPDOG

MARGARET OSBORNE

POPULAR DOGS
London

Popular Dogs Publishing Co Ltd
3 Fitzroy Square, London WIP 6JD

An imprint of the Hutchinson Publishing Group

London Melbourne Sydney Auckland
Wellington Johannesburg and agencies
throughout the world

First published (as *The Popular Shetland Sheepdog*) 1959
Second edition revised 1963
Third edition revised (as *The Shetland Sheepdog*) 1967
Fourth edition revised 1970
Fifth edition revised 1973
Sixth edition revised 1977
Seventh edition revised 1979

Printed in Great Britain by The Anchor Press Ltd
and bound by Wm Brendon & Son Ltd
both of Tiptree, Essex

ISBN 0 09 140430 4

CONTENTS

CONTENTS

ILLUSTRATIONS

Between pages 64 and 65

Between pages 96 and 97

Between pages 128 and 129

ILLUSTRATIONS

Between pages 128 and 129

Between pages 160 and 161

IN THE TEXT

*The line drawings are by Prudence Walker to whom the author
expresses her appreciation*

ILLUSTRATIONS

FOREWORD

It is many years since I first saw Miss Osborne stepping out of a car with a Sheltie on a lead; indeed, I believe she first owned a Shetland Sheepdog in 1925, when she was still a schoolgirl. Today she is well known as a breeder and exhibitor of Shelties and Collies, and as an enthusiast for Corgis, another herding breed.

Throughout the many controversies over Collie crossing and Collie type, it has always been clear to Miss Osborne that the little Shetland Sheepdog, although possessing definite points of resemblance to the Rough Collie, differs in many respects from the Show Collie, and, like all true lovers of the Sheltie, she has been anxious that the characteristics of these charming little dogs shall be preserved and not exaggerated to resemble the Collie. It is because of this knowledge and understanding that Miss Osborne is so well fitted to write a book about the Shetland Sheepdog.

Miss Osborne is a member of the Committee of the English Shetland Sheepdog Club, and is widely known in the Obedience world, her famous Moonen Shiel, C.D. ex., U.D. ex., T.D. ex., being one of the best of the Obedience Trial winners in the country, and a winner in the Shetland Sheepdog ring.

In this book Miss Osborne has touched on all aspects of Sheltie history, and has written some excellent chapters on the rearing and training of these little dogs, which have always been fortunate in having breeders who cared only for the true advancement of the breed—a breed which combines intelligence, fidelity and beauty to a marked degree. There has long been a need for a book telling the story of the Shetland Sheepdog, and at last we have it.

CLARA BOWRING

AUTHOR'S INTRODUCTIONS

*

TO THE FIRST EDITION

It has seemed to me for some time now that the delightful Shetland Sheepdog, with its very greatly increased number of admirers, has been largely neglected in literature. Except for pamphlets issued by one of the breed clubs, one handbook published recently, and a book on the breed published in the U.S.A. during the war, the Sheltie has been much neglected, and my own desire to read more about the breed I have owned for well over 30 years must surely be common to others. On this assumption I set about writing this book.

In it I have tried to offer something for everyone. I know well, from experience, the kind of questions asked by new Sheltie owners, and prospective Sheltie owners. The questions are of great variety, and many of them are weird and wonderful, but all point to the same thing: that there is no book on the breed that will serve as a guide to the Sheltie owner today. It is hoped that this book will fill that need and provide something for the one-dog pet owner, as well as for the more experienced breeder and exhibitor.

Ever since I first began spending my weekly pocket-money on canine papers, instead of on what my parents considered more 'wholesome' literature for a schoolgirl not yet counting her age in double figures, I lost a large part of my heart to the Sheltie. As long ago as 1925 I owned my first Sheltie and ventured into the ring at a Championship Show, not very successfully it must be recorded, but then we all have to learn. From that day I made two resolutions: one was that I would have the first Sheltie to win working trial qualifications, and that I must train her myself; the other was that I would breed a Sheltie Champion. I am delighted to say that I have achieved both those ambitions. That does not mean that I have done all

I want to do—not by any means. The great thing about this pastime of ours is that the more you know the more you want to learn, and, as we are dealing with live things, so we have always the chance of learning more and more. It does not matter whether your first Sheltie was acquired 30 days or 30 years ago, there is always something new cropping up, especially in our somewhat 'unpredictable' breed, and the intense interest in building up a strain of one's own is a lifetime's work—a work that is most absorbing.

The work of classifying the lines and families of the Sheltie was originally done by me in 1948 for the first post-war issue of the *Handbook* published by the English Shetland Sheepdog Club. It took a great deal of time. I found it intensely interesting, and from this self-imposed task I learned a very great deal. But there is still plenty of opportunity to go on learning.

In the choice of illustrations for this book it has been my intention to try to show the growth of, and improvement in, the breed throughout the years. Some of the photographs are of Shelties with no show careers, but they are those to which the breed owes a great deal in that they have given all that was best in themselves to the furtherance of the breed.

If *The Popular Shetland Sheepdog* makes you as happy in the reading as it did me in the writing, I know the publishers and I will be well satisfied.

1959   M.O.

TO THE SECOND EDITION

Interest in this breed is still steadily increasing, and this new edition of this book, by its alterations and additions, bring up to date the breeding details of our latest winners, and references to them will be found both in the text and in the appendices.

Ten years ago registrations in this breed were 753. For the last full year for which figures are available, (1961) the total is 3,790. A staggering and rather frightening figure. In her preface to the first edition Miss Bowring says: '(Shelties) have always been fortunate in having breeders who cared only for the true advancement of the breed'. I quote this, for I wish to stress the necessity for this. The Sheltie is not 'everybody's dog'. It is a breed which requires understanding, and a great deal of sympathy. For this reason I feel that the latest registration figure is 'frightening', because one must be concerned lest this delightful and charming little breed becomes spoiled by 'mass-production' and over popularising. I for one hope it will never head the popularity poll. If it does, or if it climbs much higher than it is at present, there is no shadow of doubt that the breed is doomed. Let us keep it as a charming, fascinating member of the canine race, in the hands of those who really understand the whims and characteristics of the breed.

The correspondence and comments which I have received since this book was first published have been delightful, and a great source of interest to me, your correspondence has been, and always will be, most welcome.

1962   M.O.

TO THE THIRD EDITION

The last four years have again seen great advances in our breed. Not, fortunately, numerically, but the establishment of several new serious kennels, the greater knowledge and popularity of the breed with the public, and the great improvement, and stabilization of the breed itself, particularly with regard to temperament.

The most important event in this period has been the acceptance by the Kennel Club of a revised, mainly amplified Standard for the breed, and I do advise everyone of you, old and new Sheltie owners alike, to read and digest this new standard very carefully.

1967   M.O.

TO THE FIFTH EDITION

We still await our first ever Best in Show award, but happily the registration position is much more stable, as can well be seen from Appendix 6. As I have said before, ours should never be a 'mass production' breed.

The increase of interest in and the quality of the blue merles in the last decade have been quite spectacular, and this fact, plus the extremely good temperaments of our present-day Shelties, reflects great credit on our breeders. However, there remains the question of size, and construction. Many, too many exhibits are above the ideal for their sex, and we still have the bug-bear of the straight shoulder and upper arm to work on. However, life would be terribly dull if we were left without a goal, wouldn't it?

1973   M.O.

TO THE SIXTH EDITION

Thankfully, the stabilisation of registrations has continued and the recent annual totals vary very little—except in 1975, which fell by over 1,000. Show entries remain very high, and quality good, but we still have many of the same problems to work on. Construction still needs much improvement so, to newcomers to the breed, there are still many goals to be aimed at. Thin, spindly bone is another point we must watch. Since, to my pleasure, this book seems to be revised every third year, it is interesting to note that during the changes which take place in these periods some things improve, and that while we are busy working on them others creep in, unnoticed at first, before we find we have to work on them instead. Such is the fascination of dog breeding. There is always an unattainable still ahead!

1976   M.O.

TO THE SEVENTH EDITION

As it is only two years since the last edition of this book appeared I have not found it necessary to make many revisions to the seventh edition. However, minor corrections have been made to the text – and the appendices have once again been brought up-to-date.

1979   M.O.

Shiel,
Copperfield Drive,
Leeds, Maidstone, Kent

I

ORIGIN AND HISTORY OF THE BREED

SHETLAND, that bleak little island lying off the north coast of
Scotland, wind-swept and sea-girt, has been known, through
the centuries, to produce a hardy race of people, making a
precarious living from the sea and land. This diminutive
country, developing everything in proportion to fit in with its
landscape, is known for its small cattle, sheep and ponies.
Just as the Shetland pony appears to be a diminutive shire
horse, so are the Shetland cattle and sheep much smaller than
their counterparts on the mainland, and thus it became
imperative that the dogs who herd should also be small; thus, a
diminutive race of working Collies emerged. These small
animals are the result of hard living in those islands.

There is no doubt that the 'Sheltie', as it is almost always
called, and will hereinafter be known, is a truly British breed,
evolved in its native island. It was a small dog of Collie type,
albeit rather nondescript, but it was certainly always the local
shepherd's dog.

The shepherd cared little for appearances, and there was no
such thing, of course, as a standard of the breed. What the shepherd wanted was a tough, courageous, intelligent little animal,
hardy, and with a coat fitted for his work. He was expected to
do his job in all weathers, drenching rain and heavy snow, and
his coat had to protect him from wet and extremes of temperature. Selective breeding must surely have been carried on to
improve or fix these properties, and these alone, and it is for
this reason that in the early days these little dogs varied
enormously in type, and the reason, too, why it was, and still is,
difficult to forecast with any certainty the results of each
mating.

The bleak country of the Shetland Islands is divided up
into 'crofts' or small farms, and these tiny hamlets are called

'Toons'. Thus, the 'toonie' dog was the dog trained to do the work around the crofts, to keep the sheep from straying off their own little piece of land on to the 'toons'.

The Sheltie is also sometimes known as the 'peerie' dog, the name I like best, for the word 'peerie' means fairy, and this description of the Sheltie as a fairy Collie seems most apt.

Where the 'first dog' in the Shetland Islands came from is quite unknown, and so the true origin of the breed will never be known either. There is no doubt, however, from the great variety of different types, that almost all the tales one hears of how the Sheltie came about may well be true, for there are dogs of types to back almost every one of these theories.

Undoubtedly there must have been some kind of dog, probably of the working Collie type and originating in the mainland of Scotland, which was used to herd the sheep in the island, and it can almost surely be assumed, with a degree of certainty, that when the fishing fleets from Scandinavia, Scotland and other north European countries came to Shetland in the summer-time they had dogs on board, and that some of these dogs stayed in Shetland, or at any rate left their offspring behind.

Another 'near certainty' too is that the Greenland whalers, when they too stopped at Shetland to pick up or land local members of their crews, had with them their 'Yakkie' dogs which also crossed with the island dogs, and distinct traces of this cross can still be seen in the dog in the show-ring of today. Those, in fact, which bear a 'smutty' muzzle; a disputed point of which more anon.

Further traces of crossing with various Spitz breeds can also be seen in the curled tails and erect ears which still occur to this day, even in the most aristocratic families.

Probable too, is it, that the Scottish Collie from the Highlands was brought over and crossed with the Toonie dogs (already many times crossed themselves) in order to improve the working capacity of these dogs. Size would speedily be reduced again by the hardship of the life and upbringing and, to a certain extent, possibly by a degree of inbreeding, probably involuntary, caused by an insufficient number of dogs in the area.

There is also evidence that in its early days the breed

carried a certain amount of the blood of a black-and-tan King Charles Spaniel, left in the islands by a visiting yacht. As his arrival coincided with the period in which the local dog was being bred more to supply a demand for lapdogs than for workers, it is well-nigh certain that a good many of the bitches were mated to him in an attempt to fulfil this demand. There is a further very interesting point raised by this probable cross and it will be dealt with in a later chapter.

An old engraving (1840) shows the town of Lerwick, capital of the island, and has, in the foreground, a Sheltie. It seems to be a small dog, similar in general type to the dogs of today, but considerably longer in body.

In the latter half of the nineteenth century, when the crofts amalgamated and became larger sheep-breeding farms, the tiny Sheltie came to be superseded by a rather larger dog. But, alongside this development, came a demand for tiny, fluffy dogs, popular as pets, and so the diversity of type continued.

At last, in 1908, in an attempt to safeguard the breed, a meeting was called in Lerwick, the 'Shetland Collie Club' was formed, and the first points standard created. In 1909 the new club requested recognition by the Kennel Club, but this, alas, was refused. Instead, however, the Scottish Shetland Sheepdog Club was formed in the same year, and because of the Kennel Club's refusal to recognize the club or the breed, the Scottish Club produced its own Stud Book. At this time there was no co-relation of standards by any governing body, and each club, in any breed, could, and did, publish its own standard for the breed—a ludicrous situation.

So while in 1908 the standard described the breed: 'The type of the Shetland Collie shall be similar to that of the Rough Collie in miniature—the height shall not exceed 15 in.'—only a year later the newly formed Scottish Club says of the dog: 'Appearance: that of the ordinary Collie in miniature; height about 12 in., weight 10–14 lb.' and the first standard drawn up by this club gave the points exactly as for the Collie, even allowing a 'Rough' and a 'Smooth'. Four years later the height standard was altered to read '12 in. is the ideal', so it will be seen that right from the beginning the size of the breed has always been a bone of contention.

The English Shetland Sheepdog Club was formed in 1914, and their first standard says, 'The general appearance of the Shetland Collie is approximately that of the Show Collie in miniature: ideal height 12 in.'

Again, in the same year, the Scottish Club altered its original wording, and it now read 'Appearance: that of the modern Show Collie in miniature (Collie type and character must be adhered to). Ideal height 12 in. at maturity, which is fixed at 10 months.' At the same time, smooth-coated Shelties were barred.

The Scottish breeders, however, more or less disregarded the height 'ideal'. They found that what might seem all right on paper did not in fact work out in practice. Collie type and 12 in. just did not go together.

As a kind of Christmas present to Sheltie breeders the Kennel Club finally granted the breed separate classification in December 1914. But, despite the efforts of the clubs, the Kennel Club refused the name Shetland Collie, so a compromise was reached and the breed became known as Shetland Sheepdog. The objectors to the original name of Shetland Collie were the Collie breeders themselves, and not the Kennel Club, but if today we were asked to change the breed's name to Shetland Collie it is well-nigh certain there would be no protests from the Collie fraternity, but that the Sheltie folk themselves would rise up in wrath!

The recognition of the breed in such a year as 1914 was rather unfortunate, for of dire necessity, shows and breeding in all breeds were severely curtailed and, later, all shows were abandoned, and breeding permitted only under licence. So the progress made by the breed immediately after recognition was obviously less than might have been expected. Fortunately for the breed there were a few breeders able to carry on, and Miss Thynne and Miss Grey kept the Kilravocks and the Greyhills going, together with one or two others.

Just before the cessation of shows in 1917, the breed's first Champion was made. He was Ch. Woodvold, whose dam was, admittedly, a small Collie.

Very soon after the war Miss Humphries decided to introduce the Collie cross into her Mountforts, and fortunately this was done quite openly. This cross, as will be seen later, did much to help stabilize type. Mr E. C. Pierce soon made a similar cross, and the Collie type became very evident in the Eltham Parks also.

In 1923 the English Shetland Sheepdog Club again altered its height clause to read 'from 12–15 in., the ideal being half-way'.

A little later the Scottish Club adopted the 13½ in. ideal also, and so, for the first time, the height clause was unanimous, and so it remained until the Kennel Club revised all the standards in 1948, when the present standard became the only one, and was accepted by all.

Assuredly the Collie cross helped to fix type, but it also made the height question a very difficult one. The more the Sheltie leant to Collie type the bigger one might generally expect it to be, and it took many, many years to arrive somewhere near a more stable size. In fact, it is only since the 1950s that height has become steadier, and even today it is not yet settled, for as we all know there are tremendous size differences in the breed, but the present ideal of 14 in. has certainly brought a much greater uniformity into the show-ring.

But while the Collie cross helped fix type it also brought a further split in the ranks of the breeders. In the early 1920s the standard of the English Club read—as regards general appearance—'*approximately* that of a Show Collie in miniature'. And it was this word 'approximately' which led to such strife a few years later, for in 1926 those breeders who did not agree with this description, and who favoured very much more the true Collie type, started their own club, the 'British Breeders Shetland Sheepdog Association', with Mr Pierce as Secretary. Their standard called for 'the ideal Collie in miniature'. The life of this club, however, was fairly short, and it was disbanded six years later.

Like everything else in life, it was understandable that the Sheltie should have 'growing pains', and these were extremely important formative years for the breed. Many of those names which are now household words in the breed came to the fore in this period.

In the early years of dog showing, the Kennel Club Rules relating to the registration of prefixes and affixes were very different from those of today, and it is therefore impossible to

put a definite date on the beginnings of some of the early
kennels. Those of Lerwick, Ashbank, Downfield and Inverness,
however, were all in existence before the 1914 war. Then, in
1914 Miss Thynne registered her 'Kilravock' prefix, as did
Miss Grey and Miss Hill their 'Greyhill'. Miss Humphries
followed with the Mountforts one year later, and in 1917 the
'Bonheurs' of the E.S.S.C. present Secretary, Miss Currie, were
first included. Mr A. Watt's 'Netherkeirs' appeared in 1920,
and a year later that wonderful stalwart and tower of strength
to the breed, Miss Clara Bowring, came in with her 'Lark-
beares', and in the same year Mr Pierce's 'Eltham Park' prefix
was registered also. Three years later Mrs Baker first registered
her 'Houghton Hill' affix, and one hardly need say more than
that. It is almost certain that no one kennel has ever done more
for the breed than Mrs Baker did through more than 30 years
of steady breeding. One year later came three new names
which are no longer active in the breed. Mr and Mrs Campbell's
Tilfords, Dr Tod's Clerwood, and Mrs Rae-Fraser's Fetlars,
though we do see the latter at shows occasionally, but almost
always without a dog. The year 1925 also brought a most
active name, Mr J. Saunders's 'Helensdale'. In 1926 came
the Cameliards of Mrs Allen and Mrs Nicholson, and in
1927 the first Exfords of Mrs Sangster, but at that time she
was Miss Baker. Mr Hendry's Aberlours first saw the light
in 1930, and one year later Miss Wright started the Michelmere, and Miss Bootle-Wilbraham the Wansdyke kennels. The
year 1932 was of great importance for this was the birth date
of the Misses Rogers' Riverhills, which have made such impact
on the prize lists ever since. In 1935 Mr E. Watt's Dryfesdales
were first registered, and one year later Miss Single's 'Tibbetts',
and the author's 'from Shiel', kennel names first went on record.
Miss Gwynne-Jones's Callarts and Mr Broughton's Fydells
came in one year later, and if we add to these Mrs Fishpool's
Ellingtons in 1938 and Miss Charley's Foulas in 1939, the
story comes up to the beginning of the Second World War.

When hostilities started, fortunately the Kennel Club took
a more rational view of the matter than they had done 20 years
previously, and realized that, to a certain extent at least, dog
showing and breeding must be carried on, if only to keep
our hobby alive. Thus, although some kennels had to close

completely, owing to the war-time occupations of their owners, others did carry on, although stock was, of course reduced. It was because of this that when Championship shows started again in 1946 Shelties were able to make a good showing, and from that moment the breed has gone ahead by leaps and bounds. In the immediate post-war years there was a certain amount of fluctuation in registrations, but since 1951 there has been a steady rise. In that year the registration total was 753, and six years later it had more than doubled itself for the 1957 figure was 1,697. Undoubtedly the Sheltie breed is still in its early youth in the popularity poll, and it is to be hoped that our breed will never reach the top limits, for, as has been seen over and over again, such a position eventually ruins a breed. It is to be hoped too that this breed will never become what might be called a 'commercial' breed, where the point is reached when all and sundry are trying to turn out Sheltie pups as from a sausage machine, regardless of pedigree, and regardless of the ultimate result. Shelties are not easy to breed. That does not mean they are not hardy, but rather that years and years of careful selective breeding have gone into the production of the dogs we know today, and it will be only too easy to take a rapid retrograde step, and find ourselves with a breed which, once again, is not breeding to type.

Further, the natural reserve of the Sheltie does not make him everyone's dog, and while we do not want our breed to be a shy one, it would no longer be a true Sheltie if this trait were bred out in the endeavour to make it a dog which would be more popular with the general public.

The breed has years of popularity ahead of it. Let us hope they will also be years of progress and success for a delightful little dog.

2

THEY HELPED MAKE THE BREED

MALE LINES

DESPITE the fact that our breed is, by many standards 'new', and has become a show breed only during the lifetime of a number of exhibitors who are still active in the breed, it will be obvious, as has already been said, that there is a great deal of mystery behind our dogs. However, a good deal is clear, and on what is clear the first lines and families were drawn up by the author almost ten years ago.

Unlike a good many other breeds which have been carefully line-bred from the early days, and so have only one or, at most, two male lines, the Shetlands have no less than seven, although five of these have been 'dead' for a number of years. Of this one suspects that there never were really seven lines at all, that, in fact, had we more details of the beginnings of lines TPR (Tresta Prince), LWW (Lassodie Willie Winkie), DL (Dornoch Laddie), LJA (Lerwick Jarl) and IH (Inverness Hoy), they would probably tie up with the two present-day lines CHE (Chestnut) and BB (Butcher Boy).

The founder dog of line BB, *Butcher Boy*, was unregistered, and the history of his parents, unknown even in name, was never traced, but he was born about 1906. Founder of line LJA, *Jake*, of CHE, *Nesting Topper* and IH, *Inverness Hoy*, seem to have been more or less contemporary with Butcher Boy, so it is surely reasonable to assume that had all the foundation dogs been registered, a good deal of common ancestry might have been traced between them, thus reducing the number of lines.

Of the five lines which now seem to be 'dead', only one, LJA, produced branches which bred on to any extent, but TPR did manage to survive for five generations, although the winner in this fifth generation was a bitch, Larkbeare Sultana Cake. LWW produced only one C.C. winner in Derian Firefly (1928), from whom we can trace back only three generations to the unregistered *Rover*, born about 1920. Line DL which, through Eltham Park Advance, produced two Champion bitches in Eltham Park Ellaline (1926) and Ch. Winstonian Pixie who won a year earlier, can be traced for only two generations to Bobby Lad, probably born about the same time as Rover. Thus, we cannot help thinking that in all probability these lines are only branches of CHE or BB, but we lack the 'clues' to prove that it is so.

An American book on the breed lists no less than ten lines, and at least one of these lines gives point to what has been said. A line was given, starting with Teddy, grandsire of Helensdale Reaf who sired Eltham Park Eofric, who sired the three Eltham Park Champion bitches, Elfine, Evette and Elda, and a Champion son, Eltham Park Evan. In fact, this is only a branch of CHE, for Teddy was sired by Greyhope Titbit, who was by Berryden Prince, the third generation of CHE.

Of the two lines still affecting us today, the first to be considered is this CHE. Its title was given to it from an early dog in the line, one that had an enormous influence on the breed, *Chestnut Rainbow*.

The line starts with *Nesting Topper*, sire of *Ashbank Olla*, who sired a C.C. winning bitch, Fulla, and *Berryden Prince* (ex Berryden Nellie).

Berryden Prince had two sons of note, *Irvine Ronnie* and the aforementioned *Greyhope Titbit* (ex Cromlet Leda), great-grandsire of *Helensdale Reaf* (ex Aberlady Princess). Reaf sired the C.C. winner *Michael of Hardingham*, and the winner producer *Eltham Park Eofric* (ex Jean of Hardingham by Ch. Specks of Mountfort), but with Eofric's Champion son, *Eltham Park Evan* (ex Eltham Park Elma), this branch of the line died.

Returning to Berryden Prince's other son, the sable *Irvine Ronnie* who sired the little tricolour who was destined to have such an influence on the breed, *Chestnut Rainbow*, we deal with the branch which still today plays such a strong part.

Chestnut Rainbow (ex Chestnut Lassie) sired five sons of great merit from a breeding point of view *Chestnut Bud*, *Chestnut Lucky Boy*, *Redbraes Rollo* and *Nut of Houghton Hill*, all four litter brothers out of Chestnut Sweet Lady, and *King Cole of Houghton Hill*, out of a different bitch of unknown pedigree.

Chestnut Lucky Boy sired *Ch. Blaeberry of Clerwood* (ex Chestnut Blossom) and he in his turn was sire of *Downfield Olaf* (ex Downfield Ethne), whose C.C. winning son *Golden Promise* (ex Glenugie Fiona) sired *Torphin of Clerwood* (ex Black Elegance), and whose Champion son *Peabody Panache* (ex Eltham Park Estelle), sired *Peabody Pannino* (ex Peabody Pauline), and the Champion bitch Peabody Peggotty.

Ch. Blaeberry sired yet another dog of special interest, *U.S.A. Ch. Wee Laird o' Downfield*, progenitor of many of today's American winners, but his interest to us is through his son Ch. Mowgli, for Mowgli sired *U.S.A. Ch. Sheltieland Laird o' Pages Hill*, a dog which came to this country just prior to the Second World War. He became the grandsire, through *Golden Rod of Marl*, of *Ch. Wonder Lad of Eleth*, but here too, for the moment, this branch has petered out as a C.C. winning line.

Redbraes Rollo sired *Ch. Gawaine of Cameliard* (ex Grizel of Clerwood), a small golden sable dog which had a big influence on the breed. He had two sons of note, *Arthur of Cameliard* and *Peabody Paul*.

Arthur (ex Ch. Ashbank Actress) sired the Champions *Tilford Tay* and *Tweed* and *Nipper of Catmore*, sire of *Ch. Catmore Chum*. *Ch. Tilford Tay* sired one C.C. winning son, *Michelmere Glengowrie*, and the two bitches, Lossie of Clerwood and Ch. Michelmere Daffin. Yet another C.C. winning son, the tricolour *Peabody Paul*, sired *Ch. Treffynon Blue Peter*.

Nut of Houghton Hill, however, was by far the most important of the litter and it is his direct descendants alone which carry on the line today, though at any moment some new star may arise tracing back to one of the other dogs.

Nut, a tricolour, sired two C.C. winning sons, the tricolour, *Nutkin of Houghton Hill* (ex Toddles of Houghton Hill), and the never-to-be-forgotten tricolour *Champion Uam-Var of Houghton Hill* (ex Lacecap of Houghton Hill), who has so far made more impact on the breed than any other dog.

Nutkin was grandsire, through *Wren of Wyndora*, of *Ch. Wrennie of Wyndora*, but since then this branch has produced only C.C. winning daughters.

Ch. Uam Var's sons which did most to carry on the line were, oddly enough, not themselves big winners.

Dolen of Houghton Hill (ex Ballet Girl of Houghton Hill) sired *Anton of Houghton Hill* who became the sire of *Ch. Marble Faun of Houghton Hill* and grandsire of the C.C. winner *Merriot Magistrate*. However, Dolen's most successful son was *Ch. Mime of Houghton Hill* (ex Sugar Cake of Houghton Hill) who sired *Ch. Tibbett's Mark* (ex Odds On of Houghton Hill); but here this branch, too, turns into one which produces only winning daughters.

Hurricane of Houghton Hill (ex Swasti of Houghton Hill) sired *Tornado of Houghton Hill*, three generations behind *Ch. Riverhill Reefer of Exford* (ex Riverhill Roguish), sire of *Jack Tar of Exford* (ex Riseboro Stupendous), who in his turn sired the Champion bitches Firebrand and Fascinator, both of Exford.

Golden Spider of Houghton Hill (ex Flyette of Houghton Hill), Uam-Var's fourth, and, to us, most important son, an oversize sable, sired *Ch. Moneyspinner of Exford* and *Spinning Coin of Exford*, brothers (ex Ballet Girl of Houghton Hill), and the C.C. winning descendants of these two, especially the former, are numerically amazing.

Spinning Coin's Champion son *Spendthrift of Exford* (ex Little Maid of Houghton Hill) sired *Delwood Bubbles*, a C.C. winner whose chances were undoubtedly spoiled by the war, and Bubbles was grandsire, through *Bubbles of Exford*, of the sable, *Magnum of Exford*, the breed's first post-war C.C. winning dog.

Coin's other son, *Fetlar Jackanapes*, sired *Ch. Fetlar Magnus*, the little tri dog who, through *Hamish of the Wansdyke*, became grandsire of *Ch. Nuthatch of Larchwood*, a dog with great influence on the breed in blue merles, and who sired *Ch. Tetrach of Barhatch*.

But it is to *Ch. Money Spinner* that we owe most, for he sired, among others, *Ch. Riverhill Rufus*, and this bright sable dog, the first Champion of the now famous Riverhill kennels, has much to his credit. It must be recorded that he was a homozygous sable (that is, he could not sire a tricolour puppy, no matter what colour the bitch to which he was mated). Rufus's son, *Rufus of Edingley*, sired *Ellington Eddy*, in turn, sire of *Ch. Delwood Terence* from whom fourteen present-day Champion dogs are descended: *Ch. Viking of Melvaig*; his sons, *Ch. Watta-woodcut* and *Ch. Dilhorne Norseman of Melvaig*; and Norseman's sons, *Ch. Pied Piper of Melvaig* and *Ch. Dilhorne Blackcap*, sire of the *Champions Eldapenny Starshine, Hildlane Twilight of Callart, Francehill Silversmith* and four champion daughters. Norseman's grand-son, *Ch. Riverhill Rogue*, sired, in his turn, *Ch. Kinreen Blue Kestrel.*

Another Terence son, *Delwood Bobby* produced *Heatherisle Hilarity* sire of *Ch. Riverhill Riddle*; while *Ch. Wattawoodcut* is sire of *Ch. Greenscrees Swordsman* who sired *Ch. Greenscrees Osmart Statesman*, and *Greenscrees Nobleman.*

Riverhill Rufus had yet another son, *Philabeg of Crawley-ridge*, whose grandson, *Burn of Exford*, sired *Ch. Exford Piskiegye Taw*, sire of *Ch. Crag of Exford* (who went to U.S.A. while still young), *Hilarity of Exford* (who at an early age went to the Shetland Islands), *Trent of Exford* (who also, as a baby, left his home for the U.S.A.) and *Ch. Lothario of Exford*, sire of *Ch. Debonair of Exford*, and *Ch. Philander of Exford.*

So turning to *Butcher Boy*, a sable dog, we trace today's most active line. Butcher Boy was sire of another sable, *Wallace*—of whose pedigree nothing was ever traced except the name of his sire and dam—and Wallace's two sons *Rip* and *War Baby of Mountfort.*

Rip himself had two sons which had a part to play, but this particular part of the line died out in the 1930s. One of these sons, Chinkie, we can discount at the moment, for all his C.C. winning descendants were bitches; the other, *Forward*, also a sable, sired *Farburn Marshall*, sire of *Helensdale Emerald*, sire of *Ch. Rob Roy o' Pages Hill*, sire of *Ch. Helensdale Rob Roy*, all these dogs being sable.

War Baby, however, had the greater influence on the breed, through his C.C. winning son, *Rufus of Mountfort*, for Rufus sired *Ch. Specks o' Mountfort* (ex Ko Ko, half-bred Collie), and as will be seen from Specks' pedigree, by today's K.C. Rules Specks should never have been registered as a pure-bred Sheltie. Yet, without him, one wonders where the breed would be today.

Of Ch. Specks' several sons only one, *Ch. Eltham Park Eureka* (ex Princess of Mountfort), need be considered here.

---

* In recent years line BB has almost completely dominated the siring in the breed, and in 1975 all the new champions were from this line and family 9!

Eureka was undoubtedly one of the pillars of the breed and today his descendants are legion.

Ch. Max of Clerwood is the first of his sons which concern us. This tricolour (ex Melita of Clerwood) sired *Mordred of Cameliard*, grandsire of *Ch. Kinnersley Gold Dust*, and Gold Dust

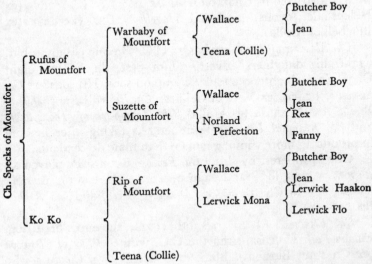

sired *Fydell Startler*. When one realizes that Startler was the sire of *Ch. Helensdale Bhan* one knows what a debt we owe this little tricolour (almost black and tan) dog. He was unfortunate in his birth date, July 1937, as the war certainly prevented him from obtaining his title, for he was still good enough in 1946, at the age of almost ten years, to win a C.C. Startler had two sons, *Ch. Fydell Round-Up* (ex Winnie of Aberlour) and *Ch. Helensdale Bhan* (ex Helensdale Gentle Lady), which made a great impact on the breed, especially the latter. *Ch. Fydell Round-Up* sired the golden sable, *Ch. Fydell Round Robin*—who left us for Sweden before making a mark as a sire—the C.C. winner *Fydell Squire*, *Ch. Parklea Playboy* and *Fydell Rob Roy*, sire of *Ch. Morula of Knockmahar*, who in turn produced a Champion son in *Garniehill Tulyar*.

However, it is *Ch. Helensdale Bhan's* son, *Ch. Helensdale Ace*, who holds pride of place in this branch of the line, for Ace sired no less than 19 individual C.C. winners, of which nine had already become Champions at the time of writing this chapter. Dealing only with those which have so far 'bred on', we have

Ch. Alasdair of Tintobank (ex Helensdale Mhairi Dhu), *Ch. Hallinwood Flash* (ex Hallinwood Elegance), *Ch. Laird of Whytelaw* (ex Merry Maid of Whytelaw), and *Helensdale Rory* (ex Helensdale Rona) who, although not in himself a particularly successful show dog, besides two C.C. winning daughters, sired the tricolour Champion *Arolla Ebony of Wallerscote* (ex Helensdale Joyous), and *Ch. Hazelhead Gay Wanderer* (ex Bluebell of Arolla).

Ch. Alasdair of Tintobank has 15 C.C. winning children, but, again, his daughters advertise him best, for he has eight Champion daughters to four Champion sons. His sons are *Ch. Struan of Callart* (ex Vora of Callart), *Ch. Ireland's Eye Trefoil of Arolla* (ex Anchusa of Arolla), *Ch. Trumpeter of Tooneytown*, and *Ch. Kendoral Ulysses*. Trumpeter is taking after his sire in producing more winning female than male descendents.

Gay Wanderer, by siring *Ch. Penvose Brandysnap*, played an important part, for Brandysnap became the sire of *Ch. Riverhill Ratafia*, sire of Ch. *Durnovaria Double-O-Seven*, and *Ch. Rodhill Burnt Sugar*.

Ch. Eltham Park Eureka's other son, the cross-bred dog, *Eltham Park Evolution*, sired the C.C. winner *Blinx of Clerwood* (ex Chestnut Blossom). Blinx sired *Ch. Euan of Clerwood* who produced a Champion son, and one son and two daughters who won C.C.s, but this branch died there. It is Blinx's other son *Harvey* (ex Speyside Osla) who has kept this part of the line alive. Harvey had a Champion son in *Wish of Wyndora* and two others which have bred on in *Sandy* and *Mac of Aberlour*. Sandy is great-grandsire of *Hector of Aberlour*, the sire of *Ch. Orpheus of Callart* (ex Heatherbelle of Callart). Orpheus sired *Ch. Riverhill Rescuer* (ex Riverhill Ragna), sire of *Ch. Budlet of Surreyhills*, and *Riverhill Ranger*, sire of *Ch. Riverhill Raider* and of *Ch. Swagman from Shiel* who sired *Ch. Riverhill Rapparee*, sire of *Ch. Durnovaria Double Agent*. *Mac of Aberlour*, through his C.C. winning son *Geordie of Aberlour*, was grandsire of *Ch. Nicky of Aberlour* (ex Nesta of Aberlour).

Ch. Nicky sired *Ch. Riverhill Redcoat* (ex Riverhill Rouge), and to this dark sable dog we owe a lot. He sired *Ch. Riverhill Rikki* (ex Ch. Riverhill Rugosa), who produced a C.C. winning son in *Lanacost of Exford* (ex Ch. Butterfly of Exford) before being exported to Kenya.

Ensign of Oastwood (yet another son of Ch. Riverhill Red-coat) sired *Ch. Brigdale Renown* (ex Brigdale Rhoda) and through him is grandsire of *Ch. Midas of Shelert* (ex Ch. Riverhill Royal Flush), sire of *Ch. Spark of Shelert* and *Ch. Monarch of Morvane.*

Ch. Redcoat's other son, *Ch. Russet Coat of Callart* (ex Wild

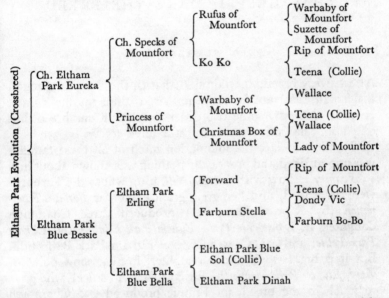

Rose of Callart), sired *Ch. Heatherisle Rufus* (ex Heatherisle Suzette) and through *Rising Star of Callart* is grandsire of *Ch. Starlight of Callart* (ex Carolyn of Callart).

Ch. Riverhill Rescuer's great-great-grandson, *Riverhill Rolling Home,* has been one of the breed's most successful sires of the last decade with three champion daughters and one champion son. However, it is his non-C.C. winning tricolour son, *Strikin' Midnight at Shelert,* who has done most for the breed. In total he sired ten champions, nine of them males and giving us three tricolours, two sables and five blue merles. A wonderful record.

And so the story comes up to date. Pages, undoubtedly, are yet to be written in Sheltie history, and many dogs have had to be omitted, but it is to be hoped that some kind of picture emerges through the years.

3

THEY HELPED MAKE THE BREED

FEMALES

As IN every breed, the families (that is, the descent through
the female side) are far more numerous than the male lines.
It seems there are some two dozen families in our breed, but
only about half this number are still 'alive' today.

Needless to say, the foundation bitch of all these families
was unregistered and practically nothing was known about her.

Family 1 starts with *Caledon Nell*, from whom the Farburns
were descended, and her great-grand-daughter *Farburn Fascination* (by Rip of Mountfort) produced three Champion
daughters in *Winstonian Pixie*, *Eltham Park Ellaline* and *Eltham
Park Petite*; and a C.C. winning son Eltham Park Perfection.
But it is her less illustrious daughter, from a show point of
view, *Eltham Park Emmie* (by Eltham Park Advance), who gave
so much to the breed, for Emmie produced two Champion
daughters, *Eltham Park Eunice* and *Eltham Park Esme*, a C.C.
winning daughter *Eltham Park Ena*, and two other daughters
E. P. Ezma and *Estelle* (by Eltham Park Erling), who became the
foundation of the Peabody kennels, and who, through *Ashbank
Dream Girl*, was responsible for much that is good in the
Helensdales, as the following shows. Five generations after
Dream Girl came *Helensdale Flash* (by Anvil Model). Flash had
two daughters, *Helensdale Mhairi Dhu* and *Helensdale Nighean
Dhu* (litter sisters by Helensdale Callum), neither winners in
their own right, but *Helensdale Mhairi Dhu* produced the C.C.
winner *Helensdale Lora* and two daughters, again litter sisters
(by Ch. Helensdale Ace), *Anna* and *Amili of Tintobank*, and their
litter brother, the illustrious Ch. Alasdair of Tintobank; *Amili*
produced a C.C. winning daughter in *Morag of Tintobank*,
while Anna, not to be outdone, had the lovely little bitch *Fiona*

30

of Tintobank (by Helensdale Rory), who unfortunately was destined to die young, but who, nevertheless, left Ch. *Beathag of Tintobank* and *Una of Tintobank*, and Una, mated to Hartfield Herald, gave the breed the tricolour Champion dog Ebony Pride of Glenhill.

Helensdale Nighean Dhu was the dam of *Helensdale Hilda* (by Ch. Helensdale Ace) and she produced the dog Ch. Franwyns Starlight. Nighean Dhu had two other daughters, bred the same way, the C.C. winner *Helensdale Lola* and the oversize bitch *Helensdale Linnet*. Linnet, mated to Ch. Riverhill Rescuer, gave us *Song Thrush* and *Stiletto from Shiel*, the latter, mated to Riverhill Roc, produced the little Champion bitch *Sheer Sauce from Shiel*. Both these Shiel bitches went to Germany at eighteen months of age, Sheer Sauce leaving this country before having a litter. *Song Thrush from Shiel* was grand-dam of the sable dog, Ch. Trumpeter of Tooneytown.

Returning to Eltham Park Emmie, in her daughter, *Ch. Eltham Park Eunice*, we find another tail female which is still breeding on, for Eunice had, among others, two daughters, *Eltham Park Elma* and *Eltham Park Eclair* (both by Ch. Max of Clerwood).

Elma gave the breed a Champion dog in Eltham Park Evan and a bitch in his sister *Eltham Park Evette* (both by Eltham Park Eofric).

Eclair's daughter, *Eltham Park Etiquette* (by Eltham Park Eurekason), was dam of the Champion litter sisters *Eltham Park Elfine* and *Eltham Park Elda* (by Eltham Park Eofric), and at this period we see the Eltham Parks at the topmost rung of the ladder.

Etiquette's other daughter, *Aldra's Golden Girl* (by Eltham Park Eofric), was dam of *Elaine* (by Eltham Park Edward), and this bitch became the foundation of the Ellington Kennel. Elaine's C.C. winning daughter, *Ellington Dainty Lady* (by Gadget of Glenholme), was dam of *Ellington Enchant* (by Ellington Envoy), and Enchant's daughter, *Ch. Ellington Easter Lady* (by Ellington Encore), was, in turn, dam of the C.C. winner *Ellington Ernestine* (by Ellington Endurer). From this same little part of the family are also descended the present-day winners *Ch. Rhapsody of Rivock*, *Ch. Ellington Wattlingate Waitress*, *Ellington Ebony Queen*, and *Minglet of Ronas Hill*.

Returning again to *Eltham Park Emmie*, her daughter

Eltham Park Ezma (by Eltham Park Eofric) has given two winning tails. The one, less strong, being responsible for *Ch. Martine of Melvaig* (by Ch. Viking of Melvaig) and *Aurora of Edenfels* (by Ireland's Eye Shevan). The other, six generations from *Ezma*, gave *Dryfesdale Daintiness* (by Ch. Helensdale Bhan) the dam of the little sisters *Alpine Rose* and *Alpine Anemone of Arolla* (by Ch. Helensdale Ace) and of their younger full sister *Aconite of Arolla. Alpine Rose* was the grand-dam of the tricolour dog Ch. Eldapenny Starshine (by Ch. Dilhorne Blackcap), whose death in a road accident when he was only four years old saddened us all. *Aconite* was grand-dam of yet another tricolour Champion dog, Graygill Nectar, and *Anemone* grand-dam of the sable Hayduc Handylad.

Family 2 starts with *Ashbank Flora*, great-grand-dam of *Kilravock Naomi* (sometimes called Kilravock Hermia) (by Elswick Beauty), and her daughter, *Farburn Bo-Bo* (by Berryden Prince) carved a great name for herself in Sheltie history through her daughter *Farburn Victrix* (by Dondy Vic).

Victrix's daughter, *Ashbank Jean* (by Ronnie of Mountfort), produced four daughters of note, the sables *Ashbank Sheila* and *Downfield Ethne* (by Ashbank Glitter), *Helensdale Rosa* (by Tilford Tam o' Shanter) and the tricolour *Nell* (also by Glitter).

Maud of Exford became grand-dam, through *Gini*, of *Ch. Butterfly of Exford. Butterfly* has a C.C. winning daughter in *Beeswing of Exford* (by Ch. Riverhill Rikki) and two Champion daughters, *Blackmoth and Honeysuckle* (both by Ch. Lothario of Exford). She is also grand-dam, through *Skylark of Exford*, of Ch. *Melody of Exford. Blackmoth* is grand-dam, through different bitches, of *Ch. Golden Thread of Exford, Sunflower of Exford* and of the tricolour dogs, Cracker and Philander of Exford; while *Ch. Honeysuckle* is dam of the C.C. winner *Honeydew* and her Champion litter brother Popgun of Exford (by Cracker).

Family 3 begins with *Fanny*, grand-dam of *Chestnut Queenie* (by Elswick Beauty), and Queenie was dam of *Chestnut Lassie*, a C.C. winner (by Berryden Prince), and the outstanding winner producer *Chestnut Sweet Lady* (also by Berryden Prince).

Chestnut Sweet lady was a tricolour bitch, but carried a great deal of the blood of the Rev. Hans Hamilton's famous Mountshannon blue merle Collies. Mated to her brother, Chestnut Rainbow she produced stock which did a great deal to improve type in the breed. This mating gave us, among others, *Ch. Redbraes Magda*, a tricolour also, four generations behind *Peabody Peggy* (a daughter of Tilford Blue Beau and *Peabody Pauline*). Peggy had two daughters of note, *Peabody Pegantwe* and *Jill of Mariemeau* (both by Ch. Tilford Tweed).

From Pegantwe we have, post-war, the two Champion bitches *Runlee Phantasy* and *Wravella of Wyndora*, but here, for the moment, this branch dies.

Jill of Mariemeau was the dam of *Mariemeau Black Bonnet* (by Playwright of Exford), and she produced two daughters through which the branch continues.

Mariemeau Katrine (by Ch. Tibbetts Mark) was dam of *Tranmere Will o' The Wisp* (later *Russet Leaf of Callart*) (by Dandy of Mariemeau), dam of *Sweet Lady of Callart* (by Blaise of Callart), and Sweet Lady produced two daughters, *Markian Magnolia* (by Ch. Fydell Round Robin) and *Fydell Maybelle* (by Ch. Helensdale Ace), each of whom in their turn produced a C.C. winning son in Fydell Monarch and Fydell Squire respectively. In direct descent from Katrine today is *Ch. Wellswood Amberrae*.

Black Bonnet's other daughter, *Rona of Pemellan*, was dam of *Ellington Edwina* (by Ellington Encore), dam of *Ch. Ellington Enjoyment* (by Ellington Encore), and of *Tibbetts Ardene Azalea* dam of *Tibbetts Jasmine* and *Ch. Ardene Asta* (also by Encore). Asta's daughter, *Althea of Oastwood* (by Ellington Escape), produced *Belle of Oastwood* (by Ellington Encore), dam of *Ch. Lovelight of Lydwell* (by Fielder of Foula), one of the most successful of the present-day Champions from a breeding point of view, for she is dam of the champions *Love Sonnet of Lydwell*, and *Love's Serenade of Lydwell* and of the C.C. winners *Love Caprice* (both these by Ch. Alasdair of Tintobank) and *Latest Love of Lydwell* (by Ch. Hallinwood Flash) who has a champion grand-daughter *Ch. Penvose Cherry Brandy*.

Family 4 begins with *Bess*, great-grand-dam of *Rubislaw Lady Fayre*, dam of *Ch. Tilford Tontine* (by Chestnut Rainbow), and this little tricolour bitch not only gained her title, but goes down as a pillar of the breed, for she was undoubtedly one of the most successful winner-producers we have ever had. Besides whelping the Champion litter brothers, Ch. Tilford Tay and Ch. Tilford Tweed, she had a Champion daughter in their full sister *Ch. Mary of Camevock* (by Arthur of Cameliard). Yet another Champion daughter, *Ch. Tilford Tinette* (by Ch. Gawaine of Cameliard), went to U.S.A., but a third daughter, *Tilford Titania* (by Ch. Euan of Clerwood), certainly did more for the breed. *Ch. Mary of Camevock*, a charming golden sable bitch, almost ahead of her day, had a daughter, *Extravagance of Exford* (by Spendthrift of Exford), and her daughter, *Gaiety of Exford* (by Bubbles of Exford), produced the lovely tricolour *Ch. Bonfire of Exford* (by Beacon of Houghton Hill), whose Champion daughter, *Firebrand of Exford* (by Jack Tar of Exford), was grand-dam of Ch. Debonair of Exford.

Tilford Titania was a most prolific bitch, yet only one of her daughters produced stock which is still breeding on, and it was from this branch, six generations later, that the lovely *Ch. Dileas of the Wansdyke* was born. In these two, Ch. Dileas and Ch. Firebrand, at the moment this part rests.

Family 5 gives food for thought. It begins with a tricolour bitch, *Lily*, and it has been suggested that this Lily is the same as the *Lily* (ex Fanny) in Family 3. There is a great deal to be said for this theory, and I for one would be ready to agree with the idea. Of course, if this could be proved beyond doubt, then Families 3 and 5 are the same, but I do not think we shall ever prove it. Not only are both these bitches—if there are two of them—contemporaries, with Lily, on the one hand, having pups about 1917, and Lily, on the other, having pups about 1920, but there is such a mingling of the blood of the one family, with the tail male of the other in the early C.C. winning descendants of both families, that I see every reason to accept that the two are one, especially as this was a period when close line- and in-breeding were being practised extensively.

Family 5 then begins with *Lily*, grand-dam of *Aberlady Wendy* (by Glendale) and of *Aberlady Spotless* (by Rip of Mountfort). Aberlady Wendy was five generations behind *Nesta of Aberlour*, dam of the C.C. winner *Nora of Aberlour* and her never-to-be-forgotten brother, Ch. Nicky of Aberlour.

Aberlour Spotless breeds on today through the Riverhills. *Riverhill Reinette* (by Ch. Riverhill Rufus) produced *Ch. Riverhill Regale* (by Ch. Riverhill Redcoat), and Regale's daughter, *Ch. Riverhill Royal Flush* (by Ch. Helensdale Ace), had two daughters, *Regalia of Shelert* (by Lyric of Melvaig) and *Fleurette of Shelert* dam of the dog Ch. Sweet Sultan of Shelert. *Regalia of*

Shelert is grand-dam of *Sequin of Shelert* dam of *Ch. Samantha of Shelert* and of *Ch. Symphony of Shelert*, herself grand-dam of the Champion dog Spark.[1]

Reinette's other daughter, *Riverhill Reina*, is grand-dam of Ch. Riverhill Rescuer and dam of the C.C. winner *Riverhill Raine* (by Burn of Exford), an ill-fated little bitch, who had an illness which deprived her of all her coat after winning her first C.C. Reina's daughter, *Riverhill Rikita* (by Ch. Riverhill Rikki), produced a C.C. winner in *Riverhill Robinetta* (by Riverhill Robbie), dam of Ch. Swagman from Shiel and grand-dam of Ch. Riverhill Ratafia.

Family 6 lives more in the history of its sons, but today it exists still through three champion bitches, *Hallinwood Sealodge Sparkle* (by Ch. Hallinwood Flash), *Hallinwood Golden Fetter* (by Hallinwood Golden Ray), *Zara of Whytelaw* and several other C.C. winners. But, in February 1967, the family hit the highspots for, at Cruft's show, Ch. *Deloraine Dilys of Monkswood, Golden Fetter's* grand-daughter (by Riverhill Rolling Home), won the Working Group and finished Best Bitch in show. No Sheltie had ever achieved this before, and it is interesting to note that, whenever something similar has been attained, it has been done by *Dilys'* immediate ancestors. The first was her great-great-grandfather Ch. Helensdale Ace, when he won Best in Show first day at Birmingham City in 1951. His granddaughter *Ch. Riverhill Rare Gold* was the next, when she was the best bitch at the L.K.A. in 1955, while still a puppy. *Dilys*, through her sire, is *Rare Gold's* grand-daughter. It must not be forgotten either that Rolling Home's son, Ch. Antoc Sealodge Spotlight, is, so far, the only other Sheltie to win a Group.[2]

Family 8 is a particularly interesting one, for the female blood in so many of today's winning kennels traces through it. Exford, Dilhorne, Brigdale, Whytelaw and Hallinwood spring to mind.

The family begins with *Gorse Blossom*, great-great grand-dam of *Ballet Girl of Houghton Hill* (by Ch. Blaeberry of Clerwood)

[1] The Champions Skirl, Sea Urchin and Strict Tempo stem from her also, plus the bitches Chs. *Samantha, Such a Frolic* and *She's My Fancy*, as well as *Ch. Gay Choice*, together with the dogs Chs. Such a Beano, Such a Spree and Such a Myth.

[2] Dilys has herself produced a Ch. son, *Monkswood Moss Trooper* (by Ch. Riverhill Raider).

and *Ch. Mazurka of Houghton Hill* (by Golden Spider of Houghton Hill), and each of these also had two most useful daughters.

Dealing first with *Ballet Girl* (who was, of course, the dam of Ch. Moneyspinner of Exford) we have *Swasti of Houghton Hill* (by Ch. Uam Var), and this tricolour bitch was five generations behind *Ch. Tibbett's Lilac* (by Ch. Nuthatch of Larchwood) and *Shiel's Frosty Day of Larchwood*, grand-dam of Ch. Dilhorne Blackcap, but with Lilac, this branch at the moment rests in tail female. Swasti's other daughter, *Trinket of Houghton Hill* (by Ian of Houghton Hill), was four generations behind *Houghton Hill Crystal* (by Riverhill Reef), herself a C.C. winner and dam of Ch. Crag of Exford. Crystal's daughter, *Prudence of Exford* (by Ch. Exford Piskiegye Taw), had a C.C. winning daughter in *Prunella of Exford*, who left for India while still in puppyhood. Prudence's other daughter, *Francehill Discreet of Exford* (by Lanacost of Exford), has so far produced *Ch. Francehill Dry Ginger* (by Ch. Kendoral Ulysses), and a C.C. winning son in Francehill Frolicsome.

Returning to Ballet Girl, we trace a fresh branch through her other daughter, *Polly Wolly of Houghton Hill* (also by Ch. Uam Var), dam of *Spinning Girl of Houghton Hill* (by Golden Spider of Houghton Hill); and her two daughters, *Loom of Houghton Hill* and *Gaby of Glenholme* (both by Gallat of Glenholme), bred on in the following way. Gaby's daughter, *Whiterocks Winnie* (by Netherkeir Flash), was dam of *Bristol Fairy* (by Ch. Garniehill Tulyar), who in turn produced a C.C. winner in *Prospect Fiona* (by Ch. Laird of Whytelaw), and she has a C.C. winning daughter, *Crochmaid Serene*.

Loom of Houghton Hill was three generations behind *Shetland Lassie* (by Titch of Brunstane), dam of the C.C. winner *Lilt of Whytelaw* (by Merriott Maxim of Dryfesdale), who was grand-dam of yet another C.C. winning bitch, *Sanda of Whytelaw* (by Glint of Whytelaw). Shetland Lassie's other daughter, *Merry Maid of Whytelaw* (by Ellington Encore), proved even more successful, for, in addition to her son Ch. Laird of Whytelaw, she was dam of the C.C. winner *Frolic of Whytelaw* (by Ch. Helensdale Bhan) who has a C.C. winning daughter in *Beauty Queen* and another daughter, *Brigdale Rhoda*, grand-dam of *Ch. Brigdale Romaris* and *Ch. Dryfesdale Gay Girl*, and dam of a Champion son in Brigdale Renown. Another daughter of *Merry Maid* the C.C. winner *Gay of Whytelaw*, gave us *Ch. Tassel of Whytelaw*, and *Merry Maid* herself is grand-dam of the C.C. winner *Bridie of Whytelaw* and of the dog, Ch. Greenscrees Swordsman, and great-grand-dam of a C.C. winner, Robin of Whytelaw. Certainly *Merry Maid* will be remembered in our breed.

Starting now to trace afresh through *Ch. Mazurka of Houghton Hill*, she also added two daughters of current interest, *Viola* is six generations behind *Ch. Blue Charm of Exford* (by Ch. Lothario of Exford), dam of *Black Perle of Exford, Mazurka's* daughter, *Sarabande of Houghton Hill* (by Anton of Houghton Hill), was dam of the black and white *Riverhill Rumba* (by Uam Var), and her blue merle C.C. winning daughter, *Riverhill Romantic* (by Peabody Silver Prince), herself produced a C.C. winner, the lovely blue merle *Riverhill Rosalind* (by Ch. Mime of H.H.), one that the war almost certainly robbed of a title. Rosalind's daughter, *Riverhill Rosaleen* (by the black and white Riverhill Rector), produced *Hallinwood Gillian* (by Ch. Riverhill Rufus). *Gillian* was the dam of *Hallinwood Merriement* (by Merriot Gold Badge), who produced a C.C. winner in *Hallinwood Token* (by Ch. Hallinwood Flash) and another daughter, *Hallinwood Amber* (by Hallinwood Sentinel), dam of *Ch. Hallinwood Amber Girl* (by Ch. Hallinwood Flash). Rosaleen's third daughter, *Hornbeam Jemima*, was the dam of *Houghton Hill Tit Bit*, a C.C. winner (by Houghton Hill Chip). Four generations from Mazurka we have *Ch. Dilhorne Blue Puffin* (by Ch. Graygill Nectar) and her daughter *Ch. Dilhorne Bluecap* (by Ch. Dilhorne Blackcap.)

Family 9[1] should appeal particularly to blue merle 'fans', for it is the earliest family in which this colour can be traced. A tricolour bitch, *Gypsy*, was the start of it all, and immediately, in the very next generation, a blue merle was produced, *Blue Floss of Houghton Hill* (by Rover), and the female blood breeds true to colour for three generations through Blue Floss's daughter, *Merle Maiden of Houghton Hill* (by Nut of Houghton Hill) and her daughter, *Blue Bean of Houghton Hill*, a result of father/ daughter mating, as she too was by Nut, to *Ch. Blue Blossom of Houghton Hill* (by Ch. Uam Var).

Few Champions have given such good breeding stock as did Blue Blossom, and this doubtless must be attributed to the

---

[1]Family 9, now the most important family in the list, has changed its pattern and is no longer almost essentially a blue one. Nowadays its boasts Champions in all three colours.

very astute piece of close line-breeding in which Mrs Baker indulged to produce her, and which, as can be seen from her pedigree, gave such a big infusion of the famous Chestnut Collie cross blood, carrying, through Chestnut Sweet Lady, the blue merle colour from the Collies also:

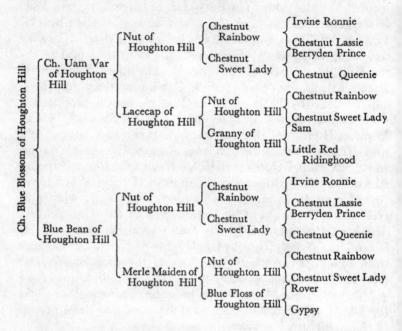

Discounting her two Champion sons, as we must when dealing with families, she gave the breed her blue merle daughter *Sweeze of Houghton Hill* (by Anton of Houghton Hill), dam of Ch. Air Mail of Houghton Hill. Another daughter of Blossom's was *Ch. Pea Blossom of Houghton Hill* (by Dolen of Houghton Hill), this time a tricolour, dam of the C.C. winner *Thrift of Houghton Hill* (by Ch. Spendthrift of Exford). Three slightly less glamorous (from a show point of view) daughters of Blossom's, who nevertheless did a great deal for the breed, were *Blue Balloon of Houghton Hill* (by Ch. Uam Var), *Blue Moon of Houghton Hill* (by Anton of Houghton Hill) and *Sugar Cake of Houghton Hill* (by Beano of Houghton Hill), all three blue merles, although Sugar Cake was almost white.

Blue Balloon, still breeding true to colour, produced the C.C. winner *Enchantress of Inchmery* (by Wren of Wyndora), dam of Ch. Nuthatch of Larchwood, and her sister *Ch. Jenny Wren of Crawleyridge*, C.D.Ex., U.D., the first C.C. winner in the breed to obtain working qualifications.

Blue Moon was dam of the tricolour *Toonie Mona* (by Ch. Mime of Houghton Hill), and Mona produced three important daughters, *Riverhill Rouge* and *Rhythmic* (both by Ch. Riverhill Rufus) and *Toonie Herepanda* (by Hamish of the Wansdyke).

Riverhill Rhythmic was dam of *Arabesque of Melvaig* (by Delwood Paddy), dam of the C.C. winner *Tiptoes of Melvaig* (by Ch. Helensdale Ace), and of *Musette of Melvaig* (by Ch. Nicky of Aberlour) dam of *Amber of Melvaig* (by Delwood Terence), dam of *Jonquil of Melvaig* (by Ch. Nicky of Aberlour), who in her turn produced Ch. Viking of Melvaig.

Riverhill Rhythmic had yet another daughter, *Makushla of Melvaig* (by Ch. Nicky of Aberlour), dam of *Alannah of Melvaig* (by Ch. Viking of Melvaig), dam of *Ch. Honeybunch of Melvaig*, grand-dam of *Ch. Gay Lass of Melvaig*.

Mona's second daughter, *Riverhill Rouge*, as well as being dam of Ch. Riverhill Redcoat, gave a daughter who has proved invaluable for *Riverhill Red Biddy* (by Hallinwood Sentinel) had three daughters of note, *Riverhill Rara Avis*, *Red Riding Hood* and *Red Gold*. The first two have both produced C.C. winning descendants, but it is *Red Gold* who has the greatest claim to fame. Her daughter, *Ch. Riverhill Rare Gold*,[1] has made a unique name for herself in the breed by producing a champion daughter in each of her first four litters to four different dogs! All these four champion daughters have bred on in their turn. *Real Gold* produced *Riverhill Ring of Gold* (by Ch. Riverhill Ratafia), *Ready Cash Rodanieh Ready Made* (by Helensdale Frolic), *Rather Rich* has been the most prolific with a tricolour daughter *Ch. Riverhill Rather Dark* (by Riverhill Ranger) and her litter brother Ch. Riverhill Raider; a sable daughter *Ch. Riverhill Rather Nice* dam of Ch. Riverhill Rapparee, now in Sweden, Ch. Riverhill Rampion (in Australia), and the latest, Ch. Riverhill Richman.

Mona's third daughter, *Toonie Herepanda*, was dam of *Golden Gleam of Callart* (by Blaise of Callart), who produced a C.C. winner in *Felicity of Merrion* (by Wrennet of Wyndora); and *Sweet Fairy of Merrion* (by Eltham Park Emperor), dam of *Freda of Merrion*, who produced a C.C. winner in *Wyndora Wroena of*

[1] See also page 35

Merrion (by Ellington Encore), and a Champion son in Francis of Merrion.

Yet another blue merle daughter of Ch. Blue Blossom of Houghton Hill, *Sugar Cake of Houghton Hill*, besides producing the dog Ch. Mime of Houghton Hill, had a daughter, *Bon Bon of Houghton Hill* (by Dolen of Houghton Hill), and her daughter, *Charmadair of Pipestyle* (by Ch. Air Mail of Houghton Hill), was dam of *Charmer of Pipestyle* (by Winkle of Wyndora), dam of *Ch. Fascinator of Exford* (by Jack Tar of Exford). *Fascinator* is dam of the C.C. winner *Ballard of Exford*, and grand-dam of *Ch. Francehill Glamorous*, and she also has a Champion son in Lothario of Exford.

Family 10 was another which, in female blood, was short-lived. It came from the small, prick-eared Rough Collie *Teena*, who had two daughters, *Ko Ko* (by Rip of Mountfort), dam of Ch. Specks of Mountfort, and *Golden Lady of Mountfort* (by Bob of Mountfort), dam of *Grizel of Clerwood* (by Ch. Specks of Mountfort), who produced Ch. Gawaine of Cameliard. Golden Lady had another daughter, *Linda of Clerwood* (by Dondy Tinto), whose daughter, *Lucilla of Clerwood* (by Ch. Blaeberry of Clerwood), produced no less than three C.C. winning bitches in *Lossie*, *Laetitia* and *Lilt of Clerwood*, and with whom, it seems extraordinary to have to record, the family died.

Family 11 is another interesting one because for the first five generations it carries one of the first kennel names in the breed, that of Inverness. Starting with *Inverness Mona* it produced, five generations later, a sable bitch, *Hailes Bunty* (by Braeheads Laddie), and Bunty had two tricolour daughters: *Hailes Babs*, grand-dam of Ch. Hurly Burly and great-grand-dam of Ch. Primus, and *Lady of Mountfort* (by Halcrow), who produced *Christmas Box of Mountfort*, a tiny sable bitch (by Wallace), dam of the dogs Ch. Nettle of Mountfort and the C.C. winner Walesby Species, as well as a sable daughter in *Princess of Mountfort* (by Ch. Specks of Mountfort), dam of Ch. Eltham Park Eureka, and dam of *Janey Marie of Mountfort*, from whom, six generations later, came *Netherkeir Susie*, dam of *Wendy of Netherkeir* and of *Netherkeir Jewel* (both by Netherkeir Dandy). Wendy was dam of *Ch. Dryfesdale Dream Girl* (by Ellington Encore) and Jewel of *Ch. Dryfesdale Daisy* (by Briar of Callart).

Family 12 is another which, for the moment at least, seems

to be dead. Starting with *Tivannix* it produced, two generations later, *Princess Nandi of Kilravock*, dam of a C.C. winning son and daughter, but also dam of *Monagard* (by Clifford Model).

Monagard, apparently a most prolific bitch, had five daughters who, for a time at least, bred on, although one, the tricolour *Larkbeare Doughnut* (by Ch. Walesby Select), produced only the C.C. winner *Larkbeare Sultana Cake* (by Ch. Larkbeare Rusk), and with her the branch petered out.

However, Monagard's other daughter, *Brenda* (or Brendagard), was dam of *Ch. Kilravock Goldfinder* (by Walesby Species), dam of *Kilravock Maree* (by Kilravock Blue Cloud), who produced a C.C. winning bitch, *Kilravock Marionette* (by Tilford Tam o' Shanter).

Yet another Monagard daughter, *Dawn of Destiny* (by Dondy Vic), was dam of *Golden Sunset of the Crest* (by Ch. Specks of Mountfort), dam of the C.C. winner *Morning Dew of Hazelcrest* (by Kilravock Specks), and from Golden Sunset, via another daughter, *Kilravock Bubbles*, we have today the C.C. winner *Willowfield Wendy*.

Monagard's last daughter to be considered is *Nan of Mountfort* (by Ch. Nettle of Mountfort), dam of Kilravock Specks and grand-dam of *Ch. Margawse of Cameliard* (by Ch. Gawaine of Cameliard), and from whose other daughter, *Pam of Stradsett* (by Ch. Specks of Mountfort), we trace a number of C.C. winning dogs, and in bitches, the *Chs. Helensdale Forget-Me-Not*, and *Michelmere Sona* and her daughter *Daffin*.

Family 13 is the one to which the Helensdales owe so much. Originating with *Fanny*, whose great-grand-daughter *Caleyvoe Rena* (by Berryden Prince) produced *Betty* (by Rip of Mountofort), dam of Ch. Kilravock Nettle and *Queenie of Redbraes* (also by Rip), grand-dam of the C.C. winner *Karen*. But it is her other daughter, *Hilton Lady* (by Chestnut Cadet), who most concerns us, for she was grand-dam of *Helensdale Kora*, in her turn grand-dam of *Lena of Aberlour* (by Harvey), dam of *Lorna of Aberlour* (by Don of Aberlour), dam of the C.C. winning brother and sister Geordie and *Gracie of Aberlour*, and of *Winnie of Aberlour* (by Ch. Wrennie of Wyndora).

Winnie was dam of *Wendy of Aberlour* (by Ch. Nicky of Aberlour), dam of Ch. Fydell Roundup; also of *Laura of Kinslady* (by Hector of Aberlour), dam of *Ch. Fair Sheena,* and dam also of *Wynford Beauty*, grand-dam of the C.C. winner *Bhan's Quinie*, and Veeantro Verb. Others descended from this branch are *Arisaig Oina* and Ch. Arolla Ebony of Wallerscote.

Winnie of Aberlour's most important daughter was, of course, *Helensdale Aviatrix* (by Hector of Aberlour), whose two C.C. winning daughters, *Helensdale Rona* and *Hazel* (both by Ch. Helensdale Bhan), have so far not bred on, but whose other daughter *Helensdale Gentle Lady* (by Ch. Nicky of Aberlour) gave the breed Ch. Helensdale Bhan and his son Ch. Helensdale Ace. Yet another Aviatrix daughter was *Fydell Satisfaction* (also by Ch. Nicky), dam of Ch. Fydell Round Robin and of *Fydell Painted Lady* (by Ch. Fydell Roundup), dam of *Ch. Fydell Frosty Moon* (by Fydell Startler) and her C.C. winning sister *Fydell Harvest Moon*. Satisfaction was grand-dam, too, of *Ch. Shady Ferne of Sheldawyn*.

Back again to Aviatrix and yet another of her daughters, *Helensdale Hostess* (by Ch. Nicky of Aberlour), dam of *Helensdale Fantasia* (by Ch. Bhan), dam of *Ch. Helensdale Wendy*, *Ch. Helensdale Waxwing* and *Helensdale Veda*, all daughters of Ch. Helensdale Ace. Another daughter of *Fantasia*, *Helensdale Wanda*, produced *Ch. Helensdale Vanessa* (by Helensdale Lorne).

Aviatrix, still not satisfied, produced *Iris of Knockmahar* (by Ch. Bhan), dam of *Ch. Cutie of Knockmahar* (by Ch. Ellington Esquire). Another great-grand-daughter of Iris, *Bell Flower of Arolla*, is behind both *Ch. Joyful of Durnovaria* (by Lonesome of Nutbush) and *Ginger of Tooneytown* (by Ch. Luna Andy of Upperslaughter).

Families 14 and 15 each existed for four generations only and 'died' in the early 1920s and so do not concern us.

Family 16 starts with a sable bitch, *Queenie*, grand-dam of *Ch. Freshfield Fad*, whose grand-daughter, *Gene of Glenholme* (by Ch. Eltham Park Eurekason ex *Gloss of Glenholm*), produced two daughters, *Glow of Glenholme* and *Aldermoss Sheila* (by Ashbank Blue Blood). The descent through Aldermoss Sheila produced, after six generations, the bitch C.C. winner *Vankiste Chonkay Willow*, and in dogs Clydell Crusader and Ch. Wonder Lad of Eleth.

The branch through Glow bred on for many generations

and then produced the charming tricolour bitch *Ch. Diadem of Callart*, grand-dam of *Ch. Star Princess of Callart* and the C.C. winner *Butterfly of Callart*, as well as three Champion dogs, Russetcoat, Orpheus and Struan, all of Callart.

The next seven families, 17 to 23 inclusive, were all so short-lived that they no longer have any influence in this country and it seems unlikely that any of them will revive.

Family 24 descends through generations of island-bred stock of which little is known to a tricolour bitch, *Voe*, dam of two blue merle daughters, *Mary of the Wansdyke* and *Riverhill Rosette* (both by Tilford Blue Beau).

Mary's daughter, *Fionie of Wyndora* (by Peabody Paul), was dam of *Wishing of Wyndora* (by Ch. Wish of Wyndora), dam of *Ch. Wevonne of Wyndora* and *Wrina of Wyndora* (both by Ch. Wrennie of Wyndora). Fionie's second daughter, *Wishes of Wyndora*, is the one from which the C.C. winning bitches *Khamsin of Callart* and *Bracken of Ronas Voe* are descended.

Returning to Voe's second daughter, *Riverhill Rosette*, we find the descent tracing alternately through blue merle and sable merle for five generations to the blue merle *Riverhill Roguish* (by Riverhill Rector ex *Riverhill Rubasse*), dam of Ch. Riverhill Reefer of Exford, and of four daughters, *Riverhill Reticent* and *Riverhill Razzle* (by Beacon of Houghton Hill), *Riverhill Romp* (by Wibbly Wob) and *Shiel's Riverhill Riotous* (by Ch. Nuthatch of Larchwood), all of them blue merles, except the first-named.

Reticent was dam of the sable bitch *Iseult of Cameliard* (by Riverhill Rival), dam of *Ch. Riverhill Rugosa* (by Ch. Fydell Roundup), and Rugosa produced a Champion son in Ch. Riverhill Rikki, and a daughter, *Riverhill Rosalie* (by Ch. Riverhill Redcoat), dam of the C.C. winner *Shot Silk of Shelert* (by Helensdale Rory). Yet another daughter of *Rugosa*, *Riverhill Rosetta*, produced *Riverhill Rock Rose* dam of Ch. Riverhill Riddle.

Riverhill Razzle was dam of *Candyda of Inchmery* (by Mickie Beaver), who went to South Africa before gaining her title or whelping a litter.

Riverhill Romp was dam of *Toddy of the Wansdyke* (by Lirima Lacquer), dam of *Vennards Mint Julep* (by Ch. Nuthatch of Larchwood), dam of *Vennards Benedictine* (by Jock of the Wansdyke).

Shiel's Riverhill Riotous was dam of the sable merle *Riverhill Remarkable* (by Swizz from Shiel), dam of the blue merle Champion *Riverhill Respectable* (by Lirima Lacquer).

And so the story of the families is brought to a temporary close. Each year the families will be extended as the history of the breed continues. Much has had to be omitted, but it is to be hoped that some picture of what is behind our charming little dogs has developed in this chapter.

4

COLOUR BREEDING

THE standard (given in Chapter 5) sets out very clearly, the different and lovely colours, in which we may expect to find the Sheltie coat, and this does not need amplification.

Breeding for colour has always been a most interesting affair, and is even more interesting in our breed than in many others because, while in Collies and Pembroke Corgis, where the colour plan is visually the same as ours, colour breeding is reasonably predictable, it is not so with the Sheltie, as various genetic changes have taken place in our breed, and as a result Shelties are a law unto themselves.

SABLE in all its shades, may be produced from the mating of sable × sable, or sable × tricolour, and, as will be seen later, sables, in our breed, may also be found in a litter from two 'visual' tricolours. It is also possible to obtain tricolours, black and white, or black and tans, from a double sable mating. However, there is a type of sable, known as homozygous, which is absolutely pure for sable, and which, when mated with a tricolour, still produce 100 per cent sable puppies.

TRICOLOUR is a pure recessive, so tricolour × tricolour will produce only tricolours, provided that the tricolour animals are truly genetically tricolours, and not just 'visually' so. It appears that there is a different type of genetic colouring in our breed, one in which, for want of a better explanation, it appears that the animal is, in fact, genetically sable, but in which the black shading has spread too far, and made that animal a tricolour to look at. Such animals are rare, but one should never be too ready to state that a 'mis-mating' has taken place if your tricolour bitch produces a sable puppy to a tricolour dog. It seems to me a reasonable possibility that this strange pattern may have evolved from the King Charles Spaniel left behind in the Islands, and referred to on page 17, for the mating of

45

black-and-tan King Charles can produce Ruby (a colour similar to sable) puppies, and I would readily accept that it is to this infiltration of 'foreign' blood that we can trace this strange genetic pattern in the Sheltie of today.

BLACK-AND-WHITE seem to be a law unto themselves, and will crop up from almost every possible colour combination, and with no real expectation.

BLACK-AND-TAN appears to have become extinct, as I do not believe one has been seen since 1937.

BLUE MERLE, although of such interest that it demands a section to itself, must never be regarded as separate from the other colours. All are Shelties, divided only by coat colour.

The blue merle is, in fact, one of the commonest original colours of the Sheepdog. In the mid-nineteenth century this colour was quite ordinary, and merle Sheepdogs were to be found in all parts of Britain.

It is a great pity that the original name of the colour— 'marled'—ever came to be changed to the word we use today, for 'marle', a corruption of marbled, so exactly describes the desired markings. A merle, on the other hand, is a blackbird!

The perfect blue merle should be a silvery blue in colour, dappled and splashed with black, nowhere in large spots. The collar, chest, feet legs and tail-tip may be white, and there may or may not be a white blaze. Although not essential, it is highly desirable that the blue merle should carry bright tan markings in the places in which we normally expect to find them in a tricolour. The eyes of the blue merle may be blue, either or both, or part of either or both. Although the nose should be black, as in the other colours, a slight amount of pink would be less-heavily penalized in the blue merle. Great attention, however, must be paid to the true silvery-blue colour. We have seen, recently, far too many 'muddy-coloured' dogs, which only deserve the designation of 'merle' without the word blue.

To me the blue merle colour is the most attractive of all, and fascinating both to the geneticist and to the practical breeder.

After forty years of being established as a show breed it is surprising that definite blue merle lines of heredity are not already more firmly established in the breed. With certain notable exceptions—unfortunately none of them still strongly existent today—there has never been a line which bred 'true blue'. This is the fault of the breeders themselves and not of the little dogs. There has always been far too much intermingling of sable blood with the blue merle. This should *never* be. No blue merle should ever be mated to a sable. To a sable-bred tricolour, yes, but not to the sable itself. The reason will become clear as you read on.

The blue merle pattern is a modification of black due to the presence of a dilution factor, and to the granules of pigmentation in each hair being less numerous than in the dog of

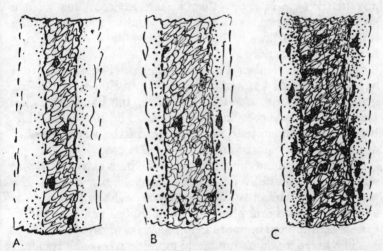

A.   B   C

Typical hairs of blue merle coat, showing pigment granules in individual hair producing blue merle pattern

whole colour; it is also due to the fact that the granules of pigmentation are arranged in a particular pattern in each hair. For this reason the *real* blue merle colour is extremely difficult to achieve in perfection, and probably because of the difficulty it presents a fascinating task to undertake.

The blue merle pattern cannot appear unless at least one parent is a blue merle. (It should, however, be stated here that two sables, mated together, when both happen to be carrying the merling or dilution factor recessively, have been known to produce mottled dogs, but these cannot be described as *blue* merles as they are usually of very poor colour.) The *blue* merle pattern cannot appear unless the bi-colour (black-and-tan pattern) is present, for the dilution factor *must* work on the bi-colour to produce blue merles. The word bi-colour denotes the black-and-tan dog, and the tricolour is just the same, but with the white collar pattern also present. Therefore, tricolours × merles produce perfectly satisfactory blue merles.

At one time it might have been necessary to mate the blue merles to sables, in order to improve type, as there have been periods when type was much better in the sables than in either tricolours or merles. As we no longer have to admit that there is any better type in sables than in the other colours, such a cross is no longer necessary, and it would be to the lasting improvement of the blue merles if the sable × merle mating in our breed was entirely abandoned.

Sable × merle always has produced rusty-coloured merles and blue-eyed sables, and always will, albeit not in the first generation perhaps, but that anathema, the blue-eyed sable, may crop up in succeeding generations. The blue-eyed sable, being genetically a merle, may produce merles when mated to any colour, but it is nevertheless to be abhorred.

The mating of merle × merle is sometimes carried out, and often most successfully indeed, but herein lies a danger—the production of defective white puppies, wholly or partially white, puppies born blind, deaf, or both, and, carried to extremes, puppies born with deformed eyes or no eyes at all.

The breeder who mates merle to merle where the resultant litter will have three or four more merle grandparents is taking a risk somewhat beyond the bounds of safety, but it is a mating which frequently produces winners—Champions have been bred that way. The defective whites born from such double-merle matings usually find their way into the bucket—or some more humane end in these enlightened days—but the blue-eyed whites could prove most useful, for, mated to tricolours, they frequently produce merles of singular colour excellence.

Shelties are so unpredictable in the colour-breeding pattern that the oddest things can happen. There has never been a very clear-cut male blue-merle line; the colour has cropped up in each of the lines for two or three generations and faded away again.

In the families, much the same thing has happened except

that Family 9 did at one time breed an extremely strong strain of blue merles, but more recently the family seems to have been better known for its C.C. winners in the other colours, until today there is no C.C. winning blue merle in direct descent from Family 9.

This is in part the fault of the breeders. Mrs Baker kept her Houghton Hill blues very pure, but others were only too ready to cross a merle with a sable. At the same time it is only fair to say that the unorganized behaviour of Sheltie genes has played a very big part in the determination of this colour. For example, some years ago the author mated a beautifully coloured blue-merle bitch to a tricolour dog with so little white that he was almost a black-and-tan. This was, then, the almost ideal mating and there was absolutely no possibility of a mismating, yet this little blue merle bitch produced four puppies, three of them orange-sable and white, and the fourth a sable merle. This latter dog, Swizz from Shiel, looked, when young, exactly like marmalade, patched orange all over; but when mature it was very difficult to tell that he was not a true-bred sable-and-white for he was a good colour except for a tiny bit of mottling on his head, and his eyes were of the darkest possible shade of brown.

Swizz was mated to another excellently coloured blue merle, Riverhill Riotous, and the litter contained one good-coloured blue, two tricolours and two sable merles, the latter both bitches. One of them, Riverhill Remarkable, was mated to a merle-bred tricolour and produced the good-coloured blue merle Ch. Riverhill Respectable. But despite numerous other matings to merles, tricolours and sables, Remarkable lived up to her name in that she always managed to throw at least one sable merle every time.

This instance is related to show how, even with the very best intentions, it is so difficult to breed the blue merles true in our breed. There was no apparent reason at all for Swizz to be anything but a real blue merle, and yet no blues were born in that litter. There seems little doubt that the question of miscoloured blue merles must be related to the visual tricolour who is in reality no such thing. This is dealt with in this chapter.

The blue merle as a show dog has long been fascinating

only to a minority of breeders, and in Shelties, success in this colour is very much more difficult to obtain than it is in Collies, for in the smaller breed there is no very clearly defined line or family from which one can expect unfailingly to breed good blue merles, good either in type or colour.

Peat goes down in history as the first blue to win a C.C., and the word blue alone is used on purpose, for he was not in fact a merle, being smoky blue all over, so the honour of being the first blue merle to win a C.C. goes to Eltham Park Bluette in bitches and to Kilravock Blue Cloud in dogs, both of them winning in 1928, but neither of them gained their titles, and Ch. Downfield Blue Mist became the breed's first blue merle Champion, one year later. Even then there was no consistency, and the next C.C. winning blue did not appear for some years and then did not trace its ancestry direct to the earlier dogs.

Today, despite the fact that we have several blue merle Champions, none trace their inheritance back to the same families as the earlier ones, though of necessity they all tie with the line CHE or BB, but not in true blue descent.

5

THE STANDARD AND ITS
INTERPRETATION

As HAS been said in the chapter on the history of the breed, the standard, at least in certain of its aspects, has at times given rise to continuous argument and change.

Fortunately the three breed clubs in the country finally agreed upon a standard, and in 1948, when the Kennel Club officially published the standards of all the breeds, it became even more difficult to alter any part of it. However, in 1964 work began on a revision, and this was passed by the Kennel Club on June 28 1965.

CHARACTERISTICS. *To enable the Shetland Sheepdog to fulfil its natural bent for sheepdog work, its physical structure should be on the lines of strength and activity, free from clodiness and without any trace of coarseness. Although the desired type is similar to that of the Rough Collie, there are marked differences that must be noted. The expression, being one of the most marked characteristics of the breed, is obtained by the perfect balance and combination of skull and foreface, size, shape, colour and placement of eyes, correct position and carriage of ears, all harmoniously blended to produce that almost indefinable look of sweet, alert, gentle intelligence.*

The Shetland Sheepdog should show affection and response to his owner; he may show reserve to strangers, but not to the point of nervousness.

GENERAL APPEARANCE. *The Shetland Sheepdog should instantly appeal as a dog of great beauty, intelligence and alertness. Action lithe and graceful with speed and jumping power great for its size. The outline should be symmetrical so that no part appears out of proportion to the whole. An abundance of coat, mane and frill, with shapeliness of head and sweetness of expression all combine to present the ideal Shetland Sheepdog that will inspire and secure admiration.*

51

The inclusion of the new paragraph 'Characteristics' and the amplification of the paragraph 'General Appearance' have in themselves gone a very long way to simplifying the interpretation of the standard. It is now quite definitely stated that the Sheltie is not, in fact, a Rough Collie in miniature, as the

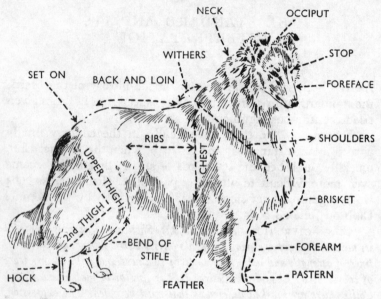

Diagram of Shetland Sheepdog

Miniature Poodle or Miniature Dachshund are an exact copy of their larger counterparts.

HEAD AND SKULL. *The skull should be refined, and its shape, when viewed from the top or side is a long, blunt wedge, tapering from ear to nose. The width of the skull necessarily depends upon the combined length of skull and muzzle, and the whole must be considered in connection with the size of the dog. The skull should be flat, moderately wide between the ears, showing no prominence of the occipital bone. Cheeks should be flat and merge smoothly into a well-rounded muzzle. Skull and muzzle to be of equal length; central point to be the inner corner of the eye. In profile the topline of the skull should be parallel to the topline of the muzzle, but on a higher plane due to a slight but definite stop. Lips should be tight.*

The clause dealing with head properties is fairly fully set out, but it still demands a good deal of explanation. (Figs. 1 and 2.)

In describing the head it is essential that the skull and foreface should be taken together, for they are indivisible. A 'two-piece' head, when the skull and muzzle do not fit, and do not mould one into the other, is most undesirable. The tendency,

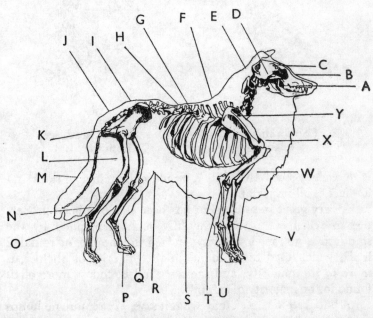

A—Muzzle
B—Stop. Foreface is muzzle, just below and in front of stop
C—Skull
D—Cheeks
E—Neck
F—Withers
G—Ribs; chest
H—Back
I—Loin
J—Croup or Rump
K—Hipbone
L—Thigh
M—Tail

N—Feathers. Breeching
O—Hock joint
P—Location of right hind dewclaw
Q—Stifle joint
R—Flank
S—Body
T—Elbow
U—Feather or foreleg
V—Knee. Between this and the foot is the pastern
W—Brisket
X—Point of shoulder
Y—Shoulder

Anatomical Diagram of Shetland Sheepdog.

Drawing by Geraldine Kerry from *The English Shetland Sheepdog Club Handbook*, 1951 immediately after the war, to breed for length of head at any price, and the longer it was the more 'Collie type' it was considered to be, led to heads with muzzles far too fine for the skull, and as I once heard it described, 'The Sheltie folk say their dogs have a Collie head when in fact all they have is an apple

1. Correct shape of   2. Correct head, seen
        head   from the front

with a cigar stuck on it!' The moulding together of skull and foreface is all-important.

A very great improvement has been made in head-properties in recent years, and the 'flat skull' demanded by the standard is no longer a rarity; indeed the 'apple', or rounded head, which used to be found in the majority of Shelties, is more in the minority, and the flat skull is, today, more often found in the majority of exhibits.

A flat skull means exactly what it says. We require no lumps or bumps, neither longways nor sideways, but instead a smooth rounded surface, and the bone above the arch of the eyes should also be moulded and not protrude, the whole making one clean line back to the occiput.

The 'apple-head' is, of course, most undesirable, as is a 'bumpy' skull. The idea to be aimed at can be clearly seen from the sketches accompanying this chapter.

It is most important also that the standard demands a skull *'moderately wide between the ears,* tapering towards the eyes' and not 'head should be as narrow as possible'. Although sometimes too wide a skull will give an impression of coarseness, very often an over-wide head is due to a rounded skull, and again is most undesirable.

'*A slight but definite stop.*' BUT THERE SHOULD BE A STOP. Too many Shelties today, as a result of the concentration of flatness and length of head, are being produced with virtually no stop at all, and in many cases, instead of there being a 'stop', there is a slight rise between the eyes. (Fig. 3.)

When the Sheltie head is viewed from the side it should not be one continuous line from occiput to nose-tip, there *must* be the slight depression between the eyes, which gives a head of two parallel lines, the line of the muzzle being just below the line of the skull.

3. No stop,
Roman nose

'*Cheeks flat.*' This is a most important point, for the flatness of cheek-bones makes all the difference between a clean and a coarse head. Flat cheek-bones give the necessary moulding between skull and muzzle, while prominent cheek-bones, which usually tend to become worse and worse with age, give a thick appearance to the head.

The standard says 'Skull and muzzle to be of equal length'. It is essential that these distances be equal, for, if not, the whole balance of head is ruined. (Fig. 4.)

Seen from on top, the head should form an elongated triangle with clean-cut side lines and no hollows or promontories; in fact, a perfect wedge. Seen from the side, again it should be a wedge, and there should be a very definite, though not prominent, chin.

The muzzle should be beautifully moulded and rounded in all directions and should show no lines, corners or flat surfaces. A 'veined' foreface is also undesirable, although it may be found that a young dog will become 'veiny' from nerves or excitement at its early shows. These veins, however, will not fill when the dog is a little older and becomes used to show going.

A weak muzzle is one in which there is insufficient mould-ing and, instead of running cleanly from nose to skull (Fig. 4), when seen from on top, there are wavy lines and indentations down its length. 'Snipy' means a weak, narrow foreface, with no moulding or strength to it, which tapers too much to the nose. 'Lippy' is when there is an excess of loose skin on the lips which is reminiscent of a hound or spaniel.

Overall, the most important point in describing the head is balance. As has already been said, the standard lays down the

4. Stop too pronounced,
receding skull, 'snipy'
jaws

balance for us—equal length from occiput to stop as from stop to nose-tip.

EYES. '*Should be of medium size, obliquely set and of almond shape, colour dark brown* (*except in the case of Merles where blue is permissible*). (*Fig.* 5.)

The standard description is full enough, and easy to under-stand, but the eyes are a most important feature, for they give expression to the dog. The tendency in the majority of Shelties is to a round eye (Fig. 6) and few still are the dogs with the desired almond eye. Without the true eye the 'alert, gentle look' cannot be present to the full, and further, the 'oblique' placement which is also demanded, cannot appear, when the eye is round, and again, without it, the beauty of expression cannot be complete. Expression is also spoilt if the eye is too small. (Fig. 7.) Eye colour is clearly defined, except that for blue merles, for in fact the impression given is that blue eyes are permissible, whereas it is more correct to say that blue, part blue or flecked eyes are permissible in a merle, and this point is much better described in the Collie standard, which says, speaking of merles, 'when the eyes are frequently, one or both, or part of one or both, blue and white or china'.

EARS. '*Should be small and moderately wide at the base, placed fairly close together on top of the skull. When in repose they should be thrown back, but when on the alert brought forward and carried semi-erect with the tips dropping forward.*'

Ears are fully described, and the correct shape and placement of ears can be seen from the sketch far better than they can

5. Correct eye and   6. Eye too round   7. Eye too small
      ear   and mean

be described in words. (Figs. 5–10.) The correct ear size, placement and carriage are extremely important, for they, too, count so much towards expression. The correct semi-erect ear must be bred for, although most puppies' ears need a little training.

It seems that in ear placement there is a deal of difference between the Collie and the Sheltie, and because of this difference the Sheltie can never, in my opinion, be a complete Collie in miniature. The Collie standard for ears, in contrast to our own, reads 'not placed too close together on top of the skull'. The closer ear placement of the Sheltie gives the breed a rather more alert look than its bigger brother's, and often when one sees a Sheltie which has a real Collie outlook it is one in which the ears are just a shade too far apart to be quite correct by Sheltie standards. Further, Sheltie ears are relatively larger than Collie ears.

TEETH. The lower incisors should fit closely behind the upper incisors, giving a 'scissor' bite. (Fig. 11.) A 'pincer' bite, in which the edges of the two sets of teeth meet, is undesirable. An overshot mouth (Fig. 12), one in which the top jaw is longer than the lower jaw, or an undershot mouth (Fig. 13), which is the reverse of overshot, is a fault.

As in a great number of other breeds, there is a tendency in Shelties for some of the teeth to be missing and special importance should be paid to this point. The missing teeth are usually

8. Correct ears   9. Incorrect ears   10. Prick ears

pre-molars (the first double teeth immediately behind the canines). Missing teeth are now counted as a fault.

NECK. '*Should be muscular, well-arched, and of sufficient length to carry the head proudly.*' Important this, for a short neck detracts a great deal from the graceful, lithe outline. Further, a short neck almost always denotes a straight shoulder, and the overall appearance it gives is one of 'stuffiness'. The arched neck is a most desirable feature, not seen nearly often enough, and its lack is a point demanding the attention of all breeders.

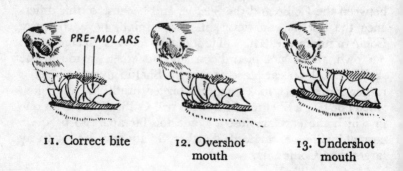

PRE-MOLARS

11. Correct bite   12. Overshot   13. Undershot
                            mouth   mouth

BODY AND QUARTERS. *From the withers the shoulder blade should slope at a 45 degree angle, forward and downward to the shoulder joint. At the withers they are separated only by the vertebrae but they must slope outwards to accommodate the desired spring of ribs. The upper arm should join the shoulder at as nearly a right-angle as possible. The elbow joint to be equidistant from the ground at the withers. The forelegs should be straight when viewed from the front, muscular and clean, with strong bone. Pasterns strong and flexible. The body is slightly longer from the withers to the root of the tail than the height at the withers, but most of the length is due to the proper angulation of shoulders and hindquarters. The chest should be deep, reaching to the point of the elbow. The ribs well sprung but tapering at their lower half to allow free play of the forelegs and shoulders. The back should be level, with a graceful sweep over the loins and the croup should slope gradually to the rear. The thigh should be broad and muscular, the thigh bones to be set into the pelvis at right angles, corresponding to the angle of the shoulder blade. The stifle joint, where the femur bone joins the tibia bone, must have a distinct angle. Hock joint to be clean cut, angular and well let down with strong bone. The hock must be straight when viewed from behind.*

The revision of the standard took a very important step when it amalgamated the three clauses in the old standard (Forequarters, Body and Hindquarters) under one heading, for the body must always be viewed as a whole.

14. Correct hock and
hindquarters

Unfortunately few Sheltie folk, even the judges, seem to understand what is meant by a well-laid shoulder, or a sloping shoulder. Our anatomical portrait shows it to perfection. The slope is in the angle the shoulder makes with the upper arm, and there should be a long, oblique line from the point of the shoulder to the withers.

In the same way, the line from the hip-joint to the point of the hindquarters should again be long and sloping and form an angle of about 90 degrees with the thighbone.

15. Straight stifles and hocks. Short tail and 'brushed-out' coat with 'sway' back

From correct shoulder and hip placement we get the correct length of body without length of back. Length of body and length of back mean two completely different things which must never be confused. An overlong or too short body is the result of wrong shoulder and hip placement, but an overlong or too short back is the result of the bones of the back itself (those bones from behind the ribs to the loin) being either too long or too short. A long back is usually a weak back and often shows that undesirable feature, a distinct dip in the middle (Fig. 15), known as 'sway-back'. Equally it is a fault, and an indication of weakness and faulty construction, for the back to curve upwards, known as a 'roach back'.

Well-sprung ribs means that the ribs, from their junction with the backbone, should curve outwards, giving a very well-rounded appearance to the body. A flat, or slab-sided, dog is one in which the ribs are not well sprung, and such a dog usually has an upright shoulder, for the lack of spring of rib interferes with the well-laid shoulder placement and, in addition, he is less able to do a full day's work for he has less lung and heart room.

Strength of loin must never be ignored, for without the lovely sweeping turn over the loin the grace of outline is lost.

Depth of chest, too, is essential, for without it the dog is insufficiently equipped to do a day's work. Viewed from the front, the edge of the brisket should be clearly apparent just below the level of the elbow. If the brisket stops before it reaches elbow level, or worse still, rises inward to a point, faulty action and inefficiency must result.

A too-narrow chest means that the forelegs must always be too close together, giving the appearance of 'both legs out of one hole', and the dog is therefore tied in elbow.

The front legs should be straight, and the 'good bone' demanded does not mean that the legs should look like tree-trunks, but that the leg bone should be of sufficient strength to support the general framework, and that it should fit into the overall balance of the dog. The bone should be well-rounded; flat, or thin bone is undesirable.

Viewed from behind, the hind legs, too, should be perfectly straight (Fig. 15), whether standing or moving, and the hocks should be turned neither in nor out. The inturned hocks are known as cow-hocks. (Fig. 16.) Viewed from the side, the hind-quarters should be a long, flowing curve of well-bent stifle, and well-let-down hocks. (Fig. 17.) The correct set-on of tail, too, is inseparable from good body outline; neither too high nor too low. (See also Fig. 23.)

TAIL. *Set on low, tapering bone must reach at least to the hock joint, with abundant hair and slight upward sweep; raised when the dog is moving, but never over the level of the back.*

FEET. '*Oval in shape, soles well padded, toes arched and close together.*' This is self-explanatory. (Figs. 18 and 19.) A thin foot

(Fig. 20), in which the pads are not springy and resilient, or a foot in which the toes are spread, or a round foot (Fig. 21) are unsuited to the breed.

16. Cow-hocks, narrow hindquarters

17. Correct tail carriage and tail length. Correct bend of stifle

GAIT. *The action of the Shetland Sheepdog should denote speed and smoothness. There should be no pacing, plaiting, rolling or stiff, stilted up and down movement.*

18. Correct foot

19. Correct ovalfoot

The writing of this new clause is a very great help, for it had never before been stated just how we expect a Sheltie to move, and the description of the absolute smoothness of action required should be very carefully noted. The floating grace of a true moving Sheltie is one of the great features of our breed, and while

20. Weak thin foot, weak pastern 'knuckled over'

21. Incorrect round foot

such action must be bred for, by using only dogs of correct conformation in one's breeding programme, a great deal will also depend upon how your puppy is reared, both how it is fed and how it is exercised.

22. Incorrect short tail, but correct stifle bend. Correctly 'fitting' coat

23. Gay tail and straight stifle

While most Shelties will put each forefoot almost into the mark made by the one before, there must be no accentuation of this action which results in plaiting.

The Sheltie is an exceptionally fast dog for its size, and a light free graceful movement at all paces is essential. The walk and trot should be slow and springy and the feet should be kept close to the ground at all times. Real 'daisy-cutting' action is highly desirable. The gallop should be flowing and effortless and full of movement. Such should be the overall conformation of the dog that there should be no jarring in movement, and untiring action should result. The jumping power of the Sheltie is very remarkable for the size of the dog, but only a Sheltie which is correctly balanced, whose shoulder placement and hip placement are correct, can have the great amount of power which is so typical of a good specimen of the breed.

COAT. *'Must be double—the outer coat of long hair of harsh texture and straight, the undercoat soft (resembling fur) short and close. The mane and frill should be very abundant and forelegs well feathered. Hind legs above the hocks profusely covered with hair, but below the hocks fairly smooth. The mask of face smooth. What are commonly known as "smooth-coated" specimens are barred.'*

Here is a good description but one might stress that the outer coat should be absolutely straight, with no waves or curls. Soft silky coat would be most unpracticable as it would rapidly become saturated with rain or mist. The undercoat is extremely important and something which, in the majority of Shelties, is sadly lacking today. This undercoat should be so short and dense that it is almost impossible to see the dog's skin through it. It is the density of this undercoat which produces the correct stand-off coat in the Sheltie. But a 'stand-off' coat should never be confused with a 'stand-up' coat. Far too many Shelties are shown with their coats brushed up, standing away from the body all round, and so ruining the outline of the dog. (Fig. 15.) The correct stand-off coat is a coat in which the outer hairs are held up by the undercoat to within an inch or so of the body, and then the tips of these hairs turn over, lie backwards and form themselves into the perfect covering in line with the body of the dog. It is so important that a coat should fit the dog. (Fig. 22.) *'The mask or face smooth.'* Here it might be added that very fine silky hair on the face and skull is a definite asset, as it tends to

Ch. Rivershill Rescuer

AND HIS GRAND-DAUGHTER

D. G. Davis, Orpington

Ch. Sheer Sauce from Shiel

Wallace, foundation dog of the male line BB

AND HIS GREAT-GRANDSON

Ch. Specks of Mountfort

Ch. Nicky of Aberlour, a 1938 representative
of line BB

H. Armstrong

Ch. Helensdale Ace, a modern representative
of line BB

Sheltie champions of yesteryear

Ch. Eltham Park Elda; Miss Rogers and Ch. Riverhill Rufus; Mrs Sangster and Ch. Spendthrift of Exford; Mrs Allen and Ch. Tilford Tweed; Lt.-Col. the Hon. B. Russell's Honey of Crawleyridge; Miss E. P. Montgomery and Peabody Pannino; Mrs Baker and Ch. Blue Blossom of Houghton Hill (almost hidden); Miss B. Thynne and Ch. Marble Faun of Houghton Hill

Ch. Alasdair of Tintobank,
son of Ch. Helensdale Ace

make the whole head look finer and better moulded. Certain strains produce this very fine head hair, others are much more bristly, and attention to breeding for this point could give happy results.

COLOUR. *'Tricolours' should be an intense black on the body with no signs of ticking; rich tan markings on a tricolour to be preferred. 'Sables' may be clear or shaded, any colour from gold to deep mahogany, but in its shade the colour should be rich in tones. Wolf sable and grey colours are undesirable. 'Blue Merles': clear, silvery blue is desired, splashed and marbled with black. Rich tan markings to be preferred, but their absence not to be counted as a fault. Heavy black markings, slate coloured or rusty tinge either in top coat or undercoat is highly undesirable. General effect should be blue. White markings may be shown in the blaze, collar, chest, frill, legs, stifle and tip of tail. All or some tan markings may be shown on eye brows, cheeks, legs, stifle and under tail. All or some of the white markings are to be preferred whatever the colour of the dog, but the absence of these markings shall not be considered a fault. 'Black and White' or 'Black and Tan' are also recognized colours. Over markings of patches of white on the body are highly undesirable. The nose black whatever the colour of the dog.*

SIZE. *Ideal height measured at the withers 14 inches for bitches, 14½ inches for dogs. Anything more than 1 inch above these heights considered to be a serious fault.*

FAULTS. *Domed or receding skull; lack of stop; large drooping or pricked ears; over-developed cheeks; weak jaw; snipy muzzle; not full complement of teeth; crooked forelegs; cow hocks; tail kinked, short or carried over back; white or white colour predominating; pink- or flesh-coloured nose; blue eyes in any colour other than blue merles; nervousness; full or light eye; under- or overshot mouth.*

Note – Male animals should have two apparently normal testicles fully descended into the scrotum.

6

HOW TO BEGIN
FOUNDING YOUR KENNEL

Dog breeding is rather like swimming. There are three ways of going about it: you can be thrown in, fall in, or actually learn the subject properly. For the purposes of this chapter I am going to assume that you have not already been thrown in or fallen in, but that you really want to learn the job thoroughly.

Assuming you have already made up your mind that it is Shelties you want to breed, then, if you possibly can, spend six months at least as a trainee in a reputable kennel of the breed, where you will have every opportunity to learn all you can. I say 'six months at least', but this is barely long enough as it does not give you time to carry through the rearing of even one litter, and the ideal period surely would be a year. Much can be learnt from books, but it is this practical experience which really counts.

It is not always easy in any breed to find the right kennel, for you want to be sure it is one where the owner is willing to pass on his or her knowledge, not only the practical knowledge of management, rearing and grooming, but—and almost more important—the knowledge of the strains and families within the breed, and a clear picture of the past which you, as a new-comer, can gain only by hearsay.

Rather naturally many breeders want to guard their secrets, but you must find one who has the interests of the future of the breed at heart, and whose only aim is not simply to defeat his fellows in the ring. There are breeders who can see far enough ahead, and who are anxious that the work they have done shall be carried on when they can no longer do it themselves. It is in a kennel such as this, and from this kind of breeder, that you want to learn, from someone who will help you to carry on where the present older generation of Sheltie breeders must, perforce, eventually leave off. Those breeders who want to see the Sheltie go forward will help you right enough. You will fairly easily discover to which of these groups a breeder belongs if you ask a few questions.

For your part, there must be a great willingness to learn. There are many novices who start out asserting they are keen to learn, but who really only want to 'get there quickly' without putting in any groundwork. A 'get-there-quick' plan is almost never a 'stay-at-the-top' plan. It is the consistent breeder who, from a small kennel and a few brood bitches, turns out top-class winners year after year, and who has undoubtedly put the greatest amount of study, brain and common sense into his breeding plan, who will consistently achieve top honours. Too much real knowledge and good hard spadework are needed in this dog business for anyone to stay at the top the easy way.

Remember too that if you are hoping to be able to learn by picking the brains of someone who has spent many years building up a successful strain, you are expecting to gain great assistance and privilege from this, and on your side you must be ready to help in every possible way in the general daily routine of the kennel. No job in the kennel is too humble to be done well by you in your training. Kennel life is not all feeding and playing with puppies and taking dogs for walks! There are plenty of irksome chores to do and there are long hours; all-night sessions with a sick dog or a bitch giving birth to her puppies; late nights and early risings, but there are also new young hopes, and show-ring prizes and great satisfaction in the work. It is a job where one never ceases to learn. Even after years and years of breeding there is always something new turning up.

Should you happen to be one of the few who can still afford to pay big prices for top-class winning stock, and should you go out and buy a certificate-winning bitch and a Champion dog, it may avail you nothing except a few more prizes in the ring, for unless you have a deep-seated knowledge behind the purchase those two high priced and beautiful animals will perhaps breed nothing better than pups for the pet market. Someone less well blessed with this world's goods, but with a great deal more knowledge of the strains and breeding programmes which have brought success, may, however, produce next year's top dogs from parents hardly fit to grace the ring, and at a fraction of the cost of your big winners.

Your first task must be to read all you can, and especially

about the standard of your chosen breed, and to learn to interpret that standard to the best of your ability. The standard is the yardstick by which any specimen of a breed must be measured. Read it and read it and read it again—then go to a show, taking a copy of the standard with you for reference, and in your own mind line up each Sheltie you see against the 'mind-dog' you have drawn from the reading of the standard. Go to show after show, and at each of them ask question after question of establishment breeders. Do remember, though, that there is a time for all things, and don't expect the harassed exhibitor arriving at the show with three or four dogs, and having a bare thirty minutes in which to get them ready before the first class will be called into the ring, to be willing at that moment to answer your queries. No, in the morning, if Shelties are first in the ring, wander round the benches if you will, but, without interrupting hard work, look at the dogs and then take a seat at the ringside, and with your catalogue in your hand, watch the judging intently. At the big Championship shows catalogues are expensive, but they are a 'must' to a would-be seeker after knowledge; you just cannot follow the judging without one.

When the judging is over the exhibitors will have time to help you, and I know they will be willing to do so. The judge, too (provided he is not rushing off to judge some other breed), will probably be only too pleased to explain his placings in a certain class if perhaps they have worried you. But again a word of warning. There are various ways of asking questions. The approach, 'I watched your judging; why did you put Mr A's Sheltie over Mrs B's Rusty?' is much less likely to meet with a kind and helpful reply than: 'I am trying my hardest to learn about the breed before starting in Shelties myself, and I was watching you judge. I wonder if you would mind telling me what you liked so much about Mr A's Sheltie?'

There are very few Sheltie breeders who will not be anxious to help you; most of us remember the days when we were beginners, too, and the questions we used to ask the then top-flight breeders.

Few of us these days have either the time or the money to start with a lot of dogs, and anyway you are much more likely to achieve success if you start with one or two. Besides, the temptation to keep several puppies from your first litters is almost beyond resisting and so, in no time at all, you no longer have just one or two.

When choosing your stock, here again be prepared to put yourself in the hands of the established winning breeders. Ask to be allowed to visit the kennels, explain that you haven't yet quite decided what stock you intend starting with, and go from kennel to kennel looking at the type and general standard of quality within each kennel before you part with any of your precious cash. But, at the same time, don't expect us not to try to sell you something while you are there—we shouldn't be human if we didn't.

You will note that between the different kennels and the different strains there is a fairly wide divergence of type. It is up to you to decide which of the types, in your opinion, comes nearly within the pattern of the standard, then to see which of the kennels has that type most clearly defined in all the dogs in the kennel. When you have decided this you will have chosen the kennel from which you wish to make your initial purchases.

Remember that the dog and bitch are to the breeder what paints and canvas are to an artist. They are the medium with which your beautiful picture, your perfect dog, will be built. You are the embryo artist when you set out to breed your first litter, but you are working with flesh and blood, and where the painter can erase his errors and horrible mistakes with a few swift strokes of the brush, your errors and mistakes will grow for all to see, and you cannot destroy them without being inhumanly ruthless. If you are planning to breed Shelties seriously, then you are taking on a great trust; the art of breeding something beautiful is almost a dedication. You must be prepared for heartbreak; you will learn the hard way if you are to learn at all, but if you set out with the desire and purpose clearly before you you will surely attain the heights and you will surely also have with you the good wishes and help of all those of us who are already trying to do the same thing.

Look to it, then, that we as creators of this beauty maintain it at the highest possible level. Our purpose must be to build on foundations already laid, until we have produced a Sheltie nearer to perfection than any which we have yet seen.

The next chapter deals with the purchase of foundation stock and the other things you will want when you obtain your first Sheltie, but here I want to make you realize just what is so much needed in any dog breeder who is not merely the owner of a 'puppy-factory'. Each one of us needs patience, perseverance, practice. Patience to give us endurance to face all our setbacks—and they will be many; perseverance to start again when all our planned matings have turned out wrongly; and practice which will come when we get plenty of these setbacks.

All that I have said already is, of course, the ideal—but now how about coming down to earth and being rather more practical. You have already 'fallen in', I expect, before having this book in your hands, and your first Sheltie may already be yours. Doubtless, then, someone will come along with the suggestion that, 'It's a nice kind of dog; why don't you show it?' Possibly the idea appeals, you immediately rush off to find details of the shows, and off you go on the due date with your Sheltie on the lead and your hopes high. Back you come at night, but your hopes have been dashed; your dog just didn't make the grade. Now you may belong to one of two groups of people, one group being those who say, 'Dog shows are silly anyway: I'm not going to bother any more.' If you belong to that group I doubt whether you would be reading this book, so more certainly you belong to the other group which says: 'That was rather fun: I'd like to go again. I'd like to do some winning and have a shot at beating the big names.' In short, you have been bitten, and the disease known as the 'dog game' is a very violent one from which the patient never recovers—he simply gets worse. Your desire now is to have a good Sheltie, or, better still, to breed a good one, and your question—'How am I to go about it?'

You must consider carefully the situation in which you are placed. Have you enough room to breed a litter and keep several of the puppies, which you will need to do if you want to find yourself with a good one to show? It takes years of practice to pick out your certain best in the litter as soon as it is born, and in the early days at least you will have to 'run on' several youngsters so that you can be sure you are not parting with a possible Champion.

Can you afford to rear a litter really well? There is no chance that you will make a fortune at the dog game, and not much that you will even make it pay its way, at least until you are

breeding stock that is able to carry your name to certain heights
in the show-ring. A Sheltie family, as you will learn in later
pages, costs a good deal to rear properly, and it is no good at
all skimping the early weeks of your puppies' lives. Your future
winners are made or marred during the first few months.

Assuming that your answer to these questions is satisfactory,
go ahead and plan for that kennel you hope to have.

Having decided upon the kennel from which you propose
to buy your first dog or dogs, it is nevertheless important, before
making your purchase, to be sure you have suitable accommodation for the puppy, or adult, when you bring it home.

A Sheltie, kept as a house pet, is ideal, but even then the
dog wants a place it can call its own, and a corner where it
will readily learn it can remain undisturbed. Whether puppy or
adult, the dog wants a bed which is cosy and out of a draught,
and to me the ideal place is a tea-chest, laid on its side, and
with a piece of wood about 4 in. wide nailed across the lower
part of the box to keep in the bedding, whatever it may be.

However, if you are planning to breed a litter from your
Sheltie you will require a place other than a box in the house,
and the most convenient, both from the point of view of the
dog and of the owner, is a shed at least 6 ft. by 4 ft. and high
enough for one to be able to stand up in without braining one-
self every time. The shed should have a run or some kind of
enclosure attached to it, and the bigger this is the better, for
the adult dog, as well as the puppies, will want to use it, and a
Sheltie litter, to do it itself well, needs plenty of playing space.

Assuming then that you have the accommodation ready,
there are two probable methods of starting your kennel. First,
and the most usual method, is to start with a puppy. Now there
is a great deal to be said both for and against this method. You
are probably longing to have a puppy to bring up yourself, to
train in your ways and to watch through all the changing
months of its early life. All these are points in favour of having
a puppy—and there is only one thing better than having a
puppy and that is having two puppies. They are less trouble
than one, they keep each other out of mischief and each acts
as the other's plaything; two puppies together are always
occupied. As a general rule, puppies do much better in pairs
or more than does one isolated baby, and you will usually find

that the bigger breeder, purchasing a puppy to add to a kennel, will nearly always buy a second, one of the same age, to 'run with' the first (unless there is already a puppy of the same age at home), and when the pups are older will discard the unwanted one. Against starting with a puppy is the long wait until you can show and breed from it. There is also the risk, ever present, that the pup may not turn out as well as was hoped, and you may then have to start all over again, for the breeder who sells you the puppy, no matter how reputable and honest, can only say what he or she thinks is likely to make a top show-specimen. You yourself may be at fault if it does not turn out right; so much depends on the rearing of a puppy.

Let us assume that you have decided to start with a puppy. You will write to the owner of the kennel whose dogs pleased you most, asking what stock the owner has for sale, and not forgetting, please, to say exactly what you want—dog or bitch puppy, approximate age, colour, show potential or not, and anything else you can think of; you have no idea of the amount of correspondence wasted when you simply write and say, 'Have you any puppies for sale?' The poor breeder may have four or five litters ready when you write, and obviously cannot detail each pup without having some idea of what you are after. He may even breed more than one breed of dog. Having discovered that the kennel in question has pups of the desired age, etc., make an appointment to call. I say 'make an appointment' not because the average kennel owner is afraid to be caught unexpectedly, but because, in these days of staff difficulties, the owner may not always be available and you may choose a moment when no one is at home. Even if kennel-maids are there, the potential purchaser will usually learn far more if the breeder himself is present.

If you have decided on a puppy of about eight to twelve weeks, then you will do best to place yourself in the hands of the breeder and say, 'Look, I want a puppy that I shall be able to show, and one that will be well worth breeding from.' Most of us are honest, and on approach like this will do our best to help. The potential purchaser who most enrages a breeder is either the one who comes along and says, 'Of course, I only want a pet,' pays a pet price and later blames the breeder when it does not win in the ring; or the complete novice who (and I quote an actual case) comes and says, 'I want the best puppy you have got, but I'm not taking the one you pick for me, I want to pick my own.' In the true story I am telling this happened when there were over twenty puppies—not Shelties —from several litters, all in one large run. I removed the two pups I was not prepared to sell at all, and let the prospective buyer spend as much time as she liked with the pups. She asked me the price for the pick of the remaining pups and I told her. Later she came along with one of the very worst puppies of the whole lot, laid the cash on the table and asked for the pedigree. I tried to point out that she had picked a pup which would never win anything and would hardly be worth breeding from, but she knew best, and was certain that my protestations were because she had chosen the best pup. The results were obvious, and needless to say the pup never did any good, but rather to my surprise she bred a winner. Do place yourself in the breeders' hands—you will almost certainly get a square deal.

One more point on the question of two puppies. The beginner is well advised not to go in for a dog puppy. So often one is asked for a dog and bitch puppy, 'suitable for mating together later'. This is a mistake. Either put the money you planned to spend on two puppies into one really tip-top bitch puppy (it will repay you hands down in the end) or, if you want two, make it two bitch puppies. After all, the very best dogs in the land are available to anyone for a reasonable fee, and you are much more likely to breed a top-class puppy in this way than if you start with a dog and bitch pup. Always remember that it is your duty to your fellow-breeders and your chosen breed to breed only from the *very best*; second-rate foundation stock is useless. A bitch with a first-class pedigree, and who in herself is good, but perhaps useless for the ring as the result of an accident, will so often be just what you want, in that she will most probably 'produce the goods', and her price will be reasonable.

Consider the possibility of starting with an adult, and here I am certainly writing only in terms of bitches, for an adult dog, if he is really a 'top-notcher', will cost a great deal of money, if he is for sale at all, and if he is not a top-notcher he is not worth purchasing for all the use he will be to you.

A good adult bitch is not come by cheaply either, but she is much more likely to repay her purchase price than is a dog.

There is yet another avenue. The average large kennel has not enough room to keep all the brood bitches it requires, and very often the owner is willing either to sell a bitch 'on part breeding terms', or to lease a bitch. The latter method is not one I like as I consider it unsatisfactory to both parties, but the 'breeding-terms' plan is usually good, and of great benefit to the novice starting out. Actual terms will naturally depend upon the quality of the bitch in question, her age, etc., but frequently you will find that a bitch, soon to be ready for mating, will be let out 'on terms' of, say, half her value in cash and a certain number of puppies from her first litter, to be selected by her original owner. Generally the agreement goes a little further and covers exactly the arrangements for the payment of the stud fee; it probably states that the stud dog is to be selected by the original owner of the bitch, has a clause covering the loss of the bitch before the terms of the agreement are fulfilled, and another stating that, when the terms have been completed, the bitch shall then become the unconditional property of the purchaser. (A specimen agreement will be found in the Appendix.) As a rule, the vendor remains the registered owner of the bitch and appears as the registered breeder of the litter, but this is a matter for mutual agreement. Whatever the arrangement, your share of the litter should be registered with your own kennel name and not that of the original owner.

To me, this is an ideal way of starting, as you are reasonably sure of getting a good beginning. The choice of the stud dog usually rests with the original owner, and as a result of this you will have his years of experience behind you; the choice is likely to be a much wiser one than you, without very much experience as yet, would be able to make for yourself. Further, if some of the puppies are to come back to him, the vendor will be most anxious that they shall be well reared, and you will receive every possible help in this direction too, ultimately possessing two real assets: probably the second-best puppy in the litter for your own and the bitch herself.

Weigh up carefully the pros and cons of each method of founding your kennel, then go ahead and do what seems to you to be the best.

7

ESTABLISHING A STRAIN

SURELY the ambition of all breeders, large or small, is to breed a Champion. 'Oh, anyone can breed a Champion,' you hear people say, and with a certain amount of truth. Anyone *can* breed a Champion, but how many can do so consistently, dogs true to type and bearing a marked resemblance to one another?

Unfortunately there are too few breeders with the necessary time, patience and money to be able to carry the task through to its conclusion. You will notice that I do not list knowledge as a necessary qualification, and there is a reason for this. If you have time and patience the knowledge can be acquired, but unless it is acquired, all other qualifications are useless. A strain cannot be established in a few months; it is the work of years. Years of study, trial, error, disappointment and final joy when the 'dog of dreams' is evolved.

When definite traits are apparent in all the dogs from a certain kennel, then, and only then, has a strain been established. A strain is not a kennel-name, tacked willy-nilly to a collection of dogs bred in that kennel—it is real live flesh and blood, a walking advertisement of a certain breeder.

How can the breeder be sure of producing certain characteristics in his own dog? The result of years of study and research by great scientists is at our disposal, and it is up to us to apply the knowledge they have left us.

Experiments carried out by Abbé Mendel have undoubtedly been the most useful for our purpose, and they are simple to understand. It was he who proved that when two individuals, each pure for a pair of opposite characteristics (such as tallness and dwarfness in the peas with which he carried out his experiments), were crossed, the first generation of the offspring would all look like the tall parent, so determining the dominant characteristic, but carrying the factor for dwarfness recessively. When two of these hybrids were crossed, the second generation produced an average of one tall, one short, breeding pure for the characteristic, and two hybrids like the parents. The two hybrids appeared tall, as did the tall offspring, the fourth appeared short, and this did not even carry the tall factor recessively. The tall hybrids carried the factor for dwarfness and themselves produced both types of offspring.

So it is with the Sheltie today, and we are lucky that other breeders, studying along Mendelian lines, have already determined for the most part which traits in our breed are carried as dominants and which are recessives. Every individual carries a pair of factors for the same characteristics, one received by him from each of his parents. An individual in which like characteristics are paired is known as an homozygous individual, and one in which unlike characteristics are paired is known as heterozygous. Recessives are *always* homozygous and always breed true to their own type, which is a test of their purity. Naturally one can determine which type of individual each animal is only by the result of test matings. Remember, too, that one individual can be homozygous for a certain characteristic and heterozygous for others. The breeder's task is to decide what kind of factors his animals carry and how they behave in combination with the factors of the individuals.

We have a harder task than Mendel with his peas. He wanted to establish only one thing—height. With our Sheltie the factors for the various characteristics are carried differently, as has been said, and while we are trying to establish one characteristic we may so easily lose another. For example, you are trying to fix natural ears, and to this end you use dog A and bitch B. Unfortunately dog A has a slightly wavy coat, bitch B a straight coat, but this is only incompletely dominant to the wave, so the resultant litter will have a large proportion of natural ears, but a percentage will also have wavy coats. Your next task, then, will be to breed out that wavy coat and yet retain the natural ears—and so the battle goes on, fixing one characteristic, possibly to lose another, then the fight to regain the second characteristic, hold the first—and all this possibly at the cost of a third. It is this which makes our task intensely interesting and, incidentally, makes perfection so very difficult to attain.

While we accept the law that like produces like, we must also accept the other which says that no two animals are ever identical. Because no two animals are ever identical, selection is possible, and because like produces like selection is effective. It is essential in trying to produce perfection that one uses not only two dogs as near perfection themselves as is possible, and that in their deficiencies each complements the other; it is also essential that a breeder should learn to 'read' a pedigree correctly. A pedigree is not just a collection of names on paper, with perhaps the Champions written in red. It is, or it should be, a whole volume. It is the dog's family tree, and each name in it should conjure up, for the intelligent breeder, a picture of each of the ancestors in question, his good points and his bad, and all that it is possible to know about him.

The new breeder cannot be expected to do this from his own knowledge, but there are plenty of 'old hands' among us today who can still 'see' the names in the pedigrees, back to many more generations than the customary five, and who are only too willing to pass on what we know if the novice really wants to learn; but, unfortunately, there are so many beginners today in our own and every other breed who 'know it all' within six months of buying their first dog.

If the pedigree you are studying contains the name of a certain animal doubled and redoubled, then you may assume that the animal to whom the pedigree belongs carries in its genetic make-up a large proportion of the genes of that particular ancestor.

It is important to consider not only the pedigree but also the owner of the pedigree itself, for despite the 'doubling' up, or line- or in-breeding as it is called, it is possible that the dog in question may not carry a large proportion of its illustrious progenitor's genes, for despite the doubling of the line this can happen; but if the animal resembles the general type one accepts from this doubled ancestor, then one can assume that he himself carries a large proportion of similar germ-plasms.

The pedigree must not be considered alone, any more than the individual animals for mating should be considered alone. The pedigrees and the dogs must be considered together, and then one should have some idea what to expect in the immediate progeny.

There are three distinct methods of breeding. Out-crossing, line-breeding and in-breeding. All three methods have their advocates, and certainly the short cut to success, if there is such a thing, is in-breeding or very close line-breeding, but although this is a successful method it demands much care and forethought and a great knowledge of the ancestors to whom one is planning the line- or in-breeding programme. Out-crossing is the mating of two unrelated, or almost unrelated, individuals, a method practised exclusively in some kennels, but which I personally do not advocate, because it is rarely that a dog or bitch, the progeny of a complete out-cross mating, who may yet be a Champion itself, proves to be a really prepotent breeding specimen. A perusal of the pedigrees of Champions in the Appendix will confirm this point. Further, in Shelties, out-crossing almost always results in the majority of the offspring being over-size. In-breeding, in its true sense, is the mating of brother and sister, father and daughter, mother and son. Except occasionally, to fix some very definite point, such intense breeding is rarely resorted to. Line-breeding is the mating of every relation between half-brother and sister up to cousins, and it is usually found that very intense line-breeding half-brother ex half-sister, grandsire ex grand-daughter—will prove most effective. Oddly enough, the mating of grandmother to grandson is rarely successful.

However, no plan of intense line-breeding should be embarked upon without a very firm intention to cull the resultant litter ruthlessly if this should be necessary.

It must be remembered that no in- or line-breeding can establish things which do not already exist in the two individuals chosen for the mating. Intense line-breeding will intensify all the points the two individuals have in common, or which their common ancestors have, and points both good and *bad* will be intensified equally.

The inexperienced dog owner usually has a deep-rooted idea that every in-bred or line-bred dog, or what the pet owner usually calls 'highly bred'—a meaningless term which always reminds me of a well-risen loaf!—must be either delicate, nervous, mentally deficient or all three.

You cannot breed in any new feature by in-breeding, but can only intensify what is already there, both the good points and the bad. No in-bred dog who comes of sensible, nerve-free stock will be nervous *because* it is in-bred. If it shows any of these tendencies they must have been present in the parents or inherent in the ancestors. These, then, are the vital needs to be absolutely certain that the dogs to which you wish to in- or line-breed, and through which you are planning to in- or line-breed, must be absolutely healthy, both mentally and physically, and as free from the faults, and as richly endowed as possible with the good points, as the standard of the breed demands. It is therefore essential to choose, for such a pro-gramme, two animals with the least possible number of common faults—and whose common ancestors are likewise as faultless as possible—and then to look at the resultant litter quite ruthlessly, and reject *at once* any progeny which shows the common fault in even the slightest degree. It is quite useless at this stage to be 'to their virtues ever kind, to their faults a little blind'; the reverse must be the case. The point that the puppy which shows the fault *even in the slightest degree* should be rejected should be stressed again; it is almost certain that this puppy will be the most prepotent for that fault. The brothers and sisters may carry the fault recessively, and only a test mating can prove that point, so do not ask for trouble by keep-ing the *apparent* offender when you may find you have an unseen 'nigger in the woodpile' too.

Whether the individual breeder decides to achieve his ideal by in-breeding or by careful selective breeding of unrelated dogs matters not so long as there is a definite plan for producing a certain type, a plan backed up by sound knowledge and the ruthless discarding of any 'doubtful' products of matings if they carry even one of the characteristics considered undesirable in the strain.

The scientific breeder tries, with every litter born, to improve his stock in at least one point. As a breeder he has an obligation to the breed he has chosen, and to his fellow-breeders—to produce only the best that his brains and know-ledge can evolve. The breeder must seek to perpetuate only those characteristics most desirable in the breed. The speed with which he can produce stock superior to that of his earlier generations is the measure of his knowledge and success.

The motto of every breeder trying to establish a strain

should be 'Patience, Perseverance, Pups'. Patience to give him calm endurance through all his setbacks; perseverance to start again when all his carefully planned matings have gone wrong; pups, for they are the proof of the rightness or the wrongness of his plan. They alone can show whether the desired characteristics are being established. As they are, so the strain will be built up, until that glorious moment when he hears someone unknown to him say, 'Look, that must be a —— Sheltie; you can tell that strain anywhere!'

Colour Breeding in Shelties

Undoubtedly one of the reasons for the appeal of the breed is the variety of colours in which it is obtainable, and the fascination of waiting to see which colour will turn up in each litter.

In view of the importance of this subject it is surprising that much greater attention has not been paid to it and a deeper study made. Experienced breeders may find little for them in this short chapter, but it is hoped that it will assist the novice.

The main groups of colour in our breed are sable, tricolour and blue merle. All these can carry the Sheepdog 'colour pattern' for white. That is to say, white collar, legs, feet, tail-tip and blaze. There are three distinct types of colour pattern: (1) a solid coloured dog with practically no white visible, except perhaps on the toes, or a hair or two at the back of the neck; (2) the Sheltie marked as we know and expect it to be; (3) the mismarked dog, in which there is more white than colour. Sometimes one finds a Sheltie of the type 3 which is almost entirely white, and has little colour other than the head, or maybe only an ear. This type of white, however, must not be confused with the almost all-white dog resulting from the merle × merle mating. This latter is a defective white, caused, probably, by a lethal factor.

Sable is a loosely used word to describe any shade of colour from clear, creamy yellow, through rich gold to deep mahogany. The colour is dominant over all other colours, and, depending on the type of the individual, the animal can throw either only sables or both tricolours and sables.

Blue merle is the modification of black, due to a dilution factor, and is dealt with fully in a previous chapter.

Tricolour is the name given to the black dog with tan markings on the cheeks, over the eyes, inside the legs, under the tail, and with the white collar pattern also present. These dogs are genetically bi-colours, with the white pattern acting on that bi-colour.

Sable, in all its shades, is fairly unpredictable, producing, as it can, all shades of sable as well as tricolour. Even two clear sables can produce a tricolour, but a sable homozygous for the colour will produce only its own colour, even when mated to tricolours. One cannot tell a homozygous sable simply by looking at it, but the purity or otherwise of any particular individual can easily be tested by mating to a tricolour partner. Conclusions cannot be drawn from one mating only, but if, over several matings with different tricolours, only sables are produced, one may assume that the sable is homozygous. Such animals are rare in our breed.

Tricolours, mated together, can produce only tricolours, for the tricolour is a pure recessive. As if to give the lie to this statement, however, one finds sable pups resulting from the mating of two individuals which *seem* to be black, tan and white. On the occasions when this happens it is certain that one of the dogs concerned is not truly a tricolour, but only *seems* so to our eye. What, in fact, has happened is this. One of the two animals concerned (and which can only be determined by further test mating) is in truth a shaded sable, but the black hair has spread beyond its usual area and the sable (but here we call it tan) is only showing at the fringes of its area, and the resultant dog is visually a tricolour. These are the cases which make all our rules of colour heredity seem false, but they are not so. I repeat, two tricolours can produce nothing but tricolours, and while in the Collie all those individuals which appear tricolour are genetically tricolours, in our breed there is yet a further colour which makes things more interesting, and which can be proved only by test.

In the first chapter reference was made to the arrival in the islands of a black-and-tan King Charles Spaniel. In my opinion he is the answer to our 'apparent' tricolours.

We all know that genes can be carried recessively for many,

many generations and that then, by the fortuitous arrival of a certain set of circumstances, these dormant genes may suddenly spring to life. It is not, therefore, too far-fetched to assume that, with many of our Shelties today probably carrying some of their inheritance from this King Charles ancestor, the circumstances arise by which his blood, though it may be many years away, is alive behind both parents of a present-day mating. Remember that he was a *black-and-tan* dog.

Now colour heredity in the King Charles Spaniel is different from that in our own breed, for in the toy breed the mating of two black-and-tans can produce a ruby (red or sable in our terminology). Surely here is the answer to our problem? When our *visual* tricolours are mated and produce sables it would seem that both parents are probably carrying genes inherited from this distant ancestor, and that they are, as we know, not true tricolours at all. That is to say they are capable, through their 'royal' ancestry, of a different type of colour inheritance from the true breeding recessive tricolour.

Tri × sable can produce both tricolours and sables (except in the case of the homozygous sable, mentioned above) and this is often a most useful mating if there has been a paling of the sable colour due to the continued crossing of sable × sable, as the introduction of the tri blood will make an enormous difference to the colour, even in the first generation, and often gives sables of very rich hue.

EYE COLOUR. A chapter on breeding for colour should not be concluded without some reference being made to the inheritance of eye colour. The desired eye in a Sheltie is dark brown, but a lightish brown eye is frequently seen, and it would be advantageous if we could know how to avoid this. The light-brown eye appears to be carried as a simple Mendelian recessive. When two light-eyed individuals are mated together all the pups will be more or less light-eyed. Two dark-eyed parents can produce some dark- and some light-eyed puppies, but more generally the resultant litter is dark-eyed. However, it is necessary, if we are to predict results with certainty, to know what type the dark-eyed parents are. If each of the pair is DD—that is to say, if each received the gene D for dark eyes from both parents—then you can safely predict 100 per cent dark-eyed pups. But if each parent is Dd, that is to say if each received one D gene from one of its own parents, and so appears dark-eyed, but at the same time received another gene, d, carrying the light-eye gene recessively, but appearing dark, then the resultant litter will have some light-eyed pups, so here again test mating alone can determine whether your dark-eyed individual is pure for this trait or not.

The inheritance of the blue, wall or china eye in the blue merle is not so easy to determine. The fact that the puppies are the result of the mating of two blue-eyed parents does not mean that the puppies will be blue-eyed also. Neither does it hold that when two brown-eyed merles are mated together the resultant litter will be wholly brown-eyed. Quite frequently one sees blue-eyed puppies from the mating of two brown-eyed blue merle parents, and it would seem that the dilution factor which is responsible for the blue merle colour is also responsible for the colour of the eyes. Therefore, eye colour in the blue merles is not carried as a purely Mendelian trait, but appears to be acted upon by the dilution factor and therefore it is well-nigh impossible to forecast eye colour in such matings. Once again, however, it should be stressed that the blue, blue-flecked or part-blue eye is highly desirable in the blue merle.

8

SHELTIE CHARACTER

IT SHOULD be clearly understood that the Sheltie with its extreme degree of intelligence and sensitivity is a dog which responds to the greatest possible amount of human companionship and individual attention. For this reason it is desirable that the Sheltie should never be kept in very large numbers, at least not unless there are plenty of people concerned with their wellbeing who are able to give them a great deal of their time, for the Sheltie is a dog which responds, possibly more than any other breed, to love, attention and affection.

Although many other breeds are 'one-family' dogs, not quite the same can be said of the Sheltie. These little people, although devoted to their family, also become 'one-person' dogs. They are essentially trainable, as witness the wonderful work so many of them are doing in obedience tests today. Their ambition is to serve. There is no doubt whatsoever that a Sheltie with a job to do is far happier than a Sheltie which is just a dog. By that I do not mean that a Sheltie needs to have its flock of sheep, but it must feel that it is serving a useful purpose in its life. Being useful to a Sheltie means being able to serve whether as a farm dog, as a constant companion, trained to the obedience ring or just taught general obedience and handiness about the house. Yes, I mean that, handiness, for a Sheltie does so love to be a help. It can be useful by being taught that when things are dropped in the house they are to be picked up, or by knowing certain items specifically by name so that it can run and retrieve them when told. A classic example of what I mean is illustrated by this story.

In the early months of the last war when petrol was rationed I always saved mine up so that at least once a week I could take my Shelties in the car to a spot where they might enjoy a really free walk. One particular afternoon, having taken them out, I locked the car, leaving my handbag in it and putting the ignition key in my pocket. Among the dogs that were with me was my beloved Moonen Shiel. She, of course, was exceptional, and was the first Sheltie trained to tracking to win the Working Trials Certificate for a tracking dog, so she knew her job. That afternoon late in autumn we had been walking some two hours in bracken which was breast high for myself, and we returned to the car just as dusk was falling. I put my hand in my pocket for my keys and they were not there. There was I, a long way from anywhere, no keys, no handbag, therefore, no money and means of telephoning. Shiel had never before been asked to search for my car keys, but I took the only course open to me. I sent her back to 'go seek'. She didn't know what she was looking for, simply that it was something belonging to me. I had no idea where I might have dropped those keys; remember we had been walking for two hours. She shot away from me and was quickly lost in the dusk and the bracken. I timed her. Just 25 minutes later the bracken started to quiver and out of it came Shiel, the keys proudly in her mouth. After all car keys are not very big and I think you will agree that that was quite an achievement. But that is the type of thing I mean by a Sheltie needing a job to do.

They are charming, gay, happy little people. Their big desire in life is to please you, and very quickly they will adapt themselves to your mood. Be it a day when you are alive and bright and ready for anything, so too will be your Sheltie. If you are feeling a little less alert and happy your dog will fit into your moods—their one desire, as I have said, being to please.

The Sheltie is usually very fond of children, many of them making themselves unofficial 'nannies', but it is up to the adults to see that the dog gets a fair deal. Often in a household of young children when a puppy or young adult is introduced it is not made sufficiently clear to the children that puppies, like babies, need plenty of rest and sleep. It would be extremely unusual for any Sheltie to defend itself against what might well be considered rough treatment by a child of the family to which it belongs. Such is the faithfulness of the little beast that it would never even scratch a young child who was giving it rather more of a rough-house than it should have, or who was expecting it to stay awake when in fact the poor little dog was so tired that all it wished to do was curl up and sleep.

Dogs with the character of Shelties are very special people, and it is a privilege to own one, or perhaps I should say to be owned by one. They are undoubtedly possessive, but not possessive to the point of aggressiveness. However, when a Sheltie decides to give its heart it gives its whole heart.

The Sheltie then is a dog of character, trainability and distinction. A dog, too, which is most pleasing to the eye, a dog which fits into one's life with great adaptability, a dog which fits into the small house or flat as well as into the small car. Its grace, happiness and beauty, its tremendous character, all tend to make it the dog of today.

9

THE SHELTIE AS AN OBEDIENCE WORKER

WHEN obedience training first became popular in this country there were no Shelties taking part. However, it was not long before one started to make a mark. This was a little sable bitch, Mrs Raike's Bundle and Go. She was the very first to bring the Sheltie as an obedience worker before the public. The next to follow her was the author's bitch Moonen Shiel, and to her went the distinction of being the first, and still the only, Sheltie to win a Working Trials Certificate. Before the Second World War, there were several other Shelties also starting to make their name. Most notable among them was Lt.-Col. The Hon. B. Russell's blue merle bitch Ch. Jenny Wren of Crawley Ridge. Jenny was the first Champion Sheltie to gain Working Trials qualifications. Considering that she was just 14 in. at the shoulder, it is highly creditable that she managed to qualify for both CD (companion dog) and UD (utility dog).

Came the war years and all thoughts of such work naturally were forgotten. After the war, however, it was not long before the Shelties once again sprang to the fore. The first of the notable workers was Mr Ratcliff's Ghillie of Mospe. When the Kennel Club instituted the Obedience Certificate and the title of Obedience Champion, Ghillie became the first Sheltie to gain this title. It was not long, however, before his son, Master Ian, also was an Obedience Champion. The first Obedience Champion bitch was Mrs Pearce's Yelruth Anfield, and so far these are the only three Obedience Champions in the breed at the moment. However, others will not be long before they join them. Mrs Glasse's Champion dog Budlet of Surreyhills already has working qualifications, is making his name remembered in the Obedience ring, and bids fair to be the breed's first dual Champion. Mrs MacMillan's little sable-and-white bitch,

Safety First from Shiel, has already won an Obedience Certificate, and surely it should not be long before she becomes our second bitch Champion in the breed. (She has gained her title since this was written.)

It is udoubtedly due in no small measure to the wonderful impact that these various Obedience workers have made upon the general public that our breed has become so increasingly popular over recent years.

The idea that the Sheltie is shy has been much dispelled by these workers. It should, however, not be forgotten that a great deal of reserve is a true part of the Sheltie character, and this reserve may well make them seem shy to the stranger. The possessiveness already referred to is all part of this reserve, and it is this possessiveness and great desire to please which makes the Sheltie the ideal Obedience worker, for nothing gives the little dog greater happiness than to be at one with its owner.

There is no doubt, however, that some of our Shelties are extroverts, and I have had some myself which have definitely declined to work really well unless there was a large enough crowd of people watching them. Further, at one time, when I was working two dogs who were constantly competing against each other, there was not a shadow of doubt that one of these dogs at least knew the differing colours of the prize cards. Should she have been placed, let us say, only third, after my other dog had won the class, and in the time-honoured manner they had been given their prize cards with which to parade around the ring, a fight always ensued, for Shiel demanded that the red card should be hers whether by right or no! Furthermore, when we got home, she would remember whether she had won or not. On each occasion the formula was different. If she had won, as soon as I opened the door of the car she would rush straight to the front door of the house and sit there waiting for me. I would then give her her prize card and she would take it in to show to my parents. On the other hand, if she had not won, as soon as the car door was opened she never made a mistake, but rushed straight to her kennel and waited there for her dinner! Conceit if you like, nevertheless very clever. In the late seventies there were many Shelties working at the very top in obedience, and they included a number of obedience champions.

10

THE STUD-DOG

IT HAS already been said that it is not an economic proposition, nor is it really advisable for the small kennel, nor the beginner, to keep a stud-dog, nevertheless the time will come when that outstanding dog puppy is bred and reared to become a stud-dog.

In the early days you should not allow yourself to be tempted either to buy a dog or to keep a dog pup, for unless you are in a position to buy a really top-notcher there is nothing whatsoever to be gained by having a male.

In fact, even with a top-grade dog there is little gain, for it is unlikely that he will be suitable for all your bitches, and if he is, he will be suitable for only one generation of your bitches, until such time as you may have grandchildren of his to put back to him. The very best dog in the land, and the most suitable for each of your bitches, can be used for a relatively small fee of about £20, that being about the scale for Sheltie fees. Your own dog, even if he mates all your own bitches, will save you nothing over a year if you take his keep into account, unless he is of such outstanding merit that his services are sought after by other breeders. This is unlikely to happen unless you are in a position to be able to show him fearlessly all over the country, and this is a job demanding plenty of time, energy and cash.

You may consider it more convenient to have your own dog, and there may be the possibility of his bringing you the odd stud fee or two from the local 'pet'-type bitches, but if you are going to look upon the mating of your bitch to the dog which is the closest at hand instead of to the dog best suited to her, then you will not get on in the dog game.

Equally, it is no use keeping a 'chance' one. That is to say, should you happen to breed a really top-class-*looking* dog, worthy maybe of gaining his title, he will in all probability be useless as a stud force, for he will not have the background essential to the ideal stud-dog. He will almost certainly not throw his like, for no stud which is not carefully and scientifically bred has the power to do this, and it is for this reason that a programme of line-breeding is usually so much more successful than a programme of out-crossing.

There are a great number of really important qualifications to which a dog should conform before he can be considered as the ideal stud. He must come of a pedigree which is such that it has been proved to carry bloodlines which have played, and are still playing, an important part in the improvement of the breed, and this pedigree should be really strong for many more generations than those which appear on the conventional five-generation pedigree form. You should assure yourself that for at least ten generations there are no weak unknown spots. By weak spots I mean that the blood carried does not go back to a line which is known to have failed, on either the male or female side, to have produced good stock. This is not easy to find in Shelties where insufficient line-breeding has been indulged in.

It will probably not be possible for you to 'see' his pedigree as a visual thing for all these generations, but by careful questioning of the old hands, and recourse to reading of the past, it should become possible for you to build up the picture you must have in your mind. It is not enough for a stud-dog to come of a Champion sire, however prepotent that sire may be; remember that the son has only half his make-up from his sire (and you can rest assured that he will not have inherited only all his father's good points, but some of his bad ones as well), the other half of his make-up comes from his dam. It is absolutely essential that she must be more than a typical member of the breed. If she is not a winner on merit, she must be a bitch who has already proved herself as being prepotent in passing on those essential qualities which go to improve the breed.

The potential stud-dog must come of stock in which there is no known inherent tendency to any particular disease or constitutional weakness, quite apart from his merit on show points. Needless to say, to be of any real economic value to you he must also be good in himself, for without some successes in the show-ring there will not be the demand for his services

unless he should happen to be a dog of outstanding pre-
potency who had his show-ring chances marred by an accident.
In such a case a dog may be sought after, but it will be appreciated that the time of waiting until his services are sought
after will be a lengthy one, for he will be able to prove himself
only through his progeny, and as one swallow does not make a
summer, nor will one youngster, no matter how good, make his
sire's name as a stud. The unshown stud-dog must be able to
turn out youngster after youngster of excellence, and of similar
type, before there will be any great demand for him. The stud
should also be a dog of excellent temperament, for the shy dog
is the greatest possible detriment to any breed. He must be a
'dog' and have no trace of femininity, and he must be capable,
sensible and virile in his stud work.

I consider that the ideal age for a Sheltie is to have his first
bitch when he is about ten months old. He should not have a
further bitch until he is twelve months of age, and from then
on, for the next eight to twelve months, he certainly should not
have more than one bitch per month, preferably only one in
two months. Because of the difficulties of these things being
seasonal, however, we often cannot choose.

The young stud should be trained from the very beginning
in the way you intend him always to mate his bitches, and you
will find it a saving both of your time and the stud-dog's
energies if he is taught to expect his bitches to be held for him.
For the first mating with a young dog it is most important that
an experienced brood bitch, known to be flirtatious and easy to
mate, should be used. The very worst thing that can happen to
a learner stud-dog is for him to fail to mate his first bitch; it
will make him uneasy, lose condition and, on a later occasion
when he is asked to do the job again, he will have lost confidence in himself. If his first bitch is easy and 'teaches him the
job' he will rapidly learn from her how to deal with the more
awkward ones he may meet later in life. It is often advantageous, too, if the bitch can be one he knows; not his own
constant companion, however, for quite often a dog who
knows a bitch too well—if they are always kennelled together
or are both house-dogs—will refuse to have anything whatever
to do with her. This is another point against the keeping of a
stud-dog by a small kennel. It is advisable that, for the first

mating at least, there should be two attendants, one to hold the bitch by her collar, the other to assist the dog.

The dog and the bitch should first be introduced to each other on the lead, so that you can be sure she is ready to meet him willingly and to indulge in a little mild flirtation. If the bitch seems happy about it the two dogs should be taken to a small run, or a shed, or to wherever you intend the mating to take place, and released there. Do not allow the play to last too long, for the dog will quickly become hot and his energies wasted.

It is very important that you assure yourself as nearly as possible that the bitch is not going to snap at the dog; a bite at this stage might put him off for months. As soon as the bitch has shown that she is really willing to stand firmly for the dog, she should be held by the collar, and the dog should be allowed to mount.

At this moment the second attendant should hold the bitch by her rear end, from underneath, and without making any fuss or getting in the dog's way, slightly raise the vulva, to make it easier for the dog to penetrate. The best way to do this is to sit on the ground, on the left-hand side of the bitch, and place the left hand flat under the bitch, from the side, and backwards between her legs, with the vulva just lying between the first and second fingers of that hand. In this manner the exact position of the penis can be felt and the dog given every possible assistance. As soon as the dog penetrates and starts to work rapidly, the right arm can be passed behind him and he can then be held firmly and gently until the 'tie' has taken place. Even a bitch which has previously been mated will usually groan or whimper slightly during the swelling of the penis as the 'tie' is being effected, and it is wise at this time to talk reassuringly, not only to the bitch, but to the dog, for he may fear he has done something wrong if the bitch is crying under him. Be sure to tell the young dog he is a clever boy! When the 'tie' is complete the dog will usually indicate that he is ready to get off the bitch and turn. He should be helped in this, for any chance of pulling away must be avoided as this can cause a rupture to the dog and/or irreparable damage to the bitch. I find that the best way to hold them while the dog is getting off and turning is to take the tails of both in the one hand—with the bitch's tail *under* the dog's leg, of course—this leaves your other hand free to assist the dog to get his leg over the bitch if necessary.

In my opinion, the ideal with our breed is to perform the mating on a table. It is so much more restful for the owner's back. Naturally no one would expect a young dog mating his first bitch to do so up on the table, but when the 'tie' has been accomplished on the ground beside a table and the dog has turned, very carefully pick up both animals. This can be done either by one person holding each dog or, and I prefer this method, take one dog under each arm, their heads beneath your elbows, and gradually raise them until both are standing on the table.

Give the dog plenty of praise when he is there, and then with his next bitch, see if he will start on the table, if not, repeat the performance with the dog.

It might be advantageous here to explain the 'tie', for it is something which is peculiar to the canine and kindred species. In other species of mammal the male is equipped with Cowper's glands, which eject the semen in a swift emission immediately the vagina is penetrated. The dog, unsupplied with these glands, can emit semen only gradually on the drip principle and, therefore, the absence of Cowper's glands has been offset by the 'tie'. As soon as the penis enters the vagina it begins gradually to swell until, at about the middle of the penis, there is a very pronounced bulbous swelling which makes it impossible for the dog to retract without doing very grave damage. To make things doubly sure, while the penis is swelling, the muscles of the bitch contract round it, and hold it firmly, and the duration of the length of the muscular contraction of the bitch controls the length of the 'tie'. It is for this reason that the length of time varies from bitch to bitch and is not always the same with the same dog. The normal length of time for the duration of a 'tie' is about 10–25 min., but it varies so much that the tie may last from moments only to as much as an hour or more. During the tie the bitch should be prevented from sitting down, fidgeting, etc., and the dog should be kept under surveillance all the time. If necessary, the bitch should be held gently.

You may find that the young dog, while not minding the

bitch being held by her collar, resents her being held by her rear. If this is so, then for this first mating he should be allowed to mate her in his own way, but the moment he penetrates he should be helped, as described above, and at the same time the left hand should be placed in the position already described so that he will be more accustomed to it for his next attempt. A great deal of time spent in getting the young dog's confidence in being handled is time well spent in this first mating; so much time will be saved on subsequent occasions, more especially when the time comes for him to have a difficult bitch brought to him, one who resents his attentions and has to be held.

It should be remembered that the young dog being used for the first time will probably emit semen in which the sperm are dead, and therefore a first mating on the dog's side should always be a dual mating. The second ejaculation is likely to be fertile, because the old wasted sperm will have been passed out, and for this reason it is always wise, if not essential, to give a second service at a first mating. The same remarks apply if the dog has not been used for a long time, and if there has been a long interval between his matings a second service should be given. With these two exceptions, if the first mating was satisfactory there is rarely, if ever, need for a second service.

It may happen that a bitch, particularly a 'maiden', though seeming to be ready and 'standing' willingly to the dog, may yet turn on him when he tries to enter. It is quite possible, in such a case, that if you separate them and let them meet again some hours later, or the next day, all will be well and she will accept him with no trouble at all, provided that she is not later than the fifteenth day in her season. On the other hand, the bitch may have a slight stricture and she should be examined for this. Particularly if it is a case of the bitch being willing and the dog, try though he may, being unable to effect penetration, should a stricture be suspected. Grease a finger (which has a short nail) and slide the finger gently into the vagina; a slight stricture can be broken down easily and almost painlessly in this way, and then the dog will have no trouble. However, if an obstruction which cannot be dealt with in this manner is found the bitch must be attended to by a veterinary surgeon before she can be mated. If the condition is detected reasonably early in the season the necessary dilation or operation can take place and a service still be obtained in that same season, but if it is not discovered until the bitch is going off, then she will have to wait until the next season. In any instance of the dog having great difficulty in penetrating, although he is attempting this correctly, a stricture should be suspected and the bitch examined at once before the dog wears himself out on a fruitless task.

The stud fee for any dog should be set, and agreed upon, before the service takes place. An established stud-dog will stand at his advertised fee, but the dog mating his first bitch always presents a slight problem. Nevertheless, the fee at which you value his services should be clearly stated prior to the service, for the fee to any dog is paid *for the service* and not for the *result* of the service. This is all very well with a proved dog, but with an unproved one it is wise to say either that you will take a puppy in lieu of fee (always very much to your financial advantage) or—and I consider this is the fairer method—the fee, as stated, shall be paid when it is known that the bitch is in whelp. By this arrangement no one stands to lose anything. With this exception, all stud fees are payable at the time of the service, unless the owner of the stud-dog has agreed to a different arrangement with the bitch's owner.

Quite often one is requested to take a puppy instead of a fee even to a proved dog, and the bitch's owner should not feel that this denotes any lack of confidence in the merits of the stud-dog, nor even in his merits to that particular bitch, if the stud-dog owner cannot agree to such a suggestion. There is nothing more awkward for the owner of a kennel than to have one 'odd' puppy of an age different from the others in the kennel, and for this reason and no other it is frequently necessary for the stud-dog owner to turn down such a suggestion. Most of us, however, try our best to be helpful, and if we cannot accept a puppy in lieu of a fee we shall probably be able to make some other suggestion.

It should be stressed that although a 'tie' is desirable it is not necessary for there to be one for the mating to be a success. There are some dogs who never 'tie' a bitch and with whom bitches rarely miss, but naturally both the owner of the stud-dog and of the bitch feel that things are more satisfactory if there has been a 'tie', and in a case where there has been no 'tie' it is usually wise, if only to create good feeling, to let the payment of the fee depend upon whether the bitch conceives or not.

Allowing for the exceptions mentioned above, it is not necessary or desirable to give two services to a bitch, but if for any reason it has been agreed that there should be two services, the second should take place as soon as possible after the first, and certainly within twenty-four hours.

Although the stud fee is payable for the service and not for the result of the service, most stud-dog owners say that, should there be no puppies, there will be a free service to the bitch next time she comes in season, provided the stud-dog is still in the same ownership. This is not compulsory in law and is simply a 'gentlemen's agreement'.

If it is agreed to take a puppy instead of a fee, this should be clearly set down at the time of mating. Special points which must be laid down are whether the pup is to be the first or second pick of the litter, and at what age it is to be selected and taken away (not always the same thing).

A dog placed at public stud should already have been proved; that is to say, there should be at least one living litter born to him. (It is important to stress that word 'living' for it does happen, in rare and isolated cases, that the dog carries a lethal factor which causes the death of all his puppies at birth.) He should have a stud-card which the owner can send out to those who enquire about him, and this card should give all the details that the bitch's owner is likely to want to know: his fee, colour, preferably a photograph, his stud-book number, if he has one, if not, then his registration number, and a copy of his pedigree, preferably to five generations. It must also carry your address, 'phone number and the name of your railway station. It is a wise precaution to state also that while every care is taken of visiting bitches no responsibility can be accepted for them. This little clause can save you a packet of trouble should an accident occur while she is in your care.

In conclusion, it is hardly necessary to say that your stud-dog must, of course, always be kept in the pink of condition and free from parasites of any kind.

Chestnut Rainbow,
after whom male line CHE is named

AND HIS GRANDSON

Ch. Uam Var of Houghton Hill,
to whom the breed owes so much

Ch. Money Spinner of Exford (grand-son of Ch. Uam Var)

AND HIS SON

Ch. Riverhill Rufus

Ellington Encore,
grandson of Ch. Riverhill
Rufus

Ch. Exford Piskiegye Taw (four generations
removed from Ch. Riverhill Rufus)

Ch. Eltham Park Eunice (Family 1)

Ch. Redbraes Magda (Family 3)

II

THE GREAT MOMENT: YOUR FIRST LITTER

As you will already have realized, quite the most important part of any kennel is its female foundation stock. However many bitches or bitch puppies you propose starting with, do make the very most of them; much better to have one really good bitch to start with than two mediocre ones, and best of all is one really good bitch which has proved herself as a producer of top-class winning stock—if you can persuade any owner to part with such a gem.

Let us take for granted that you have already followed the advice in the earlier chapters, and that now your first bitch has reached the age when you are expecting her to come into season and are hoping to mate her.

You will not have left it until now to decide to what stud-dog you are going to send her. Provided that you are free to make the choice yourself (by which I mean that you have not obtained your bitch on part-breeding terms), then you should have begun to think out, long ago, what you consider the ideal mate for her. First, study her pedigree most carefully, and find out all you possibly can about her antecedents. Discover whether there is a good dog in her pedigree which has proved himself to be prepotent for those characteristics for which you most admire him. If he is still alive and still producing stock, weigh up the possibilities of putting your bitch back to him. If it is impossible to use him, but you are still anxious to try to establish those good points of his, try to find a descendant of his, a son, or grandson, or better still a double grandson, who also excels in these good points, and whom you know, if possible, has proved himself to be a carrier of these good points also.

Now you have chosen the mate. The next thing is to write to

the stud-owner telling him when you expect your bitch to be in season, and making a tentative booking to the stud-dog. Then, as soon as she is really in season, write again *at once*, telling him the actual day on which she first came in to season, and suggesting what day you propose sending or taking her to be mated. Taking her is the ideal, but this cannot always be managed, and it is far, far better to send your bitch away to be mated to the most suitable dog than to use a less suitable one just because he happens to be handy. But if you expect to have to send her away it is essential that the necessary arrangements should be made well in advance, for you will, of course, have to send her in a box or hamper.

You will find that most stud-dog owners have a box which they are willing to lend or hire to you provided you make the request in plenty of time. You may think it is rather mercenary to say 'hire' when the dog's owner will be getting a fee, but remember that these boxes cost a fair amount of money these days and that every journey they make shortens their lives. Often the 'return empty' journey creates the most wear and tear on a box, for the railway has no respect at all for these empties, it seems. Your bitch herself may cause a great deal of damage, as she may object to being boxed, fight a battle with it at some time on the journey, and then the box is returned to its owner very much the worse for wear. I have had them come back with the bottom or sides very nearly scratched and gnawed right through. For this reason it it is very much more satisfactory to have your own box so that the bitch can sleep in it for several nights and thus get accustomed to it before making the journey. More will be said of travelling-boxes, dimensions, etc., in a later chapter.

Do not imagine for one moment that just because your bitch is now nine months old she will come into season. Even if she does, she will be too young to mate. Most general books on dogs tell us that the bitch usually comes into season at nine months of age and then at six-monthly intervals. There is only one thing wrong with this—no Sheltie I have ever met seems to have read these books. It is much more likely that a Sheltie will show no signs of coming into season until she is twelve months old or considerably more.

The first sign that can be looked for is usually a whitish,

thick, but slight, discharge from the vagina. If you have a dog he will probably show some interest in her when this first starts. Within a day or two the discharge will gradually colour until it is red, and there will be marked swelling of the vagina. A bitch herself usually indicates when she is ready to be mated by lifting her tail. This she will do when she is confronted with a dog, often for another bitch, if she is rubbed gently on the back just above the root of the tail, and if the vulva is touched gently. When I say 'lifts her tail' perhaps this should be rather more fully explained. She will not fly her tail over her back, as with a 'gay' tail, but she will lift it stiffly from the root and flick it directly over sideways, so that the tail sticks straight out at an angle of 45 degrees before dropping down with its natural weight. When rubbed, or sniffed by a dog or another bitch, she will move her tail, still in the same position, from side to side. This, undoubtedly, is the moment to take her to the dog.

Owners of stud-dogs have their own particular method of handling their own dogs, and the method of getting a mating has been dealt with in the chapter on the stud-dog. The stud-dog owner may offer you a second service, say the day after the first, but in my opinion, unless there has been an unsatisfactory short service the first time, or if there has been no 'tie', a second service is quite unnecessary, unless the dog is mating his first bitch or has not been used for a very long time. It is easy to appreciate that the owner of a top stud-dog which is in much demand and used regularly will not be anxious to give a second service if the first was satisfactory because of the risk of overusing the dog. A popular dog during the 'season' (for these things *are* seasonal) may mate three bitches a week for a short period, sometimes more, and if everyone wanted two services the poor dog would hardly ever have a day off.

It is well to let the bitch rest for a while after the service before starting the return journey, if this is possible, and she must of course be kept just as much under surveillance for the remainder of the season as she was in the first part, for a bitch, once mated, can be mated again by another dog. Then, there is no guarantee of the paternity of the puppies.

For the first four weeks after the mating there is no need to give the bitch any different treatment at all. During this period it is wellnigh impossible to know whether she is in whelp or not. The only likely indication will be an erratic appetite, on her food one day, off the next, and possibly (if she is a bitch you know really well) you may notice some slight change in her character. She may alter her habits and personality very slightly, and this is naturally more easily discernible in a bitch which is a 'house-pet' than one that leads a kennel life. At approximately 25–28 days from the date of mating, a veterinary surgeon can easily tell you whether the bitch is in whelp or not, and if she is, then from this time on she needs extra attention. Her way of life should not be altered at all; her exercise, provided it was adequate in the first place, should neither be diminished nor increased, but food is the all-important item for the next few weeks when she is carrying as many as six or eight puppies, and she must be helped in every possible way to make a good job of it with the minimum of strain on herself. Shelties, on the whole, are extremely good mothers, both when expecting and nursing, but they are also apt to be very self-sacrificing, and if the bitch is not properly looked after she will almost certainly drain her own body to give to her unborn puppies.

As soon as you know she is in whelp her feeding should be completely altered, and I consider the ideal diet for a pregnant bitch from the fourth week after mating until she whelps to be:

Breakfast. Cereals or wholemeal bread, with ½ pint milk, 1 teaspoonful cod liver oil and 1 teaspoonful calcium phosphate. A raw egg, if possible daily, and if not possible, then as often as can be managed.

Midday. 6–8 oz. raw lean meat.

6 p.m. As midday.

10 p.m. A bowl of biscuit-meal soaked in stock or milk.

The bitch will probably not be able immediately to take this complete change from her ordinary diet of two meals a day, but she should be accustomed to it by an increase of one meal the first day, then an increase in the size of the meat meal on the second day, and the fourth meal offered on the third day. By the end of 4–6 days she should be quite happy in the routine.

Don't worry unduly if occasionally she refuses a meal, or even all her meals for one day, but don't let it become a habit. If she gets a bit fussy over her food try to vary the diet. Persist with the raw meat unless she absolutely refuses to eat this, which is unlikely, but the meat can be varied. Mutton makes an occasional flavoursome change from beef or horse, or, if she is very difficult, try her with the meat lightly cooked once a day and raw for the other meal. Rabbit will almost always tempt the most difficult feeder, but if you are stuck with a problem, it is up to you to use your ingenuity and ring the changes until you find what really tempts her most. It is rare that you get an in-whelp bitch which is a 'bad feeder' but these suggestions are 'just in case'. I have one particular bitch who has a different 'fad' every time she is in whelp. (As she has had six litters I am getting used to her.) For instance, she would not eat at all before her first litter unless everything had cheese sauce on it. For her second, she would not look at cheese but wanted everything slightly flavoured with rabbit. Her raw meat was most welcome provided it had lain for a while in cold rabbit stock before being given to her—and so on. Mind you, I am quoting extreme cases; I do not believe in pandering to fads and fancies in any dog except a bitch in whelp, but if you get one of these being 'choosey', then in my opinion she must be pandered to.

Beyond keeping your bitch adequately fed, and supplied with plenty of *fresh* drinking water, there is only her exercise which needs attention. During the early days she should have plenty of unrestricted exercise, but she should never be forced to go for a long walk by being 'dragged'. Almost certainly she will gallop as usual and chase birds or whatever her favourite pastime may be. There should be no need to restrict her in any way, and she will adjust her own exercise as the days advance. Only if she is normally exercised with other dogs which are very boisterous and likely to knock her about should any alteration be made, and if this was her normal way of exercising she should be taken out either alone or with one staid Sheltie of either sex who will not chase and hustle her. Many people prefer that a bitch in the last two to three weeks of pregnancy should be exercised on a leash. This I cannot agree with, for several reasons. First, it is more tiring for any dog to exercise on the leash than free, because they have to adjust themselves to our pace, which is far from normal to them, and, secondly, a willing, friendly bitch will be much less likely to show that she does not wish to go far by hanging back on the leash than she will if she is free and can quickly but firmly indicate to you that it is 'time to go home'.

It is important that the bitch you intend breeding from is free from worms and skin disease. It is advisable to worm the bitch some two to three weeks before you expect her in season, but if she has 'caught you on the hop', as they so often do, do *not* worm her between the time of the onset of her season and the time of mating, neither should you worm her within three weeks of the date of service, but it is usually safe to use a good reliable vermifuge between the third and fifth weeks. However, to avoid accident it is best to consult your veterinary surgeon on this matter.

One other preparation which is often neglected but which (I speak from experience) if not taken care of can cause the death of a puppy. Be sure to cut the petticoats and long hair from under the tail of your bitch. I have on more than one occasion known of newborn puppies being caught in their mother's hair, and either being strangled or breaking their necks if the mother gets up quickly, or, at best, being carried out of the box to fall off into the cold. This is a most important point.

Now to the whelping arrangements. The bitch should be allowed to become accustomed to the place where she will be expected to whelp at least two weeks before the date she is due. The best place for the bitch to whelp is in an outside shed or, alternatively, an empty room in the house where she will know she will be undisturbed. While a Sheltie, as a rule, likes to know her owner is present while she is whelping, she certainly does not want to have her puppies in the lounge where all the family, as well as the visitors, will be coming and going.

Whether she is to whelp in a shed or in a spare room she must have a suitable box in which to whelp, and I do not think that the importance of such a box can be overstressed, for a great number of the puppies which die, either as soon as they are born or within a day or two after this event, do so because the whelping conditions have not been satisfactory.

A box approximately 18 in. wide by 2 ft. deep is a good

size. It should also be about 2 ft. high and should have a covered top.

A box about 20 in. × 20 in. × 24 in. is ideal. There should be a board along the bottom of the front opening at least 4 in. high. A thick blanket should hang from the top, completely covering the opening. This then makes the dark, cave-like den to which the bitch in her natural state would have taken herself, and in which every particle of heat given off by the bitch and her puppies is conserved as much as possible. Thus, the babies are living in a fairly high, even temperature.

However, these precautions for keeping the babies warm I rarely consider to be adequate. More newborn puppies die from getting chilled than from any other reason. Consider for a moment that the puppies, at birth, are suddenly and rudely shot into this world from which the temperature inside their dam of some 100°F. (38°C.), and imagine the shock it must be to their little systems to find themselves, wet and miserable in, at best, a temperature of 60°F. (16°C.), and if in the winter most probably down to, or below, freezing. Puppies for the first few days after birth lack the 'shivering mechanism', so cannot possibly warm themselves.

So into the already snug box I always place, hanging from the roof, a 12-in. tubular electric airing-cupboard heater, and this is turned on on any but the very warmest of our heat-wave summer days. If the box is a well-made one, this will keep it at approximately 70°F. (21·1°C.), so long as you do not forget your thick blanket in front. This temperature may seem high for the bitch, and indeed often makes her pant, but if she is given plenty of liquid, both milk and fresh water, I have never known it have any adverse effect on the mother. Naturally when you wish to dispense with the heater this must be done gradually, and the ideal is to have the heater thermostatically controlled. If you are not lucky enough to be able to do this, then the heater must be turned off for short spells at first, at the warmest moment of the day, lengthening these periods gradually.

Much use has been made recently of infra-red lamps for the rearing of puppies, both over the whelping-box (when the box must be an open one) and later in the kennel when the tinies start to run about. I am told that they are excellent, particularly in the latter case, but I cannot speak from experience.

The infra-red lamps need very careful adjustment and care must be taken of their possible effect on the eyes both of the mother and of the litter. Naturally the type of heater I use has no beneficial rays, but as a heat-promoting unit I consider it ideal, and there is no risk to the eyes as it gives no light. However, anyone interested in the use of infra-rays will be able to obtain full details from the various makers of lamps of this type. Some kind of heat is undoubtedly essential, and quite apart from the object of keeping the babies from getting chilled there is also another important point. It is an accepted scientific fact that quite a large proportion of the food is used to keep up the body temperature, and this part of the food is then lost to its purpose of body-building. As tiny puppies can eat only very limited amounts of food the more of it that can be used for body-building the better, and it can be assumed that if puppies are kept warm less food is needed for use as a 'heater' and more of it can go to promoting growth.

One other point on this same subject. Never feed the in-whelp bitch with really cold food; even her raw meat should just have the chill off it, for every time she consumes stone-cold food her body temperature drops, and for a while the functions of her body are concerned with turning the food into heat-promoting substances, instead of growth-promoting ones, and each intake of food therefore halts, temporarily, the growth of the unborn puppies.

I have never found it necessary to have any kind of 'guard rail' inside a Sheltie whelping-box, although I know that some people consider them absolutely essential, and for this reason I mention them here. If such a rail is thought necessary it should be placed inside each of the three complete sides of the box, about 4 in. from floor level and about 4 in. from the sides. The purpose of this rail is to prevent the bitch from crushing a puppy between her back and the wall of the kennel, should a puppy get behind her.

There are various opinions as to what is the best type of bedding to use for a bitch to whelp on, but I am certain there is nothing so satisfactory as several layers of newspapers. The bitch, before whelping, will rip up her bed anyway, and the paper can be changed frequently, and as often as it becomes wet. Straw and hay should *never* be used, for it is easy for the bitch to lose a newborn puppy in such bedding; also, straw, particularly, may prick the eyes of the tiny pups and cause damage and possibly blindness. Although wood-wool is 'safe' in regard to eye damage, it is still likely to cover up a newborn puppy while the mother is attending to the next addition to the family. Even for older puppies hay should never be used as it carries and breeds lice.

The accepted period of gestation is 63 days, but most Shelties, particularly maiden bitches, will have their puppies a day or so earlier, so one may start to expect them by about the fifty-ninth day. It is a wise move (because it is a sure guide and may well save the owner some disturbed nights) to start taking the bitch's temperature twice daily, about six days before she is due.

At this stage it will usually be found that the temperature is slightly subnormal, around 100 degrees, but before the pups are imminent the temperature will fall considerably, at least as a general rule, usually down to about 98°F. (37°C). Once the temperature reaches this low level the puppies can be expected within the next 24 hours. Occasionally a bitch's temperature will drop even lower (I had one that always went down to 96 degrees), but this is exceptional. Equally exceptional is the bitch whose temperature barely drops at all.

Another indication that whelping time is near is that the bitch when at exercise will stop to pass water very frequently. Later still she will begin to be very restless, and when this stage is reached she should be taken to her whelping-box at once. There she will probably begin almost immediately to tear up her newspaper, and she may continue with this pastime for as long as a whole day before the next stage is reached. During this period leave her quiet and look in on her every hour at least so that you may know when she begins to strain.

As the labour pains actually begin she will become more and more restless, pant a great deal and breathe very quickly. She will also turn frequently and look at, and lick, her tail. Sometimes the first puppy is born almost as soon as the pains begin, but equally frequently there is a lapse of as much as one-and-a-half hours between the onset of the pains and the first puppy. The bitch will not strain constantly during such a long period, but will alternate bouts of vigorous straining with spells of rest to regain her strength. If a period of two hours passes from the time of the onset of the pains without any signs of a puppy being born you should contact your veterinary surgeon at once. One cannot stress this point too strongly and it is for this reason that you should look in on your bitch frequently after she goes to her whelping-box, so that you may know exactly when she first shows signs of straining.

There is no doubt whatever that almost every bitch likes to have her owner with her at this time, and while they do not like being fussed about they do so much appreciate the fact that you are sitting quietly by. From time to time there is the bitch which *must* whelp in the spot she chooses, and this may be your lap, but you will almost have to put up with it, for if her mind is made up on this point you will be quite unable to change it.

Shelties, as a rule, are very easy whelpers, and no difficulties need be expected, but if a puppy gets held up, either because it is too large or wrongly presented, or because the pelvic opening is too small, that puppy naturally prevents the birth of the remainder of the litter, and any hold-up may mean death to them.

Without wanting to cast gloom on your preparations for your first whelping, it is always best to be prepared, and here is a list of those things you should have ready to hand when you think the whelping imminent: cotton wool, permanganate of potash, sterilized scissors, a bowl of hot water and a turkish towel.

When the labour pains really start, immediately turn on the heater in the box, unless the temperature of the whelping-room is above 65 degrees (most unlikely in our English climate!), so that the babies may have a warm home to be born into.

In a normal whelping you will notice first a greenish discharge staining the newspaper and then, soon after this, you will see the membraneous water-bag protruding from the bitch's vulva. Each puppy is enclosed in a separate sac. Keep your eyes open but do not attempt to help her at this stage, and if all is normal one of two things will happen; either the bitch will tear the sac as it is protruding, letting the fluid escape, to be followed almost immediately by the whole puppy, or else the puppy will suddenly shoot into the box, still enclosed in the sac. The bitch will then immediately rip the sac open and lick up the fluid. The puppy will still be attached to the placenta, or after-birth, by the umbilical cord, and this the bitch will bite and sever, and then she will eat the after-birth. This done (it usually takes place in a matter of seconds) she will immediately turn her attentions to the puppy, licking it, often quite roughly, until it breathes and gives its first cry.

Sometimes, with a first litter, the first puppy arrives and mother just doesn't know what to do. If that is the case it is up to you to do it for her, and to do it quickly. You must pick up the puppy, slit the back which, though tough, can readily be broken with the fingers, and the puppy will fall from the bag. Look quickly to make sure there is no mucus in the mouth or air passage then give it to the mother, holding it to her muzzle, when she will probably begin to lick it at once. If she still remains 'clueless', take the puppy and rub it briskly with the turkish towel. The pup will almost certainly cry and mother will equally certainly immediately say, 'Hey, give me that; that's mine', and your troubles will be over. Once her instinct is aroused she will carry on from there and deal with the remaining pups herself. However, it is always wise to stand by, for if you leave her the worst may happen, and a puppy be suffocated before it can be cleared from the sac. The mother, having claimed the first pup when it cried, will probably take over and bite through the cord and sever the pup from the afterbirth, but should she not do so the owner must do it for her. Therefore you will require your sterilized scissors with which to sever the cord about 2 in. from the puppy's body. Have ready the permanganate of potash crystals so that, should there be any bleeding from the cord, caused either by the scissors or the bitch's bite, you can apply some. This will stop the bleeding at once.

Quite frequently the puppy will appear in the box and yet be attached to the afterbirth still inside the mother's body. In such a case it is necessary to make sure the afterbirth appears; if it is retained after the birth of the last puppy it will certainly cause trouble. Sometimes, too, the mother will sever the cord with the puppy outside and the afterbirth still in the passage. Again make sure the afterbirth is passed.

The natural action of the bitch is to eat each afterbirth as it is severed from the puppy. My bitches are always allowed to do this, for this was a provision by nature for the nourishment of the bitch when, in her wild state, she had to stay in her lair after whelping and could not go hunting for food for a time. The eating of the afterbirth is beneficial to the bitch as it contains many essentials that are good for her. While providing nourishment it also acts as a laxative. There are two schools of thought on this subject, some breeders standing by and taking each afterbirth as it is severed and destroying it.

There is no regular interval between the birth of the puppies. Sometimes a matter of minutes only may elapse between the birth of the first and second puppies, sometimes an hour or more, and if it is this long period the bitch will lie quiet and rest and frequently lick the puppies she has, stimulating them to live and eat. It is an ever-recurrent miracle to me to see the new puppy, still wet, blindly struggle to the nipple within a moment or two of being born, and start in on his breakfast.

Almost always, at some time during the labour there is a very long pause between the birth of the pups, and this usually indicates that the 'half-way' mark has been reached. Do not think that by this I mean that if your bitch has already had six puppies she is going to have twelve. The bitch's uterus is made up of two separate horns and the puppies lie in each of these. When whelping begins, normally all the puppies from one horn are expelled first, then there is generally a fairly long pause while the second horn takes over the job and expels its quota of the litter. The horns do not necessarily hold an equal number of pups; in fact it can be very uneven, but there is a definite pause when one horn takes over from the other.

During the whelping the bitch may refuse all drink, but if she will take milk there is no reason why she should not have it, and if it is given it should be given as cold as possible, despite all earlier comments on warm food, for the cold will stimulate the labour pains, whereas warm milk might be conducive to sleep.

When you think she has finished whelping give her a drink of milk (I always leave a bowl in the whelping-box with her) and leave her to sleep for some hours, after having removed all damp bedding and given her fresh, dry newspaper.

A maiden bitch may not appear to have any milk at all

when the puppies are born, and she will probably produce milk as soon as the pups start to suckle. Others do not produce milk for about a day, but this is rare. However, a new-born puppy can quite well exist for 24 hours without milk, though he should not have to do so, but do remember that he cannot exist for very long at all without warmth.

The first three days in the life of a puppy are vital, and the bitch should be looked at every few hours during this period so that one may spot at once if a puppy is being pushed away by the others and not getting his fair share of food, or if he has been pushed away and has become chilled. Immediately on opening the door of the whelping-room one should be able to tell at once how the litter is doing. There is nothing more delightful than to be met with either complete silence or delicious sucking noises. One is sometimes met with crying pups; however, this need not always give you cause for alarm, for the pups may be giving hungry cries only because you have arrived at feeding time. There is one sound I never like to hear; it is the cry that sounds like a young kitten mewling. It is a very distinctive cry which denotes a hungry puppy that is weak and sickly and for which it is difficult to do very much. However, should you find a puppy pushed away and cold, despite your heating precautions, pick him up at once and take him away, wrap him in a blanket and pop him in a cool oven (with the door open of course) or under the griller of an electric cooker for a while. A puppy, apparently dead, has often been revived in this way and gone back to its mother an hour or so later and never again looked back. Just one word on taking the puppy away. Mother will almost certainly resent this, so try not to let her see. Take out two puppies together, both in the one hand if possible, slip the weak one into your pocket or down your neck and quickly put the other one back. Shelties are clever but they can't count yet.

Always watch most carefully to see that one weakly baby is not constantly being pushed out; if it it is, make sure that it gets its fair share of the milk bar by holding it on to the nipple for a definite period (ten to twenty minutes) every two hours for the first day or so. It will probably pick up, thanks to this attention, and after a couple of days be able to take its own place and keep up with its hardier brothers and sisters. Many a really good puppy has been saved in this way and the trouble entailed is more than worth while.

If, because the mother cannot care for them, or if only because the litter is very large, you have to hand-rear a puppy, it is something that can be accomplished. The complete hand-rearing of a litter is a most wearisome task, for the puppies must be fed with the greatest regularity, every two hours, day and night, for the first week at least.

I find that Lactol, which is specially prepared for puppies, and is therefore equivalent, in essentials, to bitch's milk, is the best to use. You can do no better than to follow exactly the directions given with the food. There is on the market a most excellent bottle, John Bell & Croydon's Premature Baby Feeder. This is marked off in teaspoonsful, and has a small teat, just about the size of a Sheltie's own. Further, the milk can be very gently pressed into the puppy's mouth, until it gets the idea of sucking.

If you want to help a bitch with a big litter by supplementary feeding, always select the weakest puppies in the litter and try always to feed the same puppies.

If only supplementary feeding, then the mother will look after the puppies, cleaning them and keeping them warm. However, if you are rearing a litter which has no mother, then it is essential to keep them very warm, and you must also do something to simulate the motion of the mother's tongue on them. After feeding, their tummies should be gently rubbed in a circular motion with a small piece of cotton wool dipped in olive oil, and this method continued until the bowels act. The puppies must be kept clean, by wiping with cotton wool dipped in mild antiseptic, and care must be taken to dry the puppies afterwards. They can be dusted with a plain talcum powder or boracic powder if desired.

Hand-feeding should continue, with the spaces between meals getting longer, until the puppies are three weeks old, when raw meat can be added to the diet and the usual method of weaning gradually introduced.

Everything used for these babies must be kept just as clean as if you were feeding a human baby, and all their bowls, bottles, etc., sterilized, and the bottle and teats kept immersed in cold water.

The bitch will be most reluctant to leave her litter for the first day or so after whelping, and I never make a bitch leave the nest for the first 24 hours if she does not wish to do so, but after this period has elapsed she should be encouraged to take a short spell away, just long enough to relieve her bladder twice daily. Gradually she will increase these spells of her own accord, but in my opinion no bitch should be allowed to take normal exercise until such time as she has completely finished with her litter, for too much excitement and exercise will cause the milk to dry up, and possibly cause her to collapse from calcium derangement. The idea, to my way of thinking, is for the whelping kennel to be in a run to which the bitch can have access at all times if she so wishes. A good mother will not be seen in the run very often, and then only for a few minutes at a time, while a naughty mother can be shut in with her pups if necessary.

For at least 24 hours after the last puppy has been born the bitch should have no solid food at all, being kept on milk (preferably goat's milk), Lactol and gruel. If at the end of this time she appears perfectly normal, a little solid food may be introduced in the shape of fresh raw meat, but it is preferable to keep the bitch on fluids for two days, and I feed meat during this period only if the bitch turns against milky food, which she may sometimes do. Fluids, however, can include raw eggs beaten up in milk, and if she has had rather a trying time it is always advantageous to add glucose to her liquid foods for a day or two. A dessertspoonful twice a day is sufficient.

Continue to keep the puppies bedded on newspaper. Using a blanket, even after whelping is concluded, may be risky, for the bitch may push it up into folds, and a puppy become lost in it. Frequently you will find that a bitch refuses to have any bedding at all in her box, and will either push it right out or into the corners. Undoubtedly the bitch knows best what she wants and if she insists on this all bedding should be removed. You may find that the babies, because of the strength of the pushing with their back legs to hold themselves again the teats, will develop sore pads on their back feet if they are directly on wood, but I have never known this have any lasting ill-effects and I have had a number of bitches who refused all bedding.

Once the first two days are passed the bitch must be given all the food she will eat. I always put my bitches back at once on to the four meals a day they have been accustomed to during the pre-natal period, and in addition the bitch has a bowl of milk constantly in her box with her. I am not in favour of encouraging any bitch to leave her puppies, and for the first few days at least they are fed actually in the whelping-box. By leaving the milk in the box there is, of course, the risk of its being spilt, but I have very rarely found this happen, and as a result of leaving the milk with her you will find that your bitch will drink between 2 to 3 pints a day in addition to her usual feeds, and if she has a big litter this is a great advantage. Should your Sheltie produce only one or two pups, instead of the average fix or six, she will need much less food and, anyway, unless she is a real glutton will probably adjust things herself. But with a litter of six or more, do remember that she needs a really adequate quantity of meat—at least 1 lb., preferably 1½ lb., daily. There is no food which 'makes milk' as does raw meat.

With a very big litter, or in the event of your suspecting that the quality of the milk is not very good—which you will soon detect by squeaking, discontented puppies—the addition of Lactagol to the bitch's food is a great help. This is obtainable from any chemist, and a Sheltie should be given the full human dose advised on the packet.

All puppies are born with dew-claws on their front legs. A few Shelties are born with back dew-claws as well; these *must* be removed. There is not a hard and fast rule in our breed about the removal of front dew-claws, so you can do exactly as you like in this matter. For myself, I never remove them, for I cannot see the point of putting pups to unnecessary suffering. Back dew-claws are another matter, and if you find these are present call your veterinary surgeon and have them removed when the puppies are three to four days old. It is an easy job to do, but not a nice one, and one you really cannot do yourself unless you have previously seen it done properly.

When the puppies are three weeks old (with a litter, especially if the bitch is young, even a little earlier) you can begin to wean the puppies, and their first meal should be one of raw scraped meat, about one teaspoonful per puppy. Of course you will need to feed each puppy separately, with your fingers, until after a day or two they become accustomed to the meat. At three weeks and two or three days they can have two meat meals daily, each of one heaped teaspoonful, and a day or so later yet a third meal can be offered, but this should be one of milk thickened with Farex. By the time they are four weeks old the babies should be having 1 oz. of raw meat daily, in two meals, and a meal of Farex and milk. At the beginning of the fifth week the babies can be introduced to a fourth meal, this time a starchy meal, preferably of one of the well-known brands of puppy biscuit meal, such as Saval No. 1 or Weetmeet No. 1, *very thoroughly* soaked in milk or stock. To soak meal thoroughly it should be measured out, and at least twice its volume of liquid, almost at boiling point, poured over it. It should then be covered and left to soak at least four hours before feeding to the babies. Towards the end of this fifth week their final meal can also be introduced. This can either be another meal of biscuit or (and I prefer this) a meal of barley kernels soaked in cold milk overnight. If I am giving this, then the biscuit meal is soaked in stock, so that at this age the puppies are getting two meat meals, two milk meals and one meal of biscuit and stock daily, as follows:

7 a.m.   Barley kernels soaked overnight in milk. Add a few drops cod liver oil and ¼ teaspoonful calcium per puppy.

11 a.m.   1–2 oz. raw meat.

2 p.m.   Farex and milk.

5 p.m.   1–2 oz. raw meat.

9 p.m.   Biscuit-meal soaked in stock.

As soon as you begin feeding the babies the mother will be taken away from them for increasingly long periods, until at five weeks old she is with them only at night, if at all, except for a playtime morning and evening.

I am not a believer in vegetables for dogs, whether adult or puppy, as the stomach and digestive juices of the dog are not equipped to deal with these fibrous substances, but at the same time a whole carrot makes a lovely toy, and there is some advantage to be gained from nibbling this.

It is absolutely essential that all meals should be given to an exact time-table, whether to pups or nursing mothers, and too much attention cannot be paid to this detail.

Except for meat meals, I have made no attempt to give a guide as to the size of the meals as it does vary so much from puppy to puppy, and it is a question of adapting it to each pup; but as a rough guide a Sheltie baby at five weeks should get about a quarter of a pint of milk in its Farex meal, the same with the barley kernels, of which it will need one dessert-spoonful unsoaked. Its biscuit meal, after soaking, should be about an egg-cupful, but I stress that this is not a definite amount; one pup varies so much from the next. Only your own judgment can guide you.

Daily the size of the meal should be slightly increased, but the number of meals will never go above five, at which it will remain until the puppies are ten to twelve weeks old, when it should be decreased to four, but the size of these four must be increased to offset the loss of a meal.

When eight weeks of age the babies will be taking 2 oz. of meat at each meal, and charts for feeding at various ages are set out elsewhere. Naturally, after the first few days of meat feeding it is no longer necessary to scrape the meat, and by the time the puppy is four weeks old the meat should be given chopped into small pieces. As the puppy gets older so the size of the pieces will become larger. Some breeders, and I am one, believe in feeding the meat meal in one lump for the puppy or adult to chew and tear for itself, so at eight weeks of age my puppies get their meat in a lump, and the size of the lump is increased as the puppy grows.

As soon as the puppies are on to a breakfast meal this should have added to it a few drops of cod liver oil and a quarter of calcium phosphate per puppy. The calcium phosphate should be continued until the puppy has finished teething at eight months of age, but in the early days it should be increased gradually until at four months he is receiving the adult dose of one teaspoonful. The cod liver oil should be increased gradu-ally also up to one teaspoonful, and this dose continued more or less throughout his life, except that it is advisable to cut it out for a while should we happen to get a very hot summer.

It sometimes happens that when puppies are first put on to

mixed food, as opposed to their mother's milk, they will have diarrhoea. This is nothing to become too worried about, nevertheless it must not be allowed to persist. A meal of gruel made from arrowroot and milk, with a little glucose added, is helpful, as is a meal or two of Allbran, and the addition of one-quarter teaspoonful per pup of McLean's stomach powder to each non-meat meal will also prove beneficial. I do not suggest that you use all these remedies, but here are three to choose from.

Almost every puppy has worms. No, that is not a sweeping statement, but the absolute truth. Puppies, whether they show marked symptoms of round worms or not, should *always* be wormed at six weeks of age, but puppies which show marked symptoms should be wormed two weeks earlier at least. The signs of worms are: much distension of the tummy after a meal; discharging eyes; very loose, pale-coloured motions; passing worms in the motions and vomiting worms. If puppies show any or all these signs they should be wormed early—at, say, four weeks of age. Whether they show signs or not they should always be wormed at six weeks, anyway. There are a number of excellent vermifuges on the market, or, if you prefer, you can consult your veterinary surgeon on the matter. Worm your puppy on a dry day, free from cold winds if possible, and try to avoid any chance of the puppy catching a chill for 48 hours after worming.

For no reason that I can discover, it will almost always be found that a litter from a maiden bitch is far 'wormier' than subsequent litters from the same bitch, and it is therefore specially important to watch for signs of infestation in a maiden bitch's litter.

Many bitches, when their puppies are about four weeks old, will begin to regurgitate their own part-digested food for their babies, whether you are already weaning them or not. This is a perfectly natural instinct for the bitch and should not revolt you in any way, but at the same time it is not the best thing for mother or pups. So if she starts this habit, make sure always to feed her out of sight of the puppies, and do not let her return to them for about two hours after being fed. Even this does not always suffice. I once had a bitch who, when her puppies were almost four months of age, would go out as much as four hours after being fed, jump a five-foot wire fence and present her now large babies with an extra meal. Don't worry about this habit; it is always the best of mothers who have this regurgitating instinct.

It is most important, from the time the puppies are one week old, to pay great attention to their toe-nails, which should be cut, on their front paws at least, at regular weekly intervals. The baby nails are cruel, and their regular pounding at their mother when seeking their milk will very rapidly tear and scratch her and make her very sore. Often one is rung up or written to for advice on various points, but an ever recurring question is: 'My puppies are now two weeks old, but my bitch is being horrid to them and does not seem to want them. What can I do?' My answer is always a question, 'Have you cut your puppies' toe-nails?' and the reply, nine times out of ten, is a surprised, 'No.' Here, then, is the answer; cut those toe-nails, look at the poor mother's breasts and apply a soothing cream to those scratches, and you will have no more trouble.

Now your first step has been made, your bitch, if you have fed her well and treated her as you should, will have played her part, and now it is up to you to rear those pups to the best of your ability, in the hope that in this, your first litter, you have a winner if not a Champion.

12

GROWING UP

BY THE time the babies are five weeks old the whole of their future is your responsibility, and it is up to you to rear them to the very best of your ability. It may be that there is a potential Champion in this your first litter—you would not be the first person who has produced a Champion at the first time of trying—and now you can make or mar it. The first difficulty, of course, is to pick the most 'likely looking' pup, and this comes only with years of experience. But if you have amicable relations with the owner of the stud-dog or, better still, if you have your bitch on breeding terms, the owner of either the stud-dog or the bitch will give every help in picking the litter over and helping you keep the best. If the breeding terms agreement asks you to give up the pick, the second-best will be clearly indicated to you. For myself, I like to pick a litter as soon as possible after it is born, while the pups are still wet if I can, and after that I don't like having to pick again until the babies are at least six months old. No matter what happens in between, barring accidents, your 'pick of the litter' while it is still wet, however ungainly it may become at the age of four to five months, will always end up the best of the litter. I do not pretend that at this tender age of an hour or two it is possible to say such-and-such a pup will be a Champion, but only which is the best of the lot; anyone who tries to tell you that a four-hour-old puppy is a potential Champion is just asking for trouble.

Puppies are almost always born with pink noses, and usually these turn black within a few days. However, in a sable or tricolour, with a blaze, particularly where the white hair touches the end of the nose, this part of the nose will frequently take much longer to go black. This need not give any cause for alarm, as very rarely does the nose, in these two colours, fail to change. With the blue merle, very often a much larger area of the nose is pink, and often remains so until the puppy is almost a year old. Sometimes a patch will remain pink all its life— this is so in dogs suffering from poor pigmentation—and there is not very much that can be done about it, but in blue merle it is not a disqualifying fault, nor will it be found to be strongly hereditary.

The puppies' eyes should be open about the 10th to 14th day, that is, with puppies born at approximately the right time, on the 60th to 63rd day after conception. It will usually be found that puppies born well ahead of time, say a week early, rarely open their eyes before the 18th to 20th day, while puppies born late may have their eyes open by the time they are a week old. This would seem to give credence to the theory that the determination of the time of opening the eyes is not 10 days after birth, but 73 days after conception. If, after the expected time for the eyes to open has elapsed without anything happening, or if only one eye has opened, the area could be very gently massaged all round with either butter or olive oil. This is really to make the bitch lick the spot, the use of her tongue in massage helping the eye to open. One word of warning about eyes. Should a foster-mother be necessary, and should you have to use a cat for this purpose, it is most essential to take care that the puppies are kept within their darkened box, for the extreme roughness of the cat's tongue, compared with that of a bitch, tends to cause the eyes to open too early and then the danger from light-rays is greatly increased. Special precautions are necessary if rearing on a cat under an infra-red lamp.

Eyes are always blue when first opened, and to the experienced observer there is a great difference between the blue eye which will turn brown eventually and the blue eye (of the merle) which will remain blue. When eyes start to change colour, at four to six weeks, is the time when you can assess what shade the eye will eventually be, for the eye which is the last to start changing colour will almost always be the lightest eye in the litter.

Until the puppies are at least six weeks old you will have to do your best for all of them, not just for your pick, until the litter is ready to sell. The diet already set out can be followed, with the increases already noted incorporated, and further diet sheets for various ages will be found in the Appendix. In addition, the puppies must have access to plenty of fresh, clear water from the time they are four weeks old. The puppies must either be fed separately or, if feeding several from the same dish, they must always be watched all the time, otherwise there will never be fair play. Some puppies will get too little, the greedy ones will always have more than their share.

Once the puppies are away from their dam their box can be supplied with straw or wood-wool for their bedding, preferably the latter, and the floor of the kennel should be freely sprinkled with sawdust. Sheltie babies are always clean, and by the time they are three weeks old are usually keeping their bed clean, and this will continue. Sawdust is not the very best of things for puppies to eat, and so, if it is fine weather, it is best to feed the babies in their run, and if it is not, and they have to feed on the sawdusty floor, spread sheets of newspaper as 'tablecloths' under their feeding-dishes.

Puppies, though they love playing with each other, should also have toys to play with, and those recommended are a rubber deck-tennis ring and an old stocking folded in half and knotted—this makes a delightful tug-of-war toy. Never give balls to puppies lest by accident they are swallowed and cause choking.

Once the puppies have reached the age of eight weeks any that are going to their new homes should do so as soon as possible, and it is advisable to give a feeding chart with each puppy, so that the same diet may be continued. The five meals should be continued until the puppies are three months, and then reduced to four meals, but the size of each meal should be increased, particularly the meat meal. The three-month puppy will be eating 3 to 4 oz. of meat at each of his two meat meals. The four meals should be continued as long as the puppy will co-operate, especially during the winter months, and then, when they are cut to three, which should not be before six months of age, they should be:

7 a.m.   Wholemeal bread or barley kernels or cereals, with milk, cod liver oil and calcium; ½ teaspoonful of each.

5 p.m.   6–8 oz. raw meat.

10 p.m. Bowl biscuit-meal with stock.

Three meals should be continued until teething is over at about eight months of age, and then the puppy can be put into its adult diet of two meals:

7 a.m.   Breakfast as above, but calcium can now be omitted.

6 p.m.   8 oz. raw meat or paunch, which can be varied with cooked meat and biscuit meal or cooked fish and biscuit meal, but remember raw meat is the natural diet.

During all puppyhood the babies can frequently be given big, raw bones to chew; they may well cause occasional fights, but none will prove fatal.

In addition to feeding your puppy well during the formative months, great attention must also be paid to its periods of sleep and exercise. In the early months the former is probably even more important than the latter, and so often when a puppy is sold at eight weeks of age its life becomes a misery because it is not realized that he needs just as much sleep as a human baby, and often a wee pup will be taken off to be house-pet to children, who when they are awake expect the puppy to be awake, and this is a point which should be very clearly stressed to your clients.

Correct ear carriage is a very essential part of any Sheltie's make-up; if his ear carriage is wrong his whole expression will be marred, and now is the time when you should be watching those ears and training them.

Until a puppy is about eight weeks of age his ears are generally down on the side of his head, but soon after this age they assume the 'semi-erect' position we expect. Assume it, yes, but keep it, no. Ear carriage may vary from day to day, even from hour to hour, but a puppy which, for the greater part of the time, carried his ears correctly need not give much cause for alarm. However, if at, say, ten weeks of age a puppy has given little indication that his ears are likely to go up at all, it is best to shave them, but there is always a risk in this, for the low-eared puppy may turn into the pricked-eared one after being shaved and it is a point on which I would advise the

novice to be very, very careful, taking the advice of an experienced breeder before doing anything drastic. Equally, a puppy
who, at this age, has ears which stand erect should be taken in
hand *at once,* for once erect ears are allowed to have their way
they become hard and unmanageable and the battle is as good
as lost. Almost always a Sheltie puppy will fly one or both ears
at some time during the teething period of four to eight months,
and a little advice on this subject when one is selling a puppy is
a very useful piece of knowledge to the new owner. The prick
ear should *never* have weights put on the tip. In my opinion
this only tends to strengthen the muscle, which fights constantly
against the weight, struggling to raise itself again and thereby
strengthening itself, and the struggle ends in a permanently
erect ear, which may possibly turn over long enough to see

24. Grease one-third   25. Grease one-third   26. Ear carriage after
    of inside of ear   of outside of ear   treatment

you through a class in a show, but which will be up again in no
time. The most satisfactory method, in my experience, is to
keep the tip of the ear, both inside and out, well greased. I do
this by applying a lump of Cuticura ointment, or of wool fat
(messier but less expensive), to both faces of the ear flap and for
about one-third of its length (*see* diagrams Figs. 24 to 26).
This should be a thick dollop of ointment and should not be
rubbed in. The greased part of the ear may then be dipped
into fine ash from the fire, or into bird sand, to stop the grease
getting on your clothes and furniture, and at the same time
giving just a little weight, which will not strengthen the muscle
because the grease below will keep the ear malleable. The grease
will stay on the ear for long periods, especially if the dog is
kept out of doors, and can easily be renewed whenever
necessary. To remove it when required it is best to soak the
ear in surgical spirit and then to comb out the grease very

gently with a fine-tooth comb. Vaseline may be used instead of Cuticura, but I do not find it so satisfactory as it is less sticky and melts off quicker. An ear may also go up later in life: when a bitch comes into season, when she is in whelp, when an adult casts his coat and frequently for no reason at all. In all cases the treatment is exactly the same as for the youngster whose ears are being trained. When you wish to remove grease from the ear, soak well in any proprietory brand of plaster remover, and comb gently[1].

At this stage of weaning, and just after, remember that the puppy has a great deal to do physically. In a very few months he has to grow from a fat ball of fluff to an elegant, graceful adult, a show dog we hope. He should be allowed to do this undisturbed. By this I mean that at the time he is passing through this period of intensive growth do not try to 'cram' him with too many things to do. He will have to be house-trained, he will need to be lead-trained, and if you have a car, the earlier he becomes accustomed to travelling in it the better, for if he is car-sick he is much more likely to grow out of it if he starts early. Beyond this, do nothing which will demand too much from him. Let him romp, gallop, eat and, almost most important of all, *sleep*. Many, many puppies are ruined and stunted in growth because owners do not seem to realize that the little Sheltie needs just as much sleep as a tiny human being. He cannot use his growing powers to their full extent unless he gets this sleep.

There are various views on the question of grooming, as you will note elsewhere, and it is up to you to decide whether or not your puppy is groomed daily at this time. If you belong to the 'no grooming' school of thought the daily handling of the puppy which would occur if he were groomed should be made up to him in some other way, for this handling is a very important part of his education. If he is not being groomed, see that he has a daily game with you, a rough and tumble is good for him, especially if he is the only puppy with no kennel-mates to tease and play with him. Some breeders make the mistake of always creeping about in their puppy houses, never crashing the feeding-bowl, etc. This is all wrong. The more noise a

[1]A new product has been introduced on the American market. 'Ear Tip' is well worth any trouble you may have in obtaining it.

puppy becomes accustomed to the better, and if he associates noise with the happy event of the arrival of his food, noise will soon lose its fear for him. Again, a bit of noise will help you to spot the shy puppy in the litter if there is one.

Fortunately in our breed the puppies are not scrappers and several growing youngsters can be housed together, provided the accommodation is big enough, so that if you are 'running on' two or three pups from one litter the question of an extra house does not arise, provided the first was large enough.

Although a well-reared Sheltie may remain plump from the time of its birth until maturity, it will nevertheless go through a stage when it will be 'all legs and wings' and when you will despair that it will ever be fit to show. Provided he is well covered nothing else matters, and the condition of the puppy is solely your responsibility. If he has been well supplied with bone- and body-making foods, given plenty of fresh water to drink, a warm dry house to sleep in, plenty of exercise, fresh air without draughts, and daily human companionship, you can rest assured that his deficiencies as a show specimen, if any, are not your fault, but were inherent in him.

So often it happens that one sells a puppy as a most promising show prospect, and then, when the time comes for the pup to make its show debut, it fails to win. The purchaser is disgusted with the breeder for having sold him a dud, when 99 times out of a 100 the fault lies with the owner having failed to rear the puppy correctly, despite any guidance on the subject given by the breeder.

Puppy rearing, while a most engrossing occupation, is nevertheless a scientific one, and should never be treated lightly. It is a very great responsibility. The serious breeder with a litter to rear must be always on the alert, with a ready eye to spot any sign of things going wrong; he should anticipate all those things that could happen, and always be one jump ahead of the puppy. This is more important than I can say. Time and time again an accident has happened because the person responsible has been unable to foresee a contingency: the board standing against the kennel wall which will fall if the puppy bounces on it; the toy that is getting worn and which may, at any moment, start coming away in pieces and choke the puppy; these, and a hundred other things which can so easily be foreseen if one keeps one's eyes open, are all part and parcel of successfully rearing a puppy.

Rearing one puppy is the most difficult thing of all. Always try to make it two at least. They exercise each other, keep one another out of mischief and provide a healthful competition at feeding time. The ideal, always, even if you are sure there is only one 'certain Champion' in the litter, is to keep a second puppy to 'run with' the first. You can always sell the second puppy when they are no longer in need of each other, and even if you 'sell it for a song' it will owe you nothing, for it will have saved you lots of trouble and helped you to turn out a very much better puppy, by playing companion, than if you had kept only one baby in the first place.

Puppy rearing is an exacting occupation, but it is also of the very greatest interest, and it is an occupation in which the breeder, no matter how many years of experience there may be behind him or her, can always, with every litter, find something new to learn. Every bitch, every puppy, is an individualist, and for this reason the whelping of a bitch and the rearing of a litter are the most absorbing tasks I know.

13

DAY-TO-DAY MANAGEMENT

No MATTER how many dogs one keeps, be it just the single house Sheltie or a kennel full of them, there are certain general rules which must be kept. These rules, all kept, add up to the happiness and the health of a dog.

HOUSING. Even if the dog is the only one who will be in your house all the time, it is essential that he should have a bed of his own to which he can retire at any time he chooses and to which, on occasion, he can be sent, if you wish him away from you for any reason. As has already been said, a tea-chest is loved by most Shelties, but a canvas bed of the stretcher variety raised from the floor on short legs and about 2 ft. long by 19 in. broad is also adequate. The tea-chest, because of its sides, and raised bed, by reason of the fact that it is raised, will automatically be free from draughts, and even the best constructed of dwellings usually has a draught at floor level. The house dog that has no bed of its own cannot be blamed for sitting on the sofa out of the draught.

The bed can be provided with a mattress made of a sack filled with wood-wool if desired; this keeps the bedding from straying and also is easily washed and renewed. His bed *must* be kept clean.

I do not consider that a stretcher-type bed is suitable for outdoor kennels, and here the tea-chest or similar box is practically a necessity. The box should be laid on its side so that only one end is open, and this end should have a board across it, at least 4 in. high, to keep the bedding in place. To my mind, there is no bedding so suitable as wood-wool, and unless you are in the happy position of growing your own straw you will not find wood-wool any more expensive than buying straw. It is cleaner and looks nicer, and there is considerably less risk of a bale of wood-wool being infected by rats with some disease, such as mange or leptospirosa, than there is with a bale of straw. The tea-chest should not be placed directly on the floor of the kennel but raised on a wooden platform at least 2 in. high.

The ideal kennel for a Sheltie is a wooden shed, well lined and free from draughts, about 6 ft. by 4 ft. in size, and of a height in which you can comfortably stand. Such a kennel, with two sleeping-boxes, can house two adult Shelties, and as a rule our breed is very much happier kennelled in pairs at least. Small 'loose-boxes' set in rows inside a larger building are also very useful and give added warmth.

It is not usually considered necessary to heat the kennels for a Sheltie, and except for warmth for babies I consider it unhealthful to do so. Provided the dog has a good deep bed, free from draughts, he will be contented. Should the weather be excessively cold, added warmth can be given by attaching a sack to the top of each sleeping-box and letting it hang down the front.

The flooring of all kennels should be of wood, and if, as often happens, you are converting an existing building which has a concrete floor, sections of this should be boarded over, or at least supplied with close-slatted duck-boards, so that the dogs cannot lie on the concrete.

All wooden boxes, benches, etc., should be easily removable for cleaning and the kennels themselves must be kept scrupulously clean. All woodwork should be creosoted annually, but be careful not to let the dog back until all the creosote is dry.

Kennels should be cleaned daily and thoroughly scrubbed with disinfectant at least once a week. This applies to adults; naturally baby puppy kennels require daily disinfecting and scrubbing. Not too much water should be used at any time because of the difficulty of getting the floor dry again, but if a good stiff scrubber is used and the floor mopped afterwards with an almost dry mop, any remaining surplus water can be got rid of by sprinkling the floor with a fine coating of sawdust, leaving it a few minutes, then sweeping it up and putting down a fresh supply of sawdust.

Every kennel or run in which the dog is spending a large part of his time must be supplied with a large bowl of fresh, clean water, and these water-bowls must be refilled at least twice a day.

In a large or medium-sized kennel it is necessary to have a certain number of runs. Though our breed is not quarrelsome and can readily be housed and exercised in fairly large numbers, one cannot have the entire kennel running around all day! Concrete brick or paving is ideal for the surface of runs, but obviously, because of the expense entailed, no very large runs can be so surfaced. For large runs, or all-day 'play-pens', grass is best. Shelties left in such runs are happy and play well—a Sheltie alone in a run of any size is usually miserable or, at best, bored.

If possible, every run should have a tree in it to provide shade, and if there is no natural shade then some must be provided. If the run is not attached to the dog's sleeping-quarters some kind of shed or covered protection must also be provided, especially in the case of young puppies.

EXERCISE. All exercise should be regular. Shelties do not need hours of 'road work' on a lead, and I have never found any to benefit from such exercise, though in some breeds it is essential. But the exercise must be daily, and a house dog that is never free in a run should be exercised twice daily. The best exercise for a Sheltie is free running and playing in fields, and this is simple if you have several dogs, for they exercise one another. The one dog can best be given free exercise by being taken out with a bicycle if the conditions permit, or taken to the park or similar open space and there be allowed to play ball; the dog gets lots of galloping after a ball well thrown and galloping is essential to our breed.

Naturally the town dog has less opportunity for free galloping, but things must be arranged so that he gets some.

No dog, however well trained in either town or country, should be allowed on the road off a lead. With the traffic such as it is today it is not fair either to the dog or to the driver. Too many dogs are still allowed to roam about alone, and we all know what a toll dogs take in road accidents, both to themselves and to others.

The dog should be exercised whatever the weather. In hot weather the exercise should be done in the early morning and evening. The Sheltie will not come to harm if exercised in the rain; the coat protects the dog from the elements and on return-ing home the dog can either be given a place to roll on—a big bed of straw or wood-wool—or the house dog can be wiped down, preferably with a chamois leather because this absorbs the damp and mud so well and is quickly wrung out and used again. Snow is the dog's delight and this does present some small problem because the snow balls up on their feathering and between their toes, and this must be combed off before the dog is put back in his kennel, otherwise it will melt gradually and make the bedding wet. No dog in a damp state should be put into his bed; he should be allowed to dry off first, in a rolling-place of straw or in a deep box of sawdust, before being put back into his kennel.

ALIMENTATION: FEEDING. This, too, must be regular, and the adult Sheltie usually does best on two meals a day, a light breakfast, and the main meal in the evening. The feeding of puppies was dealt with in the previous chapter, and diet sheets for various ages are set out in the Appendix.

The ideal diet for all dogs is raw meat, this, after all, being their natural food. The main meal should consist of raw, lean meat on at least five days out of seven. This can be alternated, or the other two days can be made up by giving paunches, or raw herrings.

Additions which can be made to the ordinary feeding plan, and which are very valuable in certain cases, are raw eggs and changes of food in the meat line, such as rabbit, sheep's heads, tongue, heart, etc. However, all these meat extras should be cooked; I never risk feeding offal raw (except liver sold for human consumption). They are mainly of value for broth, or because they bring a change of flavour to a difficult feeder. Another item of great value is pig's trotters, for these, boiled down, make wonderfully rich stock, especially good for puppies.

The average Sheltie requires ½ lb. of raw meat per day, and in addition a breakfast of whole-meal bread, and either milk or stock. Unfortunately the price of bread today makes things difficult in a large kennel and it is probably more economical to feed wholemeal biscuit meal than bread. There are a number of such meals on the market and these may be fed either dry or soaked according to your or your dog's

Ch. Tilford Tontine (Family 4)

Riverhill Reinette (Family 5)

Tango of Houghton Hill (Family 8)

Ch. Blue Blossom of Houghton Hill (at 12 months)
(Family 9)

Riverhill Roguish (Family 24)

C. M. Cooke

Ch. Dileas of the Wansdyke, who won
her title at 6½ years of age

Bertram Unne, Harrogate

Ch. Midas of Shelert

Ch. Riverhill Rare Gold

preference. It is always better not to feed the meat and cereal meals mixed together, but far better to give the carbohydrate in the morning, and the protein, or meat meal, alone at night.

Paunches can be fed raw or cooked, but raw is to be preferred, and if the paunches are from a human-consumption slaughter-house they are best fed not only raw but unwashed, for the value to the dog of the minerals contained in the half-digested grass found in the paunches is very great.

Herrings should be fed raw and whole. The bones will not harm a dog. However, it may be found that herrings, unless they are fed regularly so that the dog becomes accustomed to them, may prove rather rich and make the dog sick. This must be a question of trial and error. If the herring is cooked it must also be boned. It is usually found that cooked herring will not upset a dog, even if fed only rarely.

Bones must always be given raw. Cooked bones splinter and are dangerous, and all bones given should be large thin bones. The country kennel-owner will often be fortunate enough to obtain animals which have proved unsuitable to send to the slaughter-house (stillborn calves, for instance) and these can be fed cut up, just as they are, for even the smallest bones of a young calf, or newborn lamb, will not injure the dog.

Although raw food is the ideal it is sometimes not practicable, and on such occasions cooked meat, or simply the broth from the cooking, must be relied upon. If the main meal has to be one of biscuit-meal this should never be fed in a sloppy state. The meal should be soaked well in advance, by pouring boiling stock over it, covering it and leaving it to cool. The different meals on the market absorb different quantities of liquid, and it is up to you to work out proportions, but always make certain that you add only enough liquid to make a dry, crumbly meal. *Be sure there is enough* liquid, however, for a biscuit-meal that is only half soaked is dangerous, in that it usually causes indigestion.

Every dog, puppy or adult, should have the regular daily addition of cod liver oil, one teaspoonful for an adult, on one of his meals each day. Except for this, no other regular addition is needed. The money wasted on synthetic foods that are unnecessary must be very considerable. Additions to the food of the puppy, the pregnant bitch, the much-used stud-dog, and the dog which is not in tip-top condition are different matters, but for the ordinary fit dog no such additions are necessary.

All dogs, however, benefit from at least an occasional, if not a regular, course of one of the yeast preparations such as Vetzyme, loved by most dogs.

If you feed natural foods, feed regularly and feed dry; these are the foundations for a fit, healthy kennel.

LOVE. This goes almost without saying, but Shelties, because of their history of close association with man, need extra human companionship. By love I do not mean 'sloppiness', but simply letting him know that he is of use to you, and that he is appreciated.

TRAINING. This almost grows out of the last requirement, for a Sheltie lives to serve, and in his desire to serve trains himself to a certain degree. The untrained dog is a nuisance to everyone, his owner and his friends. Every puppy-dog, like every child, needs discipline, and is the better for it. Every puppy must be taught certain elementary things. He must learn his name, of course, and this is a lesson that needs little teaching; the constant use of his name when you are with him in the kennel, the call of his name before putting down his feed-bowl, will teach him in no time at all. From this point he can be taught all you wish him to know. He must learn, knowing his name, that when he is called he must come, and the best way to teach him this is to reward him every time he comes when you call him. A pocket with bits of biscuit or a Vetzyme tablet or two in it is practically a 'must' when you have puppies on the place. However, so much of his training depends on the way you go about it. Never call the puppy unless you mean him to come, and having called him insist that he *does* come. Never allow a puppy, or an older dog, to get away with anything.

Even if it takes you ten minutes, that puppy, once called, has got to come, and no matter how long he takes he is still a 'good dog' when he comes, and must still be rewarded. It is maddening, I know, but if you once scold him, *after he has come,* then you have destroyed his faith in you; to his mind, he was called, and he came. He will associate the punishment with the fact that he arrived—he cannot reason that he is being scolded for the time he took getting there. If once you scold your puppy when he comes, then you have only yourself to blame if he never comes again.

Next he must be taught to walk on a lead. This is best taught when the puppy is quite young, eight to ten weeks, and the best method is to use a slip lead for the purpose. I do not mean a chain-choke collar, for a chain should never be used on any Sheltie's neck; it will spoil his hair. The idea is a fine leather or thin cord lead of good length with a ring on one end. The free end is passed through the ring. The loop then goes over the puppy's head. The moment the puppy pulls back the lead tightens around his neck; when he is free with you he does not feel restraint at all. It is essential when giving a puppy his first lessons on the lead to have him alone somewhere where there are no distractions, where he can give you all his attention and you can give him all yours. In the very first lesson it should not matter at all in which direction the puppy goes. Don't try to make him go with you; once the lead is on and he is moving with it on, go with him. This is the simplest method of teaching him that things are not nearly so bad as they seem, and after a short period of the puppy leading he will be ready to come with you when you call his name. Do remember to talk to him reassuringly all the time, and to praise him unceasingly in this early lesson.

By the use of the slip lead and the method described I have never found a puppy who would not co-operate after a lesson of fifteen minutes. Fifteen minutes, for ordinary lessons, is too long, but the first time you decide to lead-break your puppy you must not give in until at least he is walking *his* way with the lead on. The puppy who throws himself in the air, screams and yells and generally behaves like a maniac is much simpler than the little mule who sits down, looks solemn, and says, 'If you want me, pull!'

With the exception of the first-lead lesson, no lesson for a young puppy should be longer than five or, at the outside, ten minutes in duration.

Having taught him to come when he is called and to walk on the lead, his other lessons will follow easily. He will have to learn to sit and to lie down when he is told, but beyond this, for the ordinary companion dog, or dog in a kennel, he needs to learn little else. He will teach himself the rest as he becomes 'educated'.

The golden rules for any kind of training are to get your dog's interest and trust, to be consistent, never to lose your temper, and to keep your words of command clear and simple. Don't use the word 'Down' today and 'Lie down' tomorrow; you will only confuse the dog.

The young puppy should become accustomed to seeing strangers and to being handled by strangers from quite an early age; in this way his faith in human nature will be developed. He must also be educated to traffic and other strange noises, and this is dealt with in the next chapter. With one dog in the house this sort of thing is easy, it comes as a matter of course, but if you have several dogs in a kennel do make sure that they all get their turn at being educated to the big wide world, especially if you live in the country. Take them to the main road once in a while, always on a lead of course, to let them see the world go by.

There remains only the question of house-training. This is very simple with a Sheltie, a naturally clean breed. Common sense on your part is what is most necessary. Be sure that the puppy is always taken to the same place when he is put out, so that he may learn more quickly what is required of him. He will want to relieve himself immediately after a meal, so watch him while he is feeding, and the moment he finishes put him on the chosen spot. In the same way he must be put out immediately he wakes up. If he does make a mistake in the house never do any more than scold him very gently, and take him, at once, to his proper place, praising him when you get there. Smacking is useless for such a crime.

All puppies, and a great many adults, delight in a chewing game. If you do not want the puppy to chew your shoes, stockings, etc., be sure to give him his own toys and make him realize that they are his. An old stocking knotted up is a favourite toy, and an old slipper, too, but be sure that he knows the difference between it and your best ones! His toys should be kept in a special place, so that he may know where to find them when he wants to play. Dogs, like children, can be taught to put their toys away when they have finished playing, too.

To recapitulate: keep commands concise and consistent; be

patient; be firm; keep lessons short; never try to teach a puppy anything when it has just been fed; be generous with your praise and tit-bits.

HAPPINESS. The other five requirements will by now have developed that happy, healthy dog which we all love and need to have about us. Keep your dog happy by companionship, love, a job to do, good food and exercise, and he will reward you many times over.

GROOMING. In our breed there are at least two schools of thought on this subject: the 'groom daily' school, and the 'almost never groom' school. Both have their advocates and it seems that both are successful, as Shelties treated in either way win the highest awards. If you are going to groom your dog daily this should be done with a good brush only; too much combing spoils and breaks the coat, and a comb need be used only when the dog is casting his coat. The Sheltie should be groomed right down to the skin, and the best type of brush for this seems to be one of the radial nylon brushes now available. The power of penetration of these bristles is great. If you belong to the other school and hardly ever groom your dog, it is essential to go over the dog once a week for any signs of fleas, for a long-haired dog is fairly prone to these parasites, particularly in warm weather. This second method of managing a Sheltie is really practicable only with a country-kept dog where he has plenty of opportunity to run in long grass; the town dog must certainly be groomed regularly to keep him clean.

When the Sheltie casts his coat, every grooming tool you possess must be brought into action and the dog groomed daily, twice daily if possible, until not a loose hair remains. The quicker you get rid of the dead hair the sooner the new coat will come. If your dog's coat is just 'on the blow' and you want to help it out with all speed, give the dog a bath; the unwanted hairs will then soon drop out.

Bathing a Sheltie, however, is unnecessary and, beyond perhaps washing the white parts before a show, should never be required if the dog is kept clean by grooming.

Beyond this there is little to do for your dog, so it is by no means hard work to keep a Sheltie.

14

SO YOU'RE GOING TO A SHOW

UNLESS you are breeding solely for the pet market (and if you are you would hardly have bought this book), your ultimate aim will be to show stock of your own breeding, and there is nothing that enchances a kennel's reputation, and at the same time its sales, more than consistent winning home-bred stock.

Having bred your litter, reared your puppy and got it to the age of about eight months, your thoughts will surely be turning to the idea of taking it to a show or two.

However, it will be useless, unless you happen to have an exceptional dog, to take it to a show unless the animal has had some preliminary training for the ring. Provided you have carried out the suggestions in the chapter on puppy-rearing, you will be more than half-way there already, but long before the age of eight months is reached the potential show prospect should have started his additional show training. He must have become accustomed to people, strange places, strange noises. Stores like the local Woolworths, and places such as a biggish railway station, are ideal training grounds. Teach him, too, to go up and down stairs, for at almost any show there may be stairs either at the approach to the hall or when you get inside, and a dog unaccustomed to stairs hates them. If you live in a house as opposed to a bungalow, this will present no problem, but if your home is a bungalow make use of the railway station for this lesson too.

Now, he must be taught to make the most of himself in the ring. First he will be expected to walk on a loose lead. The importance of this point cannot be stressed too much; it is impossible for the judge to assess the dog's movement if he is either strung up so tightly that he is almost hanged, and his feet are barely touching the floor, or if he is pulling away on a tight lead, and doing the oddest things with his legs. If the dog is being shown on a tight lead any judge worth his salt will ask you to walk the dog again, this time on a loose lead, and if you cannot do this your chances are practically nil. More often than not the dog being shown strung up is a shy, cringing Sheltie which cannot stand on its own legs. Of its own accord the loose lead will show this weakness up at once and repeatedly. So give your puppy confidence and get him to walk beside you under all conditions happily, and on a loose lead. Incidently, you need confidence yourself. Nerves from which you may be suffering will be transmitted at once to your dog, so if he does not show very well at his first show be sure to realize that the blame is probably as much yours as his. As your confidence increases so will his showmanship.

Besides walking confidently on a loose lead the dog will be expected to stand up and show himself. He must stand four-square, and he must be taught to take up this position as a natural thing. When standing he must use his ears, for without his expression a Sheltie is only half a dog, and his expression is lost if his ears are not at the semi-alert when the judge is looking his way. You will quickly find the best way to make him do this. He may like a certain noise that you make, he may be entranced by a bouncing ball, he may show best for a tit-bit, which you should hold low down or, better still, secrete in your pocket, giving him a tiny piece only now and again to keep his attention.

By the time he is six months old he should have a daily lesson in ring behaviour, but no lesson should last more than five minutes. It is far better to give him five minutes twice daily than one ten-minute session when he is this age, otherwise he will quickly become bored and your work will be useless.

Having taught him to walk on lead, it is now necessary to accustom him to walk on your left, neither ahead of you nor dragging behind. This is best done by talking to him to keep his attention. This will almost certainly stop him from lagging. If he pulls ahead, give him a sharp jerk on the lead (never a long steady pull) accompanied by the word 'heel' or whatever word you choose to use, but do please always use the same word. It is better to have a dog that responds to a small vocabulary than one that gets lost over a wide one. Directly he falls into the correct position he should be praised, and given a tit-bit as well if you wish. Having achieved your object of getting him to walk happily beside you on a slack lead in a straight line, the same thing must be done walking in a circle, the dog always on your left. You will be walking in an anticlockwise direction with your Sheltie always on the inside of the circle. Once he is walking well in this circle he must be taught to go in an absolutely straight line down the centre, and to turn and come back in exactly the same straight line, always on a slack lead. Reward him with praise and tit-bits when he does this. Now, having got him going straight, teach him to stand and show himself as you come to a halt; he will readily learn to stand at a word of command and it is up to you to see that he does this in the correct position, neither with his feet too close together nor too far apart, with his head held high, his ears up, and the whole of him alert and waiting for the next word of praise. Never let him get away with sitting down when you want him to stand, and if you watch him carefully for any tendency to do this you will soon be able to check it and keep him on the alert. Another tendency will be to 'settle down', by which I mean that although he is still standing he becomes slack, his neck sinking into his shoulders, his elbows spreading out, and his whole body 'settling' on to his feet rather as though he were a jelly on a hot day. This, too, must be checked. If the dog tries to sit, or if you want to alter his position in any way, don't make a big fuss over him by putting your hands on or under him; just take half a pace into a different position and he will soon set himself up again. If it is just the position of a front foot that you wish to alter, do so by just touching one paw with your toe. All these things should be done unobtrusively, for the last thing you want to do in the ring is to draw the judge's attention to a possible fault.

Very many judges prefer to see the Sheltie standing on a table. Most of them show better this way, and naturally they must become accustomed to standing on a table. This presents no difficulty if it is made a part of the usual ring-training practice.

Fortunately Shelties require little or no stripping for show preparation, and the amount of work put in on their coats depends on your own school of thought on the matter. Provided the coat has been kept free of knots and foreign bodies, live or otherwise, there should be little extra work to do except to give him a good final grooming the day before the show. It is not considered necessary or advisable to bath a Sheltie; this destroys the natural bloom on the coat, and glossiness is completely lost after a bath. However, particularly with a town dog, it is often necessary to wash at least the white parts. This, too, should be done the day before the show, and a good soapless shampoo used. The dog should be partially dried and then the white parts of the coat filled up with one of the cleaning powders. This can be one of the advertised cleaning agents or it can be precipitated chalk, a mixture of chalk, starch and whitening, or powdered magnesia, either plain or mixed with one of the other remedies mentioned. If any of these preparations are put into the damp coat they will stay there, and should be left until after the journey to the show has been made the next day, when any fresh dirt picked up en route will brush out with the cleaning powder, all of which must be removed before the dog is taken into the ring. This is a ruling of the Kennel Club.

Other than grooming, which we shall discuss elsewhere, the only preparation necessary is a little attention to the feet and legs. The feet should be trimmed all round with scissors so that the hair is cut level with the foot and gives a clear-cut outline. Further, the hair under the foot between the pads should be removed; this area should, in fact, be kept free of hair at all times, for too much hair between the pads tends to spread the foot and make it look big. The only other hair needing to be removed is that from the hock joint to the back of the foot on the hind legs. This part of the leg should be clear of long hair. Some people like to trim a Sheltie's ears, but I am of the opinion that, by the uninitiated, more ears are made 'prick' by over-trimming than one would credit, and for this reason they are best left alone. Also, ears which are trimmed too much look hard and tend to spoil the soft expression which is part and parcel of the Sheltie. However, if your dog is one of those which have very long soft, curly hair growing from the base and back of the ears, then this hair should be removed. It is best done with finger and thumb.

Doubtless you will be a subscriber to either *Our Dogs* or
Dog World, or both, and in these journals you will find
advertised the dates and places of the various shows.

It is not usually advisable to show a Sheltie before it is
seven to eight months old, for it is rarely in sufficient coat to do
itself justice before it is this age, but once it is seven months you
can start looking for an opportunity to make your show début.

You will probably want to start at a local show to make
things easier all round. It is much wiser, unless you are looking
upon the outing simply as one for a 'ring experience' for you
and your dog, to choose a show where there are classes for the
breed, for in Variety Classes—classes open to many breeds—
you may find that the judge is not very knowledgeable about
Shelties and you will not therefore profit greatly by the outing.
Far better to wait for a show where there are at least two or
three classes for the breed and where, if possible, the judge is an
acknowledged Sheltie expert. You will then reap much reward
from such a show even if you do not win.

Only dogs entered in the active register of the Kennel Club
may be shown, and full details of this new system of registration
(as from 1 October, 1978) can be found on page 158. If your
Sheltie was already in the basic register when you purchased
it, elevating it to the active register also supplies the transfer to
your name. If he was already in the active register you will still
need to transfer him to your ownership. If a dog is to be entered,
and his registration certificate has not yet been returned to
you, he must be entered with the name for which you have
applied and the initials N.A.F. (name applied for) after it. So
long as the name has been applied for before the date of the
show you are in order, but a name *must* be given on the entry
form.

Then, having decided upon the show you wish to attend,
send to the secretary of that show for a copy of the schedule.
Remember that there are three different types of show, and
while your local shows will be either Sanction or Limited
affairs[1] they will be the best kind to start at, except that these
shows will be 'unbenched' ones and the dog will have no place

<hr>

[1] *See* Chapter 16.

to call his own. Therefore, it is wise to take with you a rug or something to which he is accustomed so that he may rest happily while waiting his turn to go into the ring.

Having obtained a copy of the schedule, read it carefully, for there are different types of classes, governed either by breed or number of wins, or both, and may be governed also by age. The definitions of these classes vary with the type of show, so read them carefully before making your entries; this will prevent the disappointment that is a consequence of entering in the wrong class—and save the poor unfortunate secretary a great deal of work as well.

With a young dog it is always best not to enter in too many classes as the pup will probably become bored and tired if he is asked to keep up a sustained effort of showmanship throughout, say, ten classes, which is often a possible number in a variety classification. On the other hand, don't enter him in just one class. He may be somewhat overwhelmed at the beginning and may need a class or two before settling down. Any judge who is really on the job, if he finds a dog that he could not place in an earlier class because it would not show, but which, by reason of its having become accustomed to its surroundings, shows in a later class, will alter his earlier decision and put the dog higher than it originally was if he considers that the circumstances merit the decision. So give your Sheltie a fair run; three or four classes are ideal.

The day of the show has arrived. If it is an 'unbenched' show it is almost more important to arrive early than at a 'benched' one, as you will then be able to find a corner in which to bed-down your dog before the crush of exhibitors arrives. Even at a 'benched' show it is wise to be in plenty of time; there are always last-minute 'titivations' to make, the last grooming to do, and you do not want to rush your dog into the ring, but to give him time, after his toilet is concluded, to get accustomed to his surroundings. Even the dog which is a seasoned campaigner should have this chance, for although he may have attended many shows, the surroundings of each are different and need a bit of getting used to.

By Kennel Club rule the exhibitor is required to bench his dog on a collar and *chain*—not a lead. Like most Kennel Club rules, this one has a very good reason behind it. It is all too easy for a dog to bite through a lead and escape from its bench. Be sure to observe this rule; you make yourself liable to fine if you flaunt it, and you will most certainly cause yourself a lot of worry and heartache, and the show executive a great deal of unnecessary trouble, if your dog escapes from its bench.

You have arrived, settled down, done the necessary last-minute grooming and now you are ready for your first class. If it is a large show with a multiplicity of breeds, and therefore a number of judging rings, find out as soon as possible where the Shelties will be judged and whether they are 'first in the ring'— that is, first on the judging programme. Every ring, in addition to a judge, has one or more stewards. These are men or women who, in a purely voluntary capacity and for sheer love of the game, give their services to assist with the organization of the show. For this reason it makes me angrier when I see an exhibitor being rude to a steward than when I see an exhibitor being rude to a judge. It is the custom for one of the stewards to go round the benches before the judging of each breed begins to notify exhibitors that judging is about to start, but the onus for being in the judging ring at the right moment is on the exhibitor entirely, and it is up to you to keep a weather-eye open and see exactly what is happening so that you do not miss your class.

When you go into the ring for your first class, the steward who is marshalling the exhibits in the ring will give you your 'ring number'. This corresponds to your number in the catalogue and, if it is a benched show, is the same number as that on your bench. It is a help if you know your number when the steward comes to you—it saves a search through his catalogue after learning your name. All these little points do not seem important but they save so much time.

When all the exhibits for the first class have arrived in the ring the judging will begin, and it is usual for the judge to ask that all the exhibits be 'taken round' the ring for a start. This enables him to get a good general picture of the dogs as a whole, and usually a sound judge can have a good idea from this initial parade which dogs will be in the first three places when he has finished judging. For this first parade the exhibitors will always go round the ring in an anticlockwise direction

—that is 12, 11, 10, 9 o'clock, etc., and with the dogs on the *inside*. Remember always that it is the *dog* the judge wants to see, not your legs or your trousers, so always place the dog between you and the judge. The judge will tell the exhibitors when to stop this parade, then he will start his individual judging.

Usually the judge likes each dog to be taken into the middle of the ring in turn, and at his signal, and there he will examine each dog. Generally it is expected that you will stand the dog first of all, and make him use his ears while the judge gets an impression. This is where your training at home comes in; the dog should be ready to stand and show himself on your word or signal of command. Then the judge will inspect the exhibit part by part. Most judges, when they wish to look at the dog's teeth, will ask you to open the dog's mouth yourself. This is not because the judge is afraid your dog will bite him, it is to reduce the chances of spreading infectious disease should any dog in the ring be in the early stages of such a disease. If you are asked to open his mouth the judge will probably only say 'Mouth please', and it is important to do this correctly, and to have accustomed your dog to having it done. Do remember it is the teeth or bite the judge wants to see, not the tonsils or what he had for breakfast. The diagram (Figs. 27, 28) shows you the right and wrong way of carrying out this simple operation. A judge usually does his best to be helpful to the novice exhibitor, but it must be realized that he has a big day's work to do and he cannot spend five minutes waiting while you wrestle with a recalcitrant hound who has never been taught to have his mouth opened.

An exhibitor should not speak to the judge while the examination is going on, except to answer questions. These are likely to be only on such points as the age of the exhibit, and the judge most certainly does not want to be told the dog's parentage, nor what prizes he has won, if this is not his first show. The least said in the ring the better, for even the best-intentioned remarks will be bound to cause unfavourable comment.

Having gone over your exhibit, the judge will then ask you to move him away and back again. Now there are right and wrong ways of doing everything, and it can be extremely tiring for a judge with a big entry if every exhibitor moves the dog in the wrong direction and the poor judge has to go hopping from one corner of the ring to another to see what he wants to see. A good judge will invariably indicate the direction in which you are to go. It may be the full length of the ring, it may be diagonally across the ring; whatever the direction the

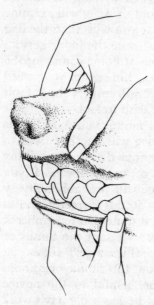

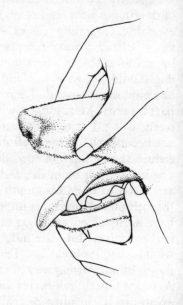

27. Correct way to show
    mouth to judge

28. Not this way!

procedure is always the same—there and back again, away from and back to the judge in as nearly a straight line as possible. Some judges also like to see the dog from the side. When he asks you to move so that he can see the dog from the side, remember that because you have trained the dog to walk on the left-hand side he will be on the *wrong* side for one length of the ring, and it is necessary for the dog to walk on your right for one length. Always remember to keep the dog between yourself and the judge and you can't go wrong.

When he has seen what he wants to see the judge will indicate, probably by a wave of the hand, that he has finished with you, and you will return to your original place unless the indication has been that you are to go to the opposite side of the ring. It is up to you to watch this. But if, before you start in your first class, you tell the steward you are a beginner, and ask him to help you, you will have done a wise thing, and you will, as a result, feel less lost and learn more quickly. The judge will then proceed in a like manner with every dog in the class, and while he is doing so let your dog rest. It does not matter if he lies down (unless there is a lot of sawdust on the floor) or sits or just lazes on his feet, but sitting or lying down are to be preferred, for the judge may turn round quickly when your dog is standing really badly (the best can do this) and then the mental picture he has made may be marred. Keep your eye on the judge, however, and when he reaches the penultimate exhibit in the class make your dog alert again, standing and showing for all he is worth when the judge looks back down the line. He will surely do this, and then, if it has been a big class, he will begin to pick the sheep from the goats, the sheep being sent to one side of the ring, the goats retained on the other. Some judges, having pulled out half a dozen promising ones, will tell the other exhibitors that they may go, but if you have not been given such a word of dismissal do not leave the ring until the prize cards have been handed out.

Let us assume that your first class was Puppy, and that you were placed third—not at all bad for your first show—and that you have also entered in Maiden and Novice. It is possible that there will be three or four new dogs, and that the dogs which were first and second in the Puppy Class are not in Maiden— probably they are no longer eligible. The steward will tell you to remain in the ring and automatically place you at the top on one side. The other exhibits which you beat in the Puppy Class will be ranged below you, and the 'new' exhibits will come in on the opposite side of the ring. With these new exhibits the procedure will be exactly the same as that outlined for your own class, and while the judge is examining these new dogs give your own exhibit a breather. As he comes to his last new exhibit alert your dog again, have him looking his very best, for although you were beaten in an earlier class here is the moment when the cherished red, First Prize, card may be yours. The judge will compare your dog—his best left from the earlier classes—with his best of the new ones, and then slip the new one into place. It may be First, it may well be down the line, and for this reason it is always up to you to be on the alert, but without overtaxing or tiring your dog. You are never beaten until you are out of the ring.

In the last paragraph it was assumed that you had gained only a yellow, Third Prize, card (the Second is blue), and later a red one—rather more than you should hope for at your first show—but in case you have had real 'beginner's luck' and gained best-of-breed, which means the best Sheltie in the show, there is yet a further step to be taken. In my opinion the winner of the best-of-breed award at any show, and particularly at a big show, should feel it is his bounden duty to take the winning exhibit into the 'Big Ring'. This is the main ring into which all the best-of-breed winners are called later in the day to compete for the Best in Show All Breeds. Even if you feel you have not a ghost of a chance your dog should be there, because of the great publicity value to the breed, and if you have had the honour and glory of being placed best-of-breed it is up to you to play your part and see that the breed is represented in the main ring, before what is bound to be the biggest audience of the day, even if it means waiting for a later train and being put to a bit of inconvenience yourself.

If your exhibit is a puppy and has won the Puppy Class in its breed and was only subsequently beaten by an adult exhibit of the same breed, then you have the right, and again I think the duty, to appear in the big ring if there is an award for Best Puppy in Show.

At most big shows, in addition to the breed classes there are usually Any Variety Classes and/or Stakes Classes. These are one and the same thing, except that the Stakes Classes usually carry increased prize money or extra prizes in kind. A Variety Class is one in which dogs of many breeds may be exhibited, and these are usually judged by a different judge from your own breed judge, and for this reason, if for no other, it is a good plan to enter in one or more, because then you will have the opportunity of more than one judge's opinion on your dog on the same day.

On returning from a show it is always wise, unless your exhibit is the only dog you own, to disinfect him and yourself.

This is best done by wiping his mouth and muzzle with a solution of T.C.P. and water and by dipping his paws in a bowl of this, as well as giving your own shoes the same treatment. Most germs of canine disease are passed through the dog's urine and excreta so those parts which come in contact with the floor are by far the most important. Needless to say, it is asking for trouble to take your dog to a show unless he has been immunized against hard-pad and distemper. In these days of 'egg-adapted' vaccines this is a simple and extremely safe procedure, costing a relatively small sum for its great 'insurance' value, and it is only kind to your dog to give him this protection. There are today several of these egg-adapted vaccines on the market and choice will entirely depend on which of them your veterinary surgeon stocks and prefers, so it is useless to enumerate them here. Be guided by him. Although your dog does not become contagious after the injection, it is best to have him treated at least 14 days before a show because it takes about this time for the vaccine to act and to give the optimum of protection. Best of all, of course, is to have your dog treated at twelve weeks of age, as I have already stated.

How the Judge Sees the Show

The best way to make an exhibitor see what is required in the ring is to let him see a class through the eyes of a judge.

The class is assembled, the steward tells the judge that the exhibits are ready, and the judge takes the centre of the ring. A quick look round and then the 'Round you go'. During this time he can sum up the qualities of most of the exhibits and only if he discovers that your dog has missing teeth, an overshot mouth, a light eye, or some other 'hidden' fault which cannot be seen without individual handling, will he find it necessary to alter drastically a first impression. During this time it is the *dog* he will be looking at, so keep him always on your left, in the centre of the circle, for you will be walking anticlockwise, and don't get between your dog and the judge. One other point: please don't bring anything into the ring except your dog on a lead. You cannot handle your dog properly and let him be seen well if you are carrying a handbag in your other hand, or tucked under your arm, nor does a judge want to be hit in the eye with a swinging bag as he bends to examine your dog's head. See that you don't wear a flapping coat, either, for it is impossible to see your dog if he is continually dragging back trying to get away from your coat which is swinging out and hitting him in the face. Circular skirts are just as bad if they are full.

When the judge has seen the dogs going round long enough —and this is no marathon—he will stop the exhibitors and will want to see each exhibit separately. He will want to know the age of your dog, so be sure you know it exactly.

Be ready to co-operate in carrying out instructions about moving your dog, etc., and if you are one of the late ones to be examined in a class you will help a very great deal if you watch the routine other exhibitors have followed. Any judge worth his salt judges each dog in exactly the same way, and if you are later than the third to be examined you should be able to fall into this routine with no difficulty and so help judge and stewards and save valuable time. If a judge has a big entry and a heavy day's work a few seconds by every exhibitor count up into a quite an appreciable number of minutes.

Your motto at a show should be: 'Keep your wits about you!'

Do not get in the way of other dogs as they are judged and don't allow your dog to be a nuisance by darting out, even in play, at other exhibits as they go past him. Concentrate on your dog, don't try to push in front of other exhibitors, don't crowd them in the ring. Even if someone else gets in front of you don't worry overmuch; a good judge won't forget a good dog just because, for the moment, he cannot see it.

Don't forget that not all judges judge to the same plan, so if you fall into one routine today don't expect it to be the same when Mr A. judges next week; his method of controlling his ring is bound to be different. This doesn't mean that one method is better than another; we are creatures of habit and each get into habits in the ring as much as anywhere else.

There are two places where I think Sheltie exhibitors, even experienced ones, sometimes fail. It is very much easier for the judge to see the dog if that dog is standing on a loose lead *away* from, and looking up at, his handler. Often a judge will step back to view the dog from a different angle, and here the

handler frequently makes the mistake of allowing, or even
encouraging, the dog to move towards him, and then it becomes
just a procession down the ring, the judge trying to get away
for a distant view and you and the dog following him step by
step! Another great point is that, more often than not, the dog
is presented with his hindquarters to the judge. This can quickly
be overcome: turn your own back on the judge, he won't
mind; it's only the dog he cares about, anyway. He won't at all
mind seeing your back if he can see your Sheltie's face. Then,
if the time comes when he wants to walk round the dog and
see him from the other end, don't follow in a circle, too, for all
will end up exactly where it started and the judge will have
seen nothing new. Also, if the judge is trying to attract your
dog's attention it is almost certainly because he wants it to look
directly at him, so that he may better assess its expression, and
it is maddening if while he is trying to do this you still persist
with pieces of liver, noises, etc., to keep the dog looking your
way. The judge in the ring is to assess the relative values of the
dogs brought before him. I, as a judge, shall be enjoying
myself, for I love judging, and I shall hope you are enjoying
yourself too. I am not a dragon, but while judging is actually
going on the ring is mine, and I do not like being interrupted.
To judge honestly and to the best of one's ability demands a
good deal of concentration, and it is concentration which
should not be allowed to relax. I shall be delighted to give a
reason for placing your dog where I did *after* I have finished
judging all the classes, but don't come to me, please, *without*
your dog and say, 'What did you think of my dog?' for it is the
dog which is in my mind's eye, *not* the exhibitor, and I may be
at a loss for an answer through not being able to connect you
with the dog you were handling. Bring the dog back to the
ring with you.

Most judges are just as anxious as anyone to see you get on,
whether you are a novice or an experienced exhibitor, and we
are almost all eager to help, but remember there are ways of
approaching your judge. Don't rush up and say, 'Why was my
dog only sixth?' when what you really mean is, 'Please can you
tell me what you liked better about the other five dogs who
went over him?' There are ways of saying all these things, and
judges, particularly after a long and tiring day's judging, can

be a bit prickly, you know. Further, I don't advise you to ask a judge's opinion unless you really want the truth. If you are seeking knowledge by which you can then improve your stock and your own knowledge of your breed, well and good. It is almost always possible to find something good to say about even the most lowly placed exhibit, but not all judges have the time to temper the wind, so if you are really lowly placed, and still want an opinion, be prepared to 'take it'!

A dog show is fun, a training ground and a meeting place; let it remain so.

15

SELLING YOUR STOCK. FREIGHT AND EXPORT

SOONER or later the problem of how to dispose of your stock will arise. In every litter there must be puppies you will not want to keep and, to save unnecessary expense, the sooner they are sold, after they are properly weaned, the better.

There are various mediums in which to advertise, and it is up to you to select the one most likely to suit the stock you have for sale. *Our Dogs* and *Dog World* are both admirable, but less suited to the pet market, for these papers rarely reach those people who are just looking for a pet. It will be found that those two periodicals are best for promising show stock. The *Tail-Waggers' Magazine* reaches a wide 'pet' public, but here the difficulty is that you must place the advertisement just about when the puppies are born if you wish it to appear when the pups are about seven weeks old, for this is a monthly publication which goes to press early the previous month. The columns of your local paper are, more often than not, the best medium for the sale of pet puppies.

Pricing the stock you have for sale is always difficult, even for the experienced breeder, and it is well to get down to the matter seriously and try to figure out just what the litter has cost you to rear. First take into consideration the stud fee, probably about £20. Next, consider what the bitch cost you while she was in whelp and while she was rearing the puppies. An additional £25 here is not out of the way; they will have cost not less than £60 to rear well to eight weeks of age, and your puppies must sell at not less than £60 each, which leaves you no profit, and should certainly not be sold for less than £65.

These prices are fair for a novice breeder to ask, for it must be remembered that the unknown breeder cannot expect to receive the price which a well-known kennel can demand for its stock. It is very much more satisfactory to be able to sell your unwanted puppies at an early age, even if for a slightly lower price than you had hoped, than to have them still runnig around at six months, when the feeding bill will have risen to astronomical proportions and the poorer-quality puppies will no longer be fat and cuddly and easy to sell, but looking their very worst, with all their faults exaggerated. By then, most probably, they will bring only the same, or at a lower price, than you had hoped for at eight weeks.

The show-ring is your natural shop window, and the value of your stock will rise gradually as your name becomes associated with winning stock, and as your kennel-name begins to carry real weight. It is absolutely essential to exhibit, and to do so regularly and frequently, if you hope to achieve a place where your kennel-name will strike a chord in the minds of the other breeders in the Sheltie world.

It stands to reason that the breeder who has built up a reputation for fair dealing and good stock will be the one who will gain the repeat orders. Such a reputation must take a few years to acquire, and the only way to achieve it is by showing and advertising so that your name becomes known, and then by backing those advertisements with really honest business.

Advertising must be clear and concise. Never advertise a dog by praising it to heaven, and forgetting that it has any faults. You most likely will not receive any reply to such advertisements, for all of us are suspicious of anything that is perfect. It is far better to state clearly what the breeding is of the particular dog or puppy, its show wins if any, and the price at which it is offered for sale, with a line intimating that the fullest details of the dog will be given on request. In replying to any advertisement yourself, be sure to ask the questions you really want answers to, and do remember that it is a great help if you enclose a stamped and addressed envelope. It will only a few pence to you, but a big kennel may get a dozen or more enquiries such as yours in a day!

While appreciating to the full the mass of correspondence that pours into a well-known kennel, it should be the aim of every breeder to try, in each instance, to reply to all enquiries by return of post. This at least gives the would-be purchaser the impression he will receive further courteous and good service.

If the enquiry comes 'out of the blue' and not in direct reply to a specific advertisement, do describe minutely the dog you are able to offer which you consider may fill the bill. Every dog has its faults, potential Champion though he may be, and it is essential that when extolling his good points those faults should also be mentioned. It is wise, when offering stock, to state 'subject to being unsold' and also to quote the price plus freight, for in these days of high rail charges the vendor is frequently out of pocket in no small way if the freight costs are not added to the purchase price. Many purchasers are unable to call to collect the dog of their choice. It is essential, when you know you are going to have a litter for sale, to be prepared to despatch the puppies in suitable hampers. At least 50 per cent of the average kennel's business is done by despatching stock by rail. For a Sheltie puppy of eight weeks a hamper measuring 14 in. by 10 in. by 12 in. high is ideal. Such a hamper costs about £20 and will last a long time. Naturally your client will be asked to return the hamper immediately. The hamper should be one that is completely closed in; hampers having an open end are uninsurable. The pup will surely be teased by fellow-passengers or railway staff in transit if the basket is open; further, it is very draughty. There is plenty of free passage of air in a closed one.

More information on this question of sending dogs by rail will be found later in this chapter.

You will find that from time to time you will receive enquiries from some of the bigger kennels unable to fill orders from their own stock, especially if you have used their stud-dogs or happen to have some of their bitches. When you receive such an enquiry do, in pricing your stock, take into consideration that the intermediate kennel must be allowed a reasonable margin of profit; state the lowest price you are willing to accept (and if by this means you can sell two or three puppies in one go you are saving yourself a great deal of trouble) and make no complaint if, at a later date, you should learn the price for which the puppy was resold. You got what you asked and should be content. It has happened to me that I have quoted a certain price and learned later that the intermediate breeder or seller has gained at least 100 per cent, sometimes more, but this is something which, though it may be irritating, must be suffered in silence.

When a client calls on you for a dog, always ask where he got your name; if from an advertisement, or from a previous satisfied client, well and good. But if you are told that another breeder was responsible for the introduction, then remember it is all a matter of business, and that it is only courteous to send a commission to the person who made the introduction. The usual commission on any such sale is 10 per cent.

It is usually the well-known kennels that receive export enquiries, but the day will surely come when a novice, building up a certain prestige, will also receive such enquiries. It is even more important to describe with the greatest accuracy any stock available for export, for while your disappointed client in this country has some redress, your overseas buyer has none, for our quarantine regulations do not allow a dog to be returned.

There are some people in all breeds who seem to consider that the foreigner's purse is bottomless, and who, as soon as an overseas enquiry comes to hand, double the price of any stock they have for sale. What a short-sighted policy this is, for it must be remembered that the overseas buyer has all the freight costs to pay as well, and that by the time a dog reaches such distant places as India or Australia a further £200 to £250 may well have been added to the bill. For myself, I would very much rather drop my price a little for an overseas order, knowing full well that a satisfied customer with a dog bearing my affix, that wins in the country of his adoption, is worth far more to me than the extra £10 I originally wanted for him.

Nothing is more satisfactory than to learn that the stock you sent out to a certain country has helped considerably in the improvement of the breed abroad.

The fact that puppies should be railed in a hamper has already been mentioned, but a puppy over three months of age is probably best sent in a travelling box. These boxes can be purchased in a variety of styles from the firms catering for the dog industry. If one does not want the expense of a special box, a small-size tea-chest is most adequate for a puppy, and a full-size one for an adult. But for sending away a bitch to be mated, for instance, a proper box is really a necessity. The box should be fastened with a padlock, and whether the key accompanies the dog or is sent in advance is a matter of personal feeling. I usually use a combination padlock, advising in advance the person to whom the dog is being sent.

If you are one of those who travel by train to shows you will find it a much more satisfactory method to box your dogs during the journey. Over a distance the freight charges will most certainly be cheaper than would a dog ticket, but far more important is that the dog sleeps in the box and arrives at the show both clean and alert. Quite a point too is that dogs are not allowed in sleeping compartments on railways, and with the dogs boxed the owner can have a sleeper and also arrive alert, but possibly not so clean!

Unfortunately British Railways are not perfect in their method of handling livestock in transit, and, despite the fact that the dog may be despatched with his selected route clearly marked on his box, it is wise to advise the stationmaster at each inter-change station that the dog will be on a particular train for change to such and such a train. This should not be necessary, but it is, and it saves many heart-burnings about the dog not arriving at his destination at the correct time. However, with a 'rush order' it is not always possible to forewarn the station staff, and a risk must be taken. It is best to consign the stock at Company's risk, but even this does not give adequate protection, and although the term 'Company's risk' might be construed as 'accepting risk to the value of the dog', this is not so, for the most that will be paid on a claim under Company's risk rate is, for one dog, a maximum of £2. It is therefore advisable to despatch livestock at a 'declared higher value'. It is not necessary to declare at full value if you do not wish, for the mere fact that even £5 has been declared, which entails only a small premium, ensures that 'declared higher value' labels are placed on the container and that a great deal more care is paid to such consignments; the guard of each train having to sign for the package is just one example.

Exporting a dog is a rather more complicated matter and it is certainly best, at any rate on the first occasion, to leave the arrangements in the hands of one of the well-known agents who deal with such things, for in certain countries there are complications and until you have gained experience it is well-nigh impossible to cope by yourself.

For every country it is essential to have a veterinary certificate of health for the dog, and, if the dog is for showing or breeding, the Kennel Club Export Pedigree. Further, if the dog is a male, the Kennel Club will not issue the Export Pedigree without the certificate of cryptorchidism or monorchidism duly signed.[1] For certain countries blood-tests are necessary, and for some Consular papers are required also. Details of what is necessary can be obtained from the Kennel Club, but if the matter is in the hands of an agent, all should be plain sailing.

Wherever possible it is most satisfactory to freight a dog abroad by air, and enquiries should be made in every case from the client as to whether shipment may be effected by this means. Naturally it is a little more expensive, but not much, when the cost of feeding, etc., is taken into account when the journey is by rail or boat, and it is an expense which is well worth while. The only countries which will not accept dogs by air are Australia and New Zealand. These countries, because of their great fear of importing rabies, will not allow dogs to enter the country by air, for it would have been necessary for the aeroplane in which the dog was travelling to have touched down in countries which are not rabies free.

Australia and New Zealand also demand that dogs, even from Great Britain, shall go through a period of quarantine, though it is considerably shorter than our own six months' period. Very few other countries demand a quarantine period for our dogs.

Dogs being shipped abroad by sea must be provided with a shipping kennel, and if by air, with a box. The selected agent will supply the kennel or box if you require it, but if you are arranging the shipment yourself then a suitable box must be acquired.

Often the question of the cost of shipment makes the chances of your overseas sales coming off a doubtful one, not because the client cannot afford the freight charges as well as the cost of the dog, but because he cannot always get sufficient currency released to cover both the cost of the dog and the freight in

[1] See *The Kennel Club and You*, Chapter 16.

sterling. This can often be overcome as some, at least, of the agents are willing to accept a dog and collect the freight and other charges on its arrival.

All these small points help to lighten the burden to the seller and to the purchaser's pocket!

16

THE KENNEL CLUB AND YOU

There is so much to learn about dog breeding and showing that the novice is always coming up against terms he does not understand. Sometimes the 'old hands' are not as clear on the subject as they might be, but if they wish to they can skip this chapter.

No one who owns a pedigree-registered dog can possibly have failed to have heard the words the 'Kennel Club', but this club has much more behind it than just the registration of your dog. Its offices are situated at 1–4 Clarges Street, Piccadilly, London W1Y 8AB and there, under one roof, everything you can possibly imagine connected with dogs and dog shows is arranged, settled and recorded.

The Committee of the Kennel Club is the governing body of the exhibition of dogs throughout the United Kingdom. The Committee is elected, not from all those of us who have dogs registered with the Kennel Club, but by the comparative few who form its own membership.

The Kennel Club is, in fact, an autocracy. But none of us quarrel with this set-up, for the Committee does a very arduous and thankless job, and does it right well, *and* in a voluntary capacity.

Despite the fact that well over 75 per cent of the dog-showing community are women, and therefore, presumably, over 75 per cent of the Kennel Club's income is derived from women, they still have no place on the Executive Committee, but although from time to time there is an outcry about this, affairs which relate to dogs proceed happily and calmly enough, and are certainly more than adequately handled by the band of men in whose hands they rest. Full membership of the Kennel Club is nowadays open to both sexes, and the Kennel Club Ladies' Branch no longer exists.

The governing body is entirely responsible for the registration and transfer of all dogs; for all shows, working- and field-trials, for the allocation of Championship status and of Challenge Certificates to the various shows and trials, for the licensing of all shows, including matches, for the recording of all registered societies (and demand an annual, up-to-date statement on the financial affairs of each club registered), for the formation of rules covering every possible side of the dog-show game, and finally for the punishment of those who infringe those rules. They are responsible for their own monthly publication, *The Kennel Gazette*, and annually the invaluable *Kennel Club Stud Book*. Both of these publications are available to everyone, not, of course, just Kennel Club members.

So you see that at any point in the dog-showing and breeding game you must come in direct contact with the Kennel Club, and a very good thing too, for without this control the dog game would be chaotic.

Occasionally, in various parts of the country, dog shows are held which are unlicensed and outside the control of the governing body. These shows are taboo and beware of them, for if it is proved that you have exhibited or officiated in any capacity at an unauthorized show you are liable to be 'warned off' for life by the Kennel Club itself, and as this 'warning off' means that you are forbidden to attend any dog activity licensed by the Kennel Club, that the stock you breed cannot be registered, that the progeny of your stud-dogs likewise cannot be registered, it results in the end of all your doggy activities. Should you happen to be one of those who tries to make a living out of dogs, your livelihood is gone. These unauthorized shows are few and far between, but do make sure that the words 'Under K.C. Rules and Regulations' appear on the schedule of any show at which you propose exhibiting. Then you are safe.

THE KENNEL CLUB LIAISON COUNCIL

The Kennel Club Liaison Council, or K.C.L.C. as it is more familiarly known, is, as its name denotes, the body which links the Kennel Club with us, the exhibiting public. The members of the K.C.L.C. are elected by nomination of the committees of the registered societies, and then by a ballot from these societies from the various nominees, who become 'Area Representatives', of the General Championship Societies. One representative for each group of dog (e.g. Sporting, Non-Sporting, etc.) forms the Council. To these representatives may be passed any suggestions or complaints from the clubs throughout the country, and these items may then be placed on the agenda of the K.C.L.C. for discussion by that body. According to the results of the Council's discussions, the items are either passed or rejected by them, and if passed are then forwarded as recommendations to the Kennel Club, who, as in everything, have the final say. Three delegates from the K.C.L.C. (one of whom is their chairman) have seats on the Committee of the Kennel Club so that the deliberations of the Council go to the Kennel Club not only as a written document but also with the backing of the delegates. Further, the Secretary of the Kennel Club is also Secretary of the K.C.L.C., providing yet another link.

REGISTRATION

As from 1 October 1978 the Kennel Club is no longer divided into the Basic Register and the Active Register but there is only:

The Active Register, into which a dog which its owner decides to show or enter for competition, breed from or export, must be advanced.

AFTER 1 OCTOBER 1978

(*a*) *If you are the breeder of a litter born on or after* this date, use the new Litter Recording Application Form.

Both the sire and the dam must be in Active Register and recorded as owned by the persons shown as their owners, or application must have been made for this.

This latest system is much less complicated than the one which was used immediately before it and which seemed to have the effect of slowing down the processes at the Kennel Club. I think that the new registration procedure will be more acceptable to most breeders who, if they are like me, favour the simplest possible approach to all forms.

When you receive the Litter Registration, you can then register the puppies yourself, unless you have already done so. Or you can hand one of the Basic Registration application forms to each person to whom you sell or give a dog from the litter in order that he or she may register it.

Note that if you wish to use your affix in naming the puppies or to place any endorsement on the registration, you must register them yourself. Bear in mind that they may be shown or entered for competition by their new owners at a later date and prove good. Remember too that they will not be 'K.C. registered' puppies before sale unless you do register them.

Once the litter has been recorded and the Litter Registration has been issued, the individual dogs in the litter can be registered *at any age* but the Basic Registration application form will be needed in order to do so.

(*b*) *Transfer of Ownership:* This will be recorded as before on application using the appropriate form.

(*c*) *Working Trials and Obedience Register:* Application for registration of dogs in order that they may be entered in only Working Trials or Obedience competition will continue to be made on the yellow Application Form 1A.

Your puppy, when you purchase it, may, and probably will, already have been registered in the *basic* register, so will already have a registered name. If it has been born since 1 April 1976 it cannot have been registered in the active register unless it has already been shown, bred from, or had an export pedigree supplied for it. If, later, you decide to show or breed with your Sheltie it *must* be advanced to the active register. If it is already in the basic register the name it received there must still be used. If it is not already in basic it must be entered there and then elevated, but you will choose the name yourself.

PREFIXES

If you are planning to breed, even in the smallest way, then you should decide, right from the outset, that all dogs of your breeding shall be known by a common prefix—a trade mark in fact. This is valuable to you even if you plan only a 'yearly litter'.

It is necessary to apply to the Kennel Club for a special form and to make application on this form for the name you wish to use. When you realize that roughly 30,000 words are on the records of the Kennel Club as names which have already been granted you will appreciate that the allocation of fresh names is not a simple task, for not only must there be no duplication, but also there must be no new one that is too similar to an existing one. Every name that the Kennel Club is considering granting is published, and the owner of an existing prefix is given the right to object to any new one suggested. Therefore it is wise to start asking for your Kennel name almost as soon as you decide to buy a puppy from which to breed a litter.

Sometimes the application will be returned a number of times before a final choice is made, and months can easily elapse.

EXPORT PEDIGREE, ETC.

If you are exporting a dog to any part of the world as either a show or breeding proposition, it will require to have the Kennel Club's official 'export pedigree', as without this the dog cannot be recorded in the stud book of the country of its adoption. This export pedigree costs £10·00 and should be applied for when sending for the transfer for the dog. When exporting a mated bitch some countries demand a 'vendor's certificate'; this is an official document, issued free by the Kennel Club, on which the vendor must give details of the mating. Other countries demand a certified pedigree of the stud-dog (£10·00) issued over the seal of the Kennel Club, and it is wise, if exporting a mated female, to enquire from the Kennel Club just which of these documents is required for the country to which the bitch is being sent. For every country in the world it is now necessary, under the rule of our own governing body, if you are exporting a male (of no matter what age), to obtain from the Kennel Club a form known as a Certificate re Monorchidism and Cryptorchidism. This form must be signed by you and returned to the Kennel Club when you are applying for the export pedigree for the dog in question. Without this certificate the Kennel Club will not issue the export pedigree.

Except for export to the U.S.A., the export pedigree need not accompany the dog, but can be sent by mail afterwards.

Bertram Unne, Harrogate

Ch. Dilhorne Blackcap

Ch. Diadem of Callart

C. M. Cooke

Ch. Riverhill Rogue

C. M. Cooke

Ch. Blue Charm of Exford

Sheltie bitch, Ch. Sheer Sauce from Shiel, and Collie dog, Skeandhu from Shiel, showing size difference betwen the two breeds

Ch. Silvasceptre from Shiel
The Collie type to be aimed at in Sheltie breeding

C. M. Cooke

Ch. Swagman from Shiel

C. M. Cooke

Ch. Monkswood Moss-Trooper

APPLICATION FOR AN EXPORT PEDIGREE

Return this form completed with the fee to:

THE KENNEL CLUB
1 CLARGES STREET
PICCADILLY,
LONDON, W1Y 8AB.

FEE
£10

Breed of dog ....

Registered name of dog ....

Registration No. .... Sex .... Colour.............

PLEASE USE BLOCK CAPITALS

	3.		7.
SIRE 1.			8.
	4.		9.
			10.
DAM. 2.	5.		11.
			12.
	6.		13.
			14.

BLOCK LETTERS PLEASE

Signature of applicant ....

Full name and address of applicant ....

....

....

Full name and address of prospective owner ....

....

....

Pedigree will be posted to applicant unless otherwise requested (below)

....

....

NOTES

In the case of an application for an Export Pedigree for a male dog, the certificate A or B must be completed.

An export pedigree cannot be issued unless the dog is registered in the name of the consignee. The application to register or transfer the dog must be completed by the time of application for the pedigree.

If the application is for a bitch in whelp the applicant should also apply for a pedigree certificate in respect of the dog to which the bitch was mated. The fee for a pedigree certificate for this purpose is £10·00

CANADIAN EXPORTS

In the case of two or more dogs (or bitches) of the same breed exported in the same consignment to Canada, each dog must be tattooed before despatch with a mark supplied by the Canadian Kennel Club to the importer. This mark must also appear on the Export Pedigree.

If such a mark has been allocated by the Canadian Kennel Club in respect of this dog give exact details for reproduction (by the Kennel Club) on the pedigree.

Certificate "A"
To be signed by veterinary surgeon or veterinary practitioner.

I certify that I have today examined the dog identified to me as over and that both testicles are fully descended in the scrotum and apparently normal.

Date .... Signature......................................

Address .... Qualification ....

....

Certificate "B"
To be signed by the vendor when the dog has not both testicles descended in the scrotum and/or are not apparently normal.

I certify that the prospective owner of the dog has been informed
(a) that both testicles are not fully descended in the scrotum and/or
(b) are not apparently normal and that with this knowledge he still instructs me to export the dog. I enclose a letter from the consignee (or some other evidence) to this effect.

Date .... Signature ....

When certificate "B" is completed the Export Pedigree will be endorsed to that effect.

TYPED	CHECKED	POSTED	NUMBER

CHALLENGE CERTIFICATES

These, the highest award a dog can obtain, are on offer at Championship Shows only, and not always every breed that is scheduled is being granted Challenge Certificates at a particular show, so read your schedule carefully. These certificates are awarded at the discretion of the judge, who is specially requested by the Kennel Club to withhold the award for want of merit. In fact, a judge has always the right to withhold any prize at any show if he does not think the quality of the exhibits merits an award. With the Challenge Certificate, however, the matter is most serious, for every certificate issued bears the signature of the judge to the declaration that such and such an exhibit 'is of such outstanding merit as to be worthy of the title of Champion'. That is a declaration which no judge should sign lightly, for on the making of Champions depends the future of the breed. Three such certificates must be won under three *different* judges before the dog can bear the proud title of Champion. The Challenge Certificate, the big green and white card which one is awarded in the ring, is not the official certificate; this follows at a later date, by post, when the win has been ratified and the eligibility of the winning exhibit is declared to be in order. When a dog has won his third certificate the Kennel Club will also forward the Champion's certificate to the owner. This certificate also comes to one automatically and should not be applied for.

BREEDER'S DIPLOMA

There is yet another award, the granting of a Breeder's Diploma to the breeder of a Champion, whether the breeder is the owner or not, and it is a very nice addition, of fairly recent origin, to the Kennel Club awards, as it acknowledges the achievement of the 'stay-at-home' breeder who may be unable to exhibit, and who always sells his best stock for others to show. This diploma, however, is not awarded automatically, and must be applied for by a letter stating the shows at which the dog concerned has won its C.C. No special application form is necessary.

JUNIOR WARRANT

This award was introduced just before the Second World

War, as recognition for an outstanding young dog who may be too immature to gain his title but who is nevertheless above the average in quality. The Warrant is gained when a dog has won 25 points between the ages of 6 and 18 months, and points are allocated thus: 1st at a Championship Show, 3 points; 1st at an Open Show, 1 point. These points are counted only if won in breed classes, and wins in classes for Collies (A.V.) or Shetland Sheepdogs do not count, as these are considered by the Kennel Club to be Variety Classes. A great deal of acclaim is often given to the Junior Warrant winner, but I do not consider this award is all it is reputed to be. It is very much easier to win in some breeds than in others. For instance, in Cockers, Boxers, Miniature Poodles, to mention only three breeds, where there is usually a multiplicity of classes for the breed, it is much easier to tot up the necessary number of points than in a breed where there are only a few classes at each show. Further, in the short-coated breeds, and in the smaller breeds, a puppy can often start his show career at 6 months of age. In our breed it is generally hopeless to start your puppy before it has had a chance to grow its coat, and he may be 9 months of age before he sees a ring. The short-coated breed can probably spend all its time between 6 and 18 months being shown. With a dog that starts at 9 months it may be that he must be temporarily retired from the ring at 12–13 months, when his coat drops, and he will be well over 18 months of age before he is again fit to show. Another point, a forward, good-coated puppy who happens to hit a string of shows may qualify easily, but that same youngster may go off early and never be heard of again after winning its Junior Warrant. In my opinion, also, a puppy of a medium or big breed may be ruined by being dragged around the country in search of those elusive points, for too many shows during the growing period are undoubtedly a mistake. An occasional outing is all right, to give the youngster a taste of what is to come, but not a general grind, when he should be at home eating, playing, sleeping and growing. Beware of that Junior Warrant!

BREEDING TERMS AGREEMENTS

These form another aspect of the game in which the Kennel

Club plays an official part. By no means all bitches who are parted with on breeding, or part-breeding, terms have this loan officially recorded at the Kennel Club; in fact it is a very definite minority, but it is well to know that the Kennel Club does issue a form of contract for the 'Loan or Use of Bitch',. which costs £1, and which, if used, covers both parties should any dispute arise, for the Kennel Club then becomes the adjudicator and final court of appeal. This document does not cover all the ways in which one can lend out a bitch on terms, and for that reason many breeders prefer to make their own agreements.[1]

STUD BOOK ENTRY

This is the official allocation to any dog or bitch of a *K.C. Stud Book* number, which then supersedes its original registration number. There is now only one way in which a dog can be admitted to the *Stud Book*: by qualification. If a dog qualifies he is entitled to free entry, and such entry is automatic. He qualifies if he: (*a*) wins a C.C. or Reserve Best-of-Sex award at a Championship Show, or if he is awarded 1st, 2nd or 3rd prize Open or Limit Class at a Championship Show, where Challenge Certificates were on offer for his breed, and provided that such classes were not restricted by weight, colour, etc.; (*b*) wins a prize, Certificate of Honour or Certificate of Merit at Field Trials held under K.C. Rules; (*c*) wins a prize or Certificate of Merit in Open Stakes at a Championship Working Trials; (*d*) wins a prize in Test C in a Championship Obedience Test.

SHOWS

As has already been stated, there are four types of show: Championship, Open, Limited and Sanction.

Championship Shows are shows where anyone may exhibit, provided the dog is registered with the Kennel Club, and where Challenge Certificates are offered. These may be multiple-breed shows or specialist club, one breed, Championship Shows. It is only at these shows that a dog can make his way towards the coveted title of Champion.

[1] *See* Appendix 3.

Open Shows. Similar to Championship Shows, but Challenge Certificates are not offered.

Limited Shows. Shows where the entry is confined to members of the promoting club or society, and restricted to a minimum number of classes.

Sanctions Shows. This is an even smaller offshoot of the Limited Show, restricted to not more than twenty classes, to medium-grade dogs and to members only.

There is one more type of show, the Exemption Show. These are usually run in connection with fêtes, etc. The Kennel Club gives permission for the holding of a show of not more than four classes. Proceeds usually go to charity. Dogs need not be K.C. registered, and entry for these shows is usually made on the day.

MATCHES

Matches are competitions between two dogs, the property of members of the promoting club, or between members of two different clubs, when the match is of an invitation variety and another club has been invited to compete. These are not shows. No prize cards may be awarded, but they are a pleasant way of spending an evening and a very good training-ground for a youngster before making his début.

This sets out then all the main parts the Kennel Club plays, and where it is most likely to affect you as an exhibitor. It should not be forgotten that today the Kennel Club runs the world's greatest dog show, Crufts, in London, in February of each year.

17

FIRST AID AND COMMON AILMENTS

*(I am indebted to Miss Copithorn, M.R.C.V.S., for checking this
chapter and making suggestions)*

FORTUNATELY the Sheltie is not subject to many complaints,
such as eczema, canker, etc., which beset so many breeds, and
for that we have much to be thankful. However, it is every bit
as necessary when dealing with a canine family to be prepared
for accident and to have the medicine chest always suitably
equipped, as it is for a human family. Most of the necessary items
for inclusion will be found in the household medicine chest.

Taking the Temperature. Every dog-owner must have a clinical
thermometer at hand, and must know how to use and read it.
An ordinary clinical thermometer is perfectly suitable, but it
should be a 'stumpy' one—that is, one in which the end con-
taining the mercury is thick and rounded, not thin and brittle.

The dog's normal temperature is 101·5°F. (38·5°C.). Dogs
that are well fed and exercised and housed have a great natural
resistance to disease, but it is a wise precaution to have a golden
rule in your kennel: 'If the dog doesn't eat, take his temperature
at once.' Don't wait until tomorrow to see if he eats then; there
are diseases in which 'tomorrow' may prove too late. To take
the temperature it is useful to have an assistant who will hold
the dog. Make sure the thermometer is shaken down to 96° or
less. Insert the thermometer, which may have been previously
smeared with vaseline, into the rectum for about half to two-
thirds of its length. Do not use force, and if there is any difficulty in getting the thermometer inserted alter the position
just a little, either up or down. Leave the thermometer in place
for one minute, even with a half-minute thermometer, and
keep hold of the end all the time. Keep the dog quiet and
under observation until further symptoms show themselves or

until his temperature is back to normal and has been that way for 24 hours. Remember never to take a dog's temperature immediately after exercise or excitement of any kind, such as a journey, for this may have raised the temperature several degrees. At least an hour should elapse after exercise before a true temperature can be determined. If the temperature is over 102°F. (39°C.) when taken one hour after exercise, wait another hour and take it again; some dogs take much longer to settle down than others. This is especially true of puppies-from six to ten months old.

The old story that a healthy dog has a cold wet nose and that the dog with a dry nose is a sick dog is not true, and the state of a dog's nose is no guide at all to his condition, except, of course, when it is in a state of discharging mucus.

A puppy may run a slight temperature for little or no reason at all, and a puppy during teething may quite often have a slight rise of temperature, but it is still wise, if the temperature persists for more than 12 hours, to call in your veterinary surgeon.

Fits

Running through everyday ailments and accidents that your dog may run into is perhaps done most easily by starting with the baby pup and following it through its life, for there are complaints which may be contracted more readily, or only, at certain periods of life. The baby puppy is most likely to be troubled with fits caused either by the presence of worms or by teething. The former kind should never appear, for a puppy so obviously 'wormy' should have been attended to before the irritation culminated in a fit. If, however, the puppy has arrived at the stage where it is having fits caused by worms it is essential to seek the advice of your veterinary surgeon, and not to handle the situation yourself unless you are very experienced, because the subsequent worm treatment might prove too much for the already-harmed system.

Sheltie puppies often have a great deal of trouble cutting their teeth, the gums often becoming very swollen and inflamed, and it is in these cases that teething fits may occur, though on the whole the condition is rare. A puppy suffering from fits must be kept quiet, and in a cool, darkened room, until such time as veterinary advice can be obtained. In fact, the best thing is to give the puppy or adult a mild sedative such as aspirin ($\frac{1}{2}$ for a puppy, 1–2 for an adult) and to shut him in a box and leave him in a dark place until the veterinary surgeon arrives. Quiet is essential. There is always the chance that fits are not caused by worms or teething, but may be a symptom of something more serious, so be sure to get advice. Remember that fits are never a disease in themselves; they are a symptom of some definite trouble.

Puppies or adults suffering from fits must be kept completely isolated, puppies even from their litter-mates, because all dogs, puppy or adult, tend to attack the abnormal one, and serious injury might be done before the sufferer can be rescued.

STRAINS AND BRUISES

Puppies will frequently hurt themselves, twisting a leg, etc., when playing, and on rushing up in answer to a frightened scream of pain one will often find a puppy apparently dead-lame, so seriously in trouble that he will tell you his leg is broken and he will surely never walk again. Take the baby away from his companions and leave him on a non-slippery floor (lino is not good) until, of his own accord, he finds his feet again. He will often be all right in as little as 30 minutes. However, if the strain or bruise is of a more serious nature, then further action must be taken, and here I swear by a homoeopathic remedy. Saturate a pad of cotton wool in cold water and squeeze it as dry as you possibly can. Now soak this pad in Tincture of Arnica Flowers, apply it to the injured part (but only when there is no skin break) and bandage lightly. It is almost certain that the patient will try to remove the bandage, so paint the outside with mustard which, in most cases, is highly discouraging. The same treatment is equally good for adults. Further, dose the patient twice daily with a dessertspoonful of water to which two drops of Tinc. Arnica has been added.

If a dog attempts to chew and tear at his bandage make sure that it is not causing pain. It may have been put on rather too tightly or the injured part may have swollen later, causing the bandage to become tight, which could be a source of great discomfort. Only when satisfied on this point should a mustard or other repellent, such as bitter aloes or tincture of ginger, be applied.

Alternative Treatment for Bruises. This should be used if the skin is broken. Soon after the injury bathe well with cold water which will help to reduce bleeding in the bruised tissue and so reduce the swelling. A few hours after the injury bathe in *hot* water, to stimulate the circulation and so help to disperse the results of the damage from the bruise. Use water as hot as you can comfortably bear on the inside of your forearm.

Car Sickness

Unfortunately, this is a weakness of Shelties. As puppies they are very prone to this, much more so than the puppies of many other breeds. Many and varied are the cures which are used, and I have tried most of them.

The most important point in the curing of this complaint is that the dog should gain confidence as quickly as possible, and it should only be taken for the shortest trips in the car at first. I have found that the proprietary medicine which gives the most satisfactory results is the human one, 'Songo', which, if not readily obtainable, will be ordered for you by your chemist. Ignoring the printed instructions on the packet, which are, naturally, for human beings, give your Sheltie one capsule, on an empty tummy, about forty-five minutes before starting a journey. In my experience, after four or five journeys with 'Songo' as an aid, the dog will outgrow the desire to be sick while travelling, and in the long run the journey can be made with no prior preparation!

Diarrhoea

This, again, is frequently a 'puppy' complaint, and may be caused by a variety of reasons.

Most usually in puppies it is caused by a sudden change of food, or by a chill. In cases of diarrhoea, whether in puppies or in adults, castor oil should *never* be administered. Liquid paraffin, however, is good, and may remove the irritation causing the condition. Liquid paraffin is a soothing mixture as well as an aperient. Castor oil is an irritant and should *never* be used except under veterinary instruction. A puppy with persistent diarrhoea should be placed on a diet of egg white and arrowroot gruel, plus a little glucose. Further treatment may consist of dosing with Boot's chlorodyne, the dose for an eight-week old puppy being five drops in half a teaspoonful of water every four hours.

Diarrhoea in adults is more often the symptom of the onset of some specific virus or bacterial disease and is usually accompanied by a rise of temperature. The treatment is the same as that for puppies, but it must be realized that diarrhoea is a condition which must be viewed seriously and, if at all persistent, veterinary advice should always be sought.

ECLAMPSIA (PUERPERAL ECLAMPSIA)

This is a condition affecting the nursing bitch and is an illness in which it is absolutely imperative that immediate action, sending for your veterinary surgeon, should be taken. The cause is the excessive drain of calcium from the blood at the time when a bitch is nursing her puppies. Good food and the administration of calcium as set out in Chapter 11 all help to ward off this condition, but all the calcium in the world will be useless if the bitch hasn't enough Vitamin D to enable her to utilize the calcium. But even the best-cared-for brood bitches may develop eclampsia and it is more common in the excessively good mother who gives all of herself to her babies. Frequently, the only symptom will be the total collapse of the bitch, without any previous warning; she may retain or lose consciousness, and in the former case she will probably get up in a few minutes. It is essential to have your veterinary surgeon on the spot with the least possible delay, for an injection of calcium will put the bitch right in as brief a space as half an hour, but neglect of this collapsed condition will lead to a worsening of the condition and death will rapidly result. Occasionally the bitch will show slight symptoms before the collapse stage. She may appear stiff in movement, pant a great deal and have a temperature. As has already been said, the presence of a temperature will demand that you seek immediate professional advice, and then all will be well, but I cannot stress too strongly the absolute necessity for *immediate* action in a suspected case of Puerperal Eclampsia.

ECZEMA

Fortunately the Sheltie does not often develop eczema, this disease being more frequently associated with other breeds. It is non-contagious and is frequently a 'seasonal' condition. There are two forms of eczema, the moist and the dry, and neither form confines itself to any special area of the body, being found anywhere. Moist eczema can appear overnight, or in less time than that. It is quite a common occurrence to put a dog into its kennel in a perfectly fit condition and to take it out in the morning with an area the size of a saucer which is red, glistening, damp and quite hairless. This sudden appearance, and the fact that these areas are sensitive to touch, are clearly symptomatic of this condition. This type of eczema cannot possibly be confused with mange in either of its forms. Moist eczema will frequently respond to treatment with calomine lotion, and this may well be tried before taking the patient to the veterinary surgeon. The dog should be placed solely on a raw-meat diet, and the addition of the juice of raw tomatoes to the food is also a great help, for the presence of wet eczema indicates a deficiency of Vitamin C which is found in tomatoes, oranges and fresh green vegetables.

Dry eczema is also non-contagious and non-parasitic, but it is very difficult to differentiate between the lesions of eczema and of sarcoptic and follicular mange, both of which are highly contagious. It is wise to take immediate professional advice if your dog is suffering from dry, scaly patches on the body, and if the surface of these bald patches is wrinkly. A condition of similar appearance can be caused by the presence of fleas and lice, but a close examination of the coat will soon reveal these. However, only a microscopic examination of deep scrapings will reveal whether the sarcopt or demodect is present, and as this is the main distinguishing feature between dry eczema and mange the advice to take your dog to the veterinary surgeon if dry eczema is suspected cannot be over-emphasized.

Many dogs will take finely chopped lettuce mixed with their food, when this is available. Vitamin C can also be given in tablet form and is exceedingly helpful in treating both skin diseases and septic wounds.

ENTERITIS (Inflammation of the bowel)

Again, this is a serious condition. Its symptoms are loss of appetite, vomiting and thirst, accompanied sometimes by a very high temperature, but more normally by a temperature of no more than 102–104°F. (39–40·5°C.). Enteritis usually accompanies a specific disease but it can also be caused by worms, chills, decomposed foodstuffs, poisoning of the irritant kind, and by the swallowing of foreign bodies. The treatment is warmth and rest, and purgatives should *never* be given; above all *never give castor oil*. The dog should be given no food in the early stages, but he may be allowed liquids such as milk, egg and milk, glucose and water. Benger's Food, groats and arrowroot gruel. If vomiting is a prominent sympton he should be given barley water only. A dose of liquid paraffin may be administered (but, again, *never* castor oil) and if the condition does not improve, the veterinary surgeon must be sent for.

EYE INJURIES

It is very easy for a dog to injure an eye, whether the injury is to a puppy by a puppy, or to an adult out at exercise or work. Immediately an injury is noticed the cause should be sought. It may be a foreign body, such as a grass seed, in the eye. This should be removed at once and the eye bathed with a solution of boracic, or with cold tea (without milk). I prefer the latter. An eye can often be scratched and in such a case it is as well to put penicillin eye ointment into the injured eye, for if it proves to be a more severe injury than was at first suspected this medicament does not preclude further treatment of another kind. However, if it is intended to use penicillin, and it is also considered desirable to wash the eye out first, then the eye should be bathed only with plain warm water, as use of any chemical (e.g. boracic) might inhibit the action of the penicillin.

Foreign Body in the Eye. When attempting to wash out a foreign body from an eye it is necessary to hold the dog's head slightly on one side, raise the lower eyelid a little so that it makes a tiny cup, flood this with lukewarm water, then let the dog's head go so that he can blink and wash the liquid round the eyeball. This will often wash out a grass seed or a bit of grit. If you cannot wash a foreign body out of the eye, do not probe it. Put a few drops of liquid paraffin into the eye, and arrange to take the dog to your veterinary surgeon as soon as possible.

GASTRITIS (Inflammation of the stomach)

The principal symptom of gastritis is excessive thirst accompanied by vomiting, mainly of a white or yellow frothy gastric mucus. The dog is restless, seeks cold places to lie in, yet rarely does his temperature exceed 102°F. The condition calls for skilled treatment but, pending the arrival of this, the dog should be given nothing but barley water to drink, access to fresh water being definitely forbidden, and a dose of chlorotone (5 gr.) may be administered. The dog may be given ice to lick or small pieces may be forcibly administered. If this is done the barley water need not be given, but he must be compensated in some way for the loss of fluid which occurs through continuous vomiting. The dog must be kept warm, and hot-water bottles (well covered) may be placed at the pit of the stomach to relieve pain and sickness. (Refer to the last section of this chapter, 'Home Nursing'.) Rest the stomach by withholding all food, and keep the dog warm and dry indoors.

FLEAS AND LICE

Most dogs, however well cared for, get fleas at some time in their lives, and it is necessary to keep these well under control if only because the flea is the host of the tapeworm egg. Anyway, it does not improve a long-coated dog if he is constantly scratching.

Prevention and treatment are the same: dusting with one of the gammexane powders until the whole dog is covered. All kennels and bedding should also be dusted with the powder, including the cracks between floor-boards and corners of sleeping boxes, for it must be remembered that a flea does not breed on the dog but in cracks and chinks in wood.

Lice are small bluish-grey insects which attach themselves to the skin and the blood of the dog. An effective remedy is to bathe the dog in Izal shampoo, but it is essential to see that the coat is soaked right down to the skin—not at all easy in our breed—and the shampoo should be left in contact with the skin for about 15 minutes before being rinsed off. During this time the shampoo must continue, and friction be kept up on the skin in order to keep the dog warm. After that time has expired the coat can be rinsed and allowed to dry in the usual way.

An alternative method for lice is to dust gammexane powder thoroughly on the coat, making sure that it reaches right down to the skin. This dusting should be repeated every fourth day until the dog has been treated five or six times. The first thorough dusting will kill all the lice, but as it does not kill the nits it has to be repeated several times to catch them as they hatch.

A most effective method of getting any kind of powder well into the coat is the use of a 'puffer' similar to those used for certain kinds of talcum powder. By this means the powder can be blown right down to the roots, and the consequent saving of powder which would otherwise be wasted is quite important.

Harvest Mites or Harvesters are tiny little orange-coloured insects with the same habits as lice. As their name denotes, they are usually found during summer and autumn, and it is not often that they are found anywhere except between the toes and, in puppies, possibly on the head and round the eyes. These respond to Izal shampoo. If it is preferred not to bathe the dog, a dusting with gammexane powder blown directly in to the clump of mites will kill them at once, though the bodies may not drop off for a day or two.

TICKS

Dogs running in the country, and all who are bedded on straw, are likely to pick up a cattle tick at some time or other. If so do not pull it off; if you do, the head will remain and may cause a nasty sore. Put a drop of methylated spirit round the head of the tick and after a few seconds try to ease it out gently (with forceps or tweezers for preference). If you cannot get it off in this way leave it alone; it will do less harm if it drops off naturally in its own time than if you pull it off. If a tick fastens on to a dog's eyelid or lip, or if the dog is very upset about it wherever it is, you had better ask for veterinary help. In some countries ticks can carry diseases that may be serious to dogs, such as the tick causing paralysis, but fortunately these diseases are not prevalent in this country.

JAUNDICE

Ordinary jaundice is usually the result of some other disease and can often arise as the result of a chill. There is, however, another type, known as *Leptospiral Jaundice*, and this is the type contracted from the urine of infected rats and mice. It is often thought that this disease is likely to be found only in rat-infested kennels. This is not so. The presence of one infected rat, even if he only passes by *en route* for somewhere else, or the introduction into the kennel of a bale of straw over which an infected rat has urinated, are all that is necessary to introduce the virus to the dog. This is a most invidious disease as the early symptoms are often not noticed at all; the first sign the owner has is that the dog is somewhat lethargic. Temperature is usually normal or subnormal, and thirst accompanies this condition. In the later stages the dog will vomit, but more often than not by the time the symptoms are such that a veterinary surgeon is called, even by the most careful and conscientious of owners, the spirochaetes (the microscopic organs which invade the blood-stream in this disease) have already set themselves up in the kidneys, where the nephritis they cause has already done so much damage that a cure is well-nigh impossible.

However, it is now possible to have one's dog immunized against this disease. It is not an expensive treatment, and is therefore recommended if there is any chance of dogs being in a rat-contact area.

Yet another type of jaundice exists—*Leptospira Canicola*, or canicola jaundice. This is thought to be the cause of a lot of the kidney trouble in older dogs. The infection takes place in young dogs, often with no obvious symptoms, and the consequent damage to the kidney tissue frequently does not show until the dog arrives at middle age and develops 'chronic nephritis'. Immunization against this type of jaundice is also possible and gives a good measure of protection.

Hard Pad and Kindred Diseases

It is not considered that this is the right place for a discussion of the symptoms or treatment of these diseases, which are essentially a matter for the professional to deal with. Symptoms are so varied in the same disease that it is almost useless to list them, and beyond saying that a cough should make one suspicious of something, and a cough plus rise of temperature, certain, there can be no better advice than to tell you to call your veterinary surgeon if the dog appears off colour, refuses food, has a slight rise of temperature or coughs. Best of all, be certain to have your dog immunized against hard pad with one of the several 'egg-adapted' vaccines on the market, whichever one is favoured by your own veterinary surgeon.

MANGE

There are two kinds of mange, sarcoptic and follicular. The former is caused by a mite, a microscopic parasite, the sarcopt, which burrows under the skin. There the female lays her eggs which, taking only about a week to hatch, rapidly produce the condition of sarcoptic mange. Follicular mange is also caused by a mite, demodex folliculorim. Streptococci and other bacteria often invade the skin damaged by the demodex and cause the boils and pus often associated with this disease. This type of mange may cause serious illness and even death from toxemia and exhaustion.

If mange is suspected, it is essential to obtain laboratory confirmation, by the microscopal examination of deep skin scrapings, and the treatment, which in all cases must be very thorough indeed, must be left to your veterinary surgeon.

STINGS

Dogs, being ready at almost all times to chase and play, are frequently stung by the bees and wasps which they consider fair game. Remember that a bee leaves his sting in the skin; wasps rarely do so. You will probably not have seen the actual stinging, so if your dog comes to you with a swollen face or other part of his body (during the 'wasp season') and a sting is suspected, it is wise, first of all, to look for the centre of the swelling and if the sting can be seen there to remove this with a pair of tweezers. Half an onion or a blue bag can then be applied to the seat of the sting. If the sting is in the mouth, however, do not apply a blue bag there. A piece of onion can be rubbed gently on the inside of the mouth, or, alternatively, the pain can be relieved by the application of a little bicarbonate of soda. It is not necessary to make a solution of this; a little rubbed gently on to the spot with the fingers works wonders. Watch the dog carefully until you are satisfied that the swelling is not increasing, for it is possible, though not common, for a dog to be suffocated by the pressure of the swelling from a sting in the throat. If in doubt, take the dog to a veterinary surgeon as an injection can be given which will reduce the swelling.

Wounds

Dogs are very liable to get minor cuts, scratches or bites from another dog. A laceration which bleeds freely is usually 'safe' in that it will heal quickly and cleanly. A wound that is more in the nature of a puncture, that is deep-seated and that bleeds little or not at all, is the kind that requires greater care, for this type of wound will often heal from the surface, instead of from the bottom outwards, and therefore will have imprisoned in it bacteria and pus which cause trouble later. Treatment of any type of wound is first to stop the bleeding which may, in the case of a deep cut, necessitate the application of a tourniquet. Next comes the extraction of any foreign body there may be in the wound. Then the wound must be cleansed with a weak solution of T.C.P., Dettol or similar antiseptic. Lysol and carbolic must *never* be used. It is almost certain that it will be necessary to cut the hair from the area round the wound, and this is particularly necessary with a long-coated dog such as ours. The wound should be kept dressed with penicillin ointment and a punctured wound kept open so that it may heal cleanly from the bottom up. When the time is reached where it is desired to 'dry up' an open wound, to accelerate the healing it is advisable to apply sulphathyzamide powder. Both this and penicillin ointment can be obtained only from your veterinary surgeon or on his prescription, but they are wonderful things to have in your medicine chest at all times.

Urticaria (Nettle Rash)

This is frequently met with and may at first be confused with a sting, for the dog will appear swollen. The raised patches on the skin are, however, flat, and vary in size from a pea to a five-shilling piece. There are no scabs and no irritation, and with our breed (unless the condition is seen on the face and legs) it is difficult to notice, but on these short-haired areas the hairs stand straight out. Urticaria is usually caused by an internal toxic condition and the best remedy is a sharp purgative; in the case of an adult Sheltie the administration of a good half-teaspoonful of Epsom salts usually has a satisfactory effect. One dose is generally sufficient. The dog should be kept on a laxative diet for a few days. This condition is rarely as serious as it looks, but if it recurs in the kennel, or in the same dog, a cause must be sought. Very often it is some particular food to which the dog is sensitive—bacon rinds and bloaters (neither the ideal dog food) have been known to cause it. One repeated case was traced to a gravy salt used in boiling up bones to make a tasty soup for the dog's biscuit meal.

CHOKING

Choking may occur if a dog tries to swallow too large an object; for instance, any dog is apt to bolt whatever he has in his mouth if approached by a strange dog while he is eating. Many dogs, unless properly trained, will try to swallow any 'find' they may have made rather than give it up to their owner when asked to do so.

If the obstruction is in the upper part of the throat the dog may suffocate in a very few minutes, so *action* must be the word! Open his mouth—even if he tries to bite it's worth the risk—try to catch hold of the object and if you cannot get a hold and pull it up try to push it down gently. If the object goes to the lower part of the gullet the immediate risk of death is over. The foreign body might have to be removed surgically afterwards, but that is a matter for your veterinary surgeon to decide, and at least your dog is alive to swallow something else.

SHOCK

Any injury is followed by a certain amount of shock. The dog will appear dazed and stupid; he may be shaky and weak or even become unconscious. His breathing will be shallow and rapid, his mucous membranes, as seen in his gums and inside his eye-lids, pale, and he will feel cold to the touch. As a rule animals will not take hot drinks, but offer all drinks warm. Give glucose or sugar if possible, wrap the patient up in a coat or blanket and try to get him warm. Do not, of course, try to force any liquids down the throat of an unconscious dog.

BURNS AND SCALDS

Shock always follows these two accidents and it is frequently severe. Unless the damage is very slight, never attempt home treatment. Cover the injured area by bandaging very lightly, or, if necessary, wrap the dog entirely in a blanket, leaving only the tip of his nose exposed, and get him to a veterinary surgeon as soon as you possibly can. Your main object must be to exclude air from all the burnt areas and to treat the dog for severe shock. Do not put oil or grease on a burn.

Scalds are more difficult to treat than burns, because with a Sheltie the dog's thick coat holds the hot liquid on to the skin; therefore the best method is to douche the area with lukewarm water as a first measure. Never use *cold* water—this might increase the shock.

Burns and scalds which cover only a very small area can be treated by covering with a paste made of soda bicarbonate (baking soda) and water. Spread this thickly over the injured area and don't let the dog lick it off.

COLLAPSE

If an old dog should collapse suddenly, perhaps on a very hot day, move him to the coolest place you can find, make sure he has plenty of fresh air, open his mouth and pull his tongue out and to one side so that his 'air passage' is clear. Rest him on his right side, with his head a little lower than his body.

If collapse occurs in cold weather it is essential that the dog should be wrapped up warmly (although he must still be allowed plenty of fresh air) while you await the arrival of your veterinary surgeon.

FOUL BREATH

So long as there is no possibility of its being attributed to a specific disease such as hard pad or jaundice, bad breath is almost always due to teeth, or to tartar on the teeth. Teeth can be cleaned with hydrogen peroxide solution, or with an ordinary toothpaste, but it is best to let your veterinary surgeon look at them as some may need to be removed.

HOME NURSING OF DOGS

(Kindly contributed by a Veterinary Surgeon)

All animals, and especially dogs, are creatures of habit, and many of them are seriously disturbed when their routine is upset. Because of this, almost all animal patients do best when nursed at home in their own familiar surroundings. Of course this is not always possible; infectious cases must be separated from other dogs, and some, particularly surgical cases, may have to become in-patients in a veterinary hospital for a time.

Whether your veterinary surgeon will agree that your Sheltie can be satisfactorily nursed at home depends largely on you. Shelties are very sensitive dogs, very much one-man dogs, and I think that most of you would prefer to keep your Sheltie at home, so let us look into the question of canine home nursing.

The essential needs of any sick animal are quietness, warmth, suitable bed, suitable food and drink, correct veterinary treatment and last, but by no means least, the love, care and encouragement of a sensible owner. All of us who have ever loved and been loved by a Sheltie know the queer telepathy (I can call it nothing else) that exists between a much-loved Sheltie and the owner, so be careful not to think defeatism, be as cheerful and hopeful with your sick Sheltie as you would with a sick child.

Speaking from a veterinary surgeon's point of view, I find that Shelties, on the whole, are very good patients. They make a great fight for life, however injured or ill, and are sensible patients, allowing themselves to be helped. But if separated for too long from the person to whom they have become attached they tend to lose interest in life.

Nurse a sick dog in a room in the house or in a kennel close to the house, or an outbuilding nearby—somewhere you can easily get at him day or night, and where you can hear any cries or barks from the patient. The kennel needs to be weather-proof and the bed warm, and protected from draughts, whether in a kennel or in the house.

In the house a good warm corner can be contrived for the sick bed by hanging an old blanket or other covering over a clothes-horse and using this screen to surround the bed on the sides exposed to doors and windows. Do not put the screen too close to the dog's bed, so that he feels shut in, but get down on the floor yourself and feel where the draughts are coming from, and then arrange your screen to stop them. I stress this because I find that many owners who pooh-pooh the idea of draughts in their houses are horrified when they are persuaded to try resting on floor-level themselves.

If possible, use the dog's own bed, but this must depend on the patient—e.g. if partly paralysed, or with a fractured pelvis, the dog cannot get on to a raised bed; for such a patient several layers of sacks or blankets, or a sack filled with wood-wool not packed too tightly, make a good bed. Many layers of newspaper under the sacks help to preserve the warmth. Many patients whose vitality is low tend to get chilled at night and in the early hours of the morning, so it is well worth while to get up once or twice in the night to renew hot-water bottles, but try to keep an even temperature as far as possible. While I am on the subject, may I remind you that hot-water bottles must be covered, and covered so that no kicking or scratching can uncover them! Neglect of this precaution can result in nasty burns.

Quietness really means that the dog patient must not be disturbed more than is absolutely necessary. Frequent visits and unnecessary fussing and petting may well do more harm than good. Attend to the patient at regular intervals, as determined by the needs to give medicine, food, etc., but in between *let him rest*.

If your dog is dangerously ill, try to arrange some way of peeping in at him frequently without having to go in to him and arouse him, perhaps from a healing sleep. If the dog is partly paralysed, or so weak that he is unable to move himself, remember to turn him over gently at least twice a day, so that he does not lie for hours in the same position.

Unless decreed otherwise by the veterinary surgeon in charge of the case, all sick animals should have plenty of fresh drinking water. A small quantity, renewed several times a day, will be fresher and more attractive to the patient than a large bowlful which is allowed to go stale before it is recharged.

Owners are often worried if the sick dog does not take food for a day or two. Most animals can well bear a few days self-imposed starvation and are often all the better for it. If your patient does not want food, coax him by all means but do not force him. If he is still on hunger-strike after several days have gone by it may be advisable to try forced feeding, but never be in a big hurry over this.

If an animal is only off-colour for a few days little grooming need be attempted, but in dealing with a longer illness some attention to the toilet each day will make a lot of difference to the comfort of the patient. Eyes should be washed out daily with a little warm water, and the eyelids smeared with a little olive oil or liquid paraffin to prevent the hairs on the lids sticking down. The nose, if discharging, should be cleaned several times a day with a swab of cotton wool dipped into warm (not hot) water, and afterwards wiped with a little olive oil too. A similar cotton swab in warm water should be wiped round the face and ears and also round the tail and back feathering each day. If necessary, wash any soiled fur with a wet cloth wrung out with cleansing solution and then dried off, rather than soak the feathering itself.

If you are keeping a record of the patient's temperature always remember that it must be taken before the patient is disturbed or excited in any way. Nervousness, excitement and exertion can quickly cause a rise in temperature and if your Sheltie is of a very excitable temperament you may get a wrong impression if you take his temperature after his morning toilet instead of before.

Giving medicine is important. If he is to have a dose, make sure that he gets it; be firm with him and let him see that you intend him to have it. Tablets can often be given in food or in a tit-bit of meat or chocolate (one of my patients, a Peke, always takes his tablets in marmalade) if it is easier. Crush the tablets and give the dog the resulting powder on the back of his tongue. Firm pressure with your fingers just behind the big canine teeth will usually make any dog open his mouth. Press upwards, keeping the dog's lips between his teeth and your fingers, and when his mouth is well opened throw in the dose.

If the patient has been put on to a medicine which you are directed to 'give every four hours', or some similar direction, do please give the dose at the proper intervals. Many in use at the present time depend for their value on keeping the level of the drug in the patient's blood constant all the time, and the timing of doses is worked out to achieve this result. If this blood level is allowed to fall too soon, or become irregular, it may undo all the good that has been, or can be, done by the medicine.

If these notes give any helpful ideas or useful advice towards easing the lot of the animal patient and helping the 'nurse in charge' they will have achieved their object.

APPENDIX I

Champions 14 June 1947 to 31 December 1978

Colour Key: T—Tricolour. S—Sable. BM—Blue merle. B & T—Black and tan. B & W—Black and white.

Name	Sex	Line	Family	Colour	Sire	Dam	Breeder	Owner
1947								
Ellington Enjoyment	B	CHE	3	S	Ellington Encore	Ellington Edwina	R. A. Hogger	Mrs C. Fishpool
Exford, Bonfire of	B	CHE	4	T	Beacon of Houghton Hill	Gaiety of Exford	Mrs F. P. B. Sangster	Breeder
Fydell Round-up	D	BB	13	S	Fydell Startler	Fydell Satisfaction	A. Broughton	Breeder
Larchwood, Nuthatch of	D	CHE	9	BM	Hamish of the Wandsdyke	Enchantress of Inchmery	Mrs G. Hunter	Breeder
1948								
Crawleyridge, Skellum of	D	CHE	14	T	Tabor of Crawleyridge	Tabor of Crawleyridge	Lt Col The Hon. B. Russell	Breeder
Ellington Easter Lady	B	CHE	1	S	Ellington Encore	Ellington Enchant	Mrs C. Fishpool	Breeder
Fydell Frosty Moon	B	BB	13	T	Fydell Startler	Fydell Painted Lady	A. Broughton	Breeder
Fydell Round Robin	D	BB	13	S	Ch. Fydell Round-up	Fydell Satisfaction	A. Broughton	Breeder
Riverhill Redcoat	D	BB	9	S	Ch. Nicky of Aberlour	Riverhill Rouge	The Misses P. M. & F. M. Rogers	Breeders
Riverhill Reefer of Exford	D	CHE	24	T	Riverhill Reef	Riverhill Roguish	The Misses P. M. & F. M. Rogers	Mrs F. P. B. Sangster
Tibbett's Lilac	B	CHE	8	BM	Ch. Nuthatch of Larchwood	Tibbett's Wild Swan of Larchwood	Miss I. Single	Breeder
1949								
Ardene Asta	B	CHE	3	S	Ellington Encore	Ellington Edwina	R. A. Hogger	R. Bainbridge

Name	Sex	Line	Family	Colour	Sire	Dam	Breeder	Owner
Delwood Terence	D	CHE	4	S	Ellington Eddy	Delwood Pippin	Mrs H. Wilberforce	Breeder
Dryfesdale Dream Girl	B	CHE	11	S	Ellington Encore	Wendy of Netherkeir	E. Watt	Breeder
Ellington Esquire	D	CHE	1	S	Ellington Encore	Ellington Even	Mrs C. Fishpool	H. Irvine
Exford, Butterfly of	B	BB	2	S	Riverhill Rival	Gini	Mrs J. H. K. Richardson	Mrs F. P. B. Sangster
Helensdale Bhan	D	BB	13	S	Fydell Startler	Helensdale Gentle Lady	J. G. Saunders	Breeder
Riverhill Rugosa	B	BB	24	S	Ch. Fydell Round-up	Iseult of Camelaird	Mmes Allen & Nicholson	The Misses P. M. & F. M. Rogers
Runlee Phantasy	B	CHE	3	T	Runlee Post Patrol	Runlee Process	Miss M. H. Burnett	Mrs A. M. Miller
Runlee Pro Patria	D	CHE	3	S	Runlee Patron	Runlee Proquest	Mrs A. M. Miller	Breeder
1950 Callart, Orpheus of	D	BB	16	S	Hector of Aberlour	Heatherbelle of Callart	Miss O. Gwynne-Jones	Breeder
Dryfesdale Daisy	B	BB	11	S	Briar of Callart	Dryfesdale Netherkeir Jewel	E. Watt	Breeder
Eleth, Wonder Lad of	D	CHE	16	S	Golden Rod of Marl	Golden Fluffy of Eleth	O. T. Jones	Breeder
Exford, Firebrand of	B	CHE	4	T	Jack Tar of Exford	Ch. Bonfire of Exford	Mrs F. P. B. Sangster	Breeder
Exford Piskiegye Taw	D	CHE	9	S	Burn of Exford	Charmer of Pipestyle	Miss K. M. Downes-Shaw	Mrs F. P. B. Sangster
Fair Sheena	B	CHE	13	S	Sandy of Kinslady	Laura of Kinslady	J. Campbell	E. Falconer
Helensdale Ace	D	BB	13	S	Ch. Helensdale Bhan	Helensdale Gentle Lady	J. G. Saunders	Breeder

Name	Sex	Line	Family	Colour	Sire	Dam	Breeder	Owner
Rivock, Rhapsody of	B	CHE	1	S	Ellington Encore	Ellington Enticing	M. Slater	S. Meek
1951								
Ellington Wattlingate Waitress	B	BB	1	S	Sheltiedell Robert Bruce	Wanda of Wallerscote	D. Kitchen	Mrs C. Fishpool
Exford, Crag of	D	CHE	8	T	Ch. Exford Piskiegye Taw	Houghton Hill Crystal	Mrs F. P. B. Sangster	Breeder
Exford, Fascinator of	B	CHE	9	T	Jack Tar of Exford	Charmer of Pipestyle	Miss K. M. Downes-Shaw	Mrs F. P. B. Sangster
Hallinwood Flash	D	BB	8	S	Ch. Helensdale Ace	Hallinwood Elegance	Mrs M. Bellas-Simpson	Breeder
Knockmahar, Morula of	D	BB	3	S	Fydell Rob Roy	Sprite of Orangefield	A. Barton	H. W. Irvine
Melvaig, Viking of	D	CHE	9	S	Delwood Bobbie	Jonquil of Melvaig	Mrs J. G. Charlton	Breeder
Riverhill Regale	B	BB	5	S	Ch. Riverhill Redcoat	Riverhill Reinette	Misses P. M. & F. M. Rogers	Breeders
Riverhill Rikki	D	BB	24	S	Ch. Riverhill Redcoat	Ch. Riverhill Rugosa	Misses P. M. & F. M. Rogers	Breeders
Riverhill Royal Flush	B	BB	5	S	Ch. Helensdale Ace	Ch. Riverhill Regale	Misses P. M. & F. M. Rogers	Misses B. & J. Herbert
Wyndora, Wravella of	B	CHE	3	S	Prince of Merrion	Placid Pauline	D. M. David	J. B. Taylor
1952								
Barhatch, Tetrarch of	D	CHE	4	BM	Ch. Nuthatch of Larchwood	Cara of the Wansdyke	Miss Y. Bootle-Wilbraham	Mr & Mrs L. Codd
Callart, Russet Coat of	D	BB	16	S	Ch. Riverhill Redcoat	Wild Rose of Callart	Miss O. Gwynne-Jones	Breeder

Name	Sex	Line	Family	Colour	Sire	Dam	Breeder	Owner
Ellington Easter Parade	D	CHE	3	S	Ellington Epicure	Ch. Ellington Enjoyment	Mrs C. Fishpool	Breeder
Helensdale Wendy	B	BB	13	S	Ch. Helensdale Ace	Helensdale Fantasia	J. G. Saunders	Breeder
Lydwell, Lovelight of	B	BB	3	S	Fielder of Foula	Belle of Oastwood	Mrs A. Greig	Breeder
Riverhill Rescuer	D	BB	5	S	Ch. Orpheus of Callart	Riverhill Ragna	Misses P. M. & F. M. Rogers	Breeders
Tintobank, Alasdair of	D	BB	1	S	Ch. Helensdale Ace	Helensdale Mhairi Dhu	W. E. Guthrie	Breeder
Wansdyke, Dileas of the	B	BB	4	S	Ch. Riverhill Redcoat	Hazel of the Wansdyke	Miss Y. Bootle-Wilbraham	Breeder
1953 Exford, Lothario of	D	CHE	9	T	Ch. Exford Piskiegye Taw	Ch. Fascinator of Exford	Mrs F. P. B. Sangster	Breeder
Garniehill Tulyar	D	BB	11	S	Ch. Morula of Knockmahar	Netherkeir Katrine	J. Shearer	Breeder
Hartfield Harbinger	B	BB	2	T	Ch. Riverhill Redcoat	Scalloway	Mrs W. K. Thatcher	Breeder
Knockmahar, Cutie of	B	CHE	13	S	Ch. Ellington Esquire	Iris of Knockmahar	H. W. Irvine	Breeder
Merrion, Francis of	D	BB	9	S	Helensdale Herald	Fauna of Merrion	Mr & Mrs E. J. Allsop	Breeders
Riverhill Respectable	B	CHE	24	BM	Lirima Lacquer	Riverhill Remarkable	Misses P. M. & F. M. Rogers	Breeders
Sheldawyn, Shady Ferne of	B	BB	13	S	Ch. Helensdale Ace	Flick of Tynewyn	Miss P. A. Todd	Breeder
Surreyhills, Budlet of	D	BB	9	S	Ch. Riverhill Rescuer	Beaumaris of Scatho	Mrs C. G. Glasse	Breeder

Name	Sex	Line	Family	Colour	Sire	Dam	Breeder	Owner
Whytelaw, Laird of	D	BB	8	S	Ch. Helensdale Ace	Merry Maid of Whytelaw	Miss M. Heatley	Breeder
1954								
Callart, Diadem of	B	BB	16	T	Ch. Alasdair of Tintobank	Heatherbelle of Callart	Miss O. Gwynne-Jones	Breeder
Exford, Melody of	B	CHE	2	T	Ch. Exford Piskiegye Taw	Skylark of Exford	Mrs Maxwell-Hyde	Mrs. F. P. B. Sangster
Franwyns What Ho	D	BB	13	S	Ch. Helensdale Bhan	Helensdale Wishful	Mr & Mrs F. Davies	Breeders
Hallinwood Amber Girl	B	BB	8	S	Ch. Hallinwood Flash	Hallinwood Amber	Mrs P. F. Humphries	Mr & Mrs G. Bellas-Simpson
Hallinwood Sealodge Sparkle	B	BB	6	S	Ch. Hallinwood Flash	Riverhill Rattle	Miss J. Armstrong	Mr & Mrs G. Bellas-Simpson
Riverhill Rare Gold	B	BB	9	S	Ch. Alasdair of Tintobank	Riverhill Red Gold	Misses P. M. & F. M. Rogers	Breeders
Whytelaw, Zara of	B	BB	6	S	Ch. Laird of Whytelaw	Lassie of Lingey	Mrs E. Metcalfe	Miss M. Heatley
1955								
Arolla Ebony of Wallerscote	D	BB	13	T	Helensdale Rory	Helensdale Joyous	E. Walker	Mrs M. W. Hingley
Brigdale Renown	D	BB	8	S	Ensign of Oastwood	Brigdale Rhoda	Miss M. Solley	G. Watt
Callart, Starlight of	D	BB	9	S	Rising Star of Callart	Carolyn of Callart	Miss O. Gwynne-Jones	Breeder
Dilhorne Norseman of Melvaig	D	CHE	8	T	Ch. Viking of Melvaig	Dilhorne Starlight	Mrs C. Charlesworth	A. J. Brisby
Exford, Blue Charm of	B	CHE	8	BM	Ch. Lothario of Exford	Houghton Hill Bellringer	Mrs F. P. B. Sangster	Breeder
Exford, Debonair of	D	CHE	4	T	Ch. Lothario of Exford	Blue Flame of Exford	Mrs F. P. B. Sangster	Breeder

Name	Sex	Line	Family	Colour	Sire	Dam	Breeder	Owner
Franwyns Starlight	D	BB	1	S	Ch. Helensdale Bhan	Helensdale Hilda	J. G. Saunders	Mr & Mrs F. Davies
Helensdale Waxwing	B	BB	13	S	Ch. Helensdale Ace	Helensdale Fantasia	J. G. Saunders	Breeder
Ireland's Eye Trefoil of Arolla	D	BB	13	S	Ch. Alasdair of Tintobank	Anchusa of Arolla	Mrs M. W. Hingley	Miss E. Finch
Melvaig, Honeybunch of	B	BB	9	S	Ch. Alasdair of Tintobank	Alannah of Melvaig	Mrs J. G. Charlton	Breeder
Parklea Playboy	D	BB	9	S	Ch. Fydell Round-up	Bryony of Bothkennar	W. E. Dascombe	M. Kinniburgh
Tintobank, Beathag of	B	BB	1	S	Ch. Alasdair of Tintobank	Fiona of Tintobank	W. E. Guthrie	Breeder
1956 Callart, Straun of	D	BB	16	S	Ch. Alasdair of Tintobank	Vora of Callart	Miss O. Gwynne-Jones	Breeder
Crochmaid Starlight	B	BB	1	S	Ch. Alasdair of Tintobank	Crochmaid Susan	Mmes McArthur-Onslow & Kewley	Breeders
Dilhorne Blackcap	D	CHE	8	T	Ch. Dilhorne Norseman of Melvaig	Dilhorne Blue Brocade	Mrs C. Charlesworth	Breeder
Dryfesdale Gay Girl	B	BB	8	S	Dryfesdale Dalesman	Beauty of Mount Sydney	Miss E. C. McQuade	E. Watt
Hallinwood Golden Fetter	B	BB	6	S	Hallinwood Golden Ray	Riverhill Rattle	Miss J. A. Armstrong	Mrs A. Speding
Hazelhead Gay Wanderer	D	BB	13	S	Ch. Helensdale Ace	Bluebell of Arolla	Miss J. Gordon	C. V. Smale
Heatherisle Rufus	D	BB	2	S	Ch. Russetcoat of Callart	Heatherisle Suzette	Mrs M. Hawkins	Breeder
Helensdale Lena	D	BB	1	S	Ch. Helensdale Ace	Helensdale Lola	J. G. Saunders	Breeder

Name	Sex	Line	Family	Colour	Sire	Dam	Breeder	Owner
Lydwell, Love Sonnet of	B	BB	3	S	Ch. Alasdair of Tintobank	Ch. Lovelight of Lydwell	Mrs A. Greig	Mrs J. Stern
Melvaig, Pied Piper of	D	CHE	8	BM	Ch. Dilhorne Norseman of Melvaig	Pipestyle June Fairy	W. George	Mrs J. G. Charlton
Riverhill Real Gold	B	BB	9	S	Riverhill Robbie	Ch. Riverhill Rare Gold	Misses P. M. & F. M. Rogers	Breeders
Shelert, Midas of	D	BB	5	S	Ch. Brigdale Renown	Ch. Riverhill Royal Flush	Misses B. & J. Herbert	Breeders
Shelert, Symphony of	B	BB	5	S	Ch. Brigdale Renown	Carillon of Shelert	Misses B. & J. Herbert	Breeders
1957								
Exford, Black Moth of	B	CHE	2	T	Ch. Lothario of Exford	Ch. Butterfly of Exford	Mrs F. P. B. Sangster	Breeder
Exford, Honeysuckle of	B	CHE	2	S	Ch. Lothario of Exford	Ch. Butterfly of Exford	Mrs F. P. B. Sangster	Breeder
Glenhill, Ebony Pride of	D	BB	1	T	Hartfield Herald	Una of Tintobank	Mrs Lane	Mr & Mrs McIntosh
Helengowan Striking	D	BB	11	S	Ch. Laird of Whytelaw	Garniehill Gaytime	J. Shearer	Mr & Mrs J. McAdam
Shelert, Sweet Sultan of	D	BB	5	S	Sovereign of Shelert	Fleurette of Shelert	Misses B. & J. Herbert	Breeders
Shiel, Sheer Sauce from	B	BB	1	S	Riverhill Roc	Stiletto from Shiel	Miss M. Osborne	Breeder
1958								
Crochmaid Sunstar	B	BB	1	S	Ch. Helensdale Ace	Crochmaid Susan	Mmes. McArthur-Onslow & Kewley	Breeders
Easton Emperor	D	BB	1	S	Hartfield Herald	Una of Tintobank	Mrs Lane	F. Clegg
Heathlow Luciana	B	BB	1	S	Ch. Francis of Merrion	Heathlow Hippolyta	Mrs H. Lowe	Mr & Mrs A. T. Jeffries

Name	Sex	Line	Family	Colour	Sire	Dam	Breeder	Owner
Hightown Majestic Lad	D	BB	13	S	Glyntirion Wee Laird of Marl	Hazelhead Golden Ray	Mrs J. Halstead	Breeder
Oastwood Lady Gay	B	BB	13	S	Badger of Antoc	Sue of Tullyvin	Miss Holton	A. Bainbridge
Penvose Black Velvet	B	BB	1	T	Hjatland Tomtit	Penvose Sherry	C. V. Smale	Breeder
Riverhill Ready Cash	B	BB	9	S	Riverhill Raq	Ch. Riverhill Rare Gold	Misses P. M. & F. M. Rogers	Breeders
Riverhill Rogue	D	CHE	24	BM	Riverhill Reckless	Riverhill Roselle	Misses P. M. & F. M. Rogers	Breeders
Upperslaughter, Luna Andy of	D	BB	16	S	Luna of Callart	Eriska of Callart	Mrs E. Busby	Breeder
Whytelaw, Tassel of	B	CHE	8	S	Ch.Wattawoodcut	Gay of Whytelaw	Miss M. Heatley	Mrs Morris
1959 Eldapenny Starshine	D	CHE	1	T	Ch. Dilhorne Blackcap	Eldapenny Evening Star	Mrs J. Stuart-White	Breeder
Exford, Golden Thread of	B	BB	2	S	Ch. Ebony Pride of Glenhill	Tawny Gold of Exford	Mrs F. P. B. Sangster	Breeder
Kendoral Ulysses	D	BB	9	S	Ch. Alasdair of Tintobank	Stillmerri Snow Shoes	Mrs D. A. Baxendale	Breeder
Melvaig, Gay Lass of	B	BB	9	S	Helensdale Frolic	Fair Maid of Melvaig	Mrs K. Charlton	Mrs E. V. Harker
Melvaig, Martine of	B	CHE	1	S	Ch. Viking of Melvaig	Candy Floss of Glenawind	Miss M. Crowley	Mrs M. Charlton
Penvose Brandy Snap	D	BB	13	S	Ch. Hazelhead Gay Wanderer	Penvose Goldilocks	C. V. Smale	Breeder
Plovern, Pippet of	B	BB	13	S	Helensdale Frolic	Kinklebridge Foam	Mrs J. Turner	Breeder
Riverhill Rather Rich	B	BB	9	S	Ch. Midas of Shelert	Ch. Riverhill Rare Gold	Misses P. M. & F. M. Rogers	Breeders

Name	Sex	Line	Family	Colour	Sire	Dam	Breeder	Owner
Shelert, Spark of	D	BB	5	S	Ch. Midas of Shelert	Scintilla of Shelert	Misses P. M. & F. M. Rogers	Breeders
1960								
Antoc Handclap	B	BB	6	S	Granary Hartfield Handful	Ch. Hallinwood Golden Fetter	Mrs A. Speding	Breeder
Callart, Miel of	D	BB	16	S	Ch. Straun of Callart	Candy of Callart	Miss O. Gwynne-Jones	Breeder
Cheluth Twinkleberry	D	BB	1	S	Ch. Francis of Merrion	Heathlow Mopsa	Miss R. Matthews	Mrs R. Matthews
Francehill Glamorous	B	BB	9	BM	Roundabout of Melvaig	Francehill Glamorous of Exford	Miss M. Bagot	Breeder
Graygill Nectar	D	BB	1	T	Nightstar of Callart	Graygill Jasmine	H. D. Graham	S. J. Meek
Helensdale Vanessa	B	BB	13	S	Helensdale Lorne	Helensdale Wanda	J. G. Saunders	Mrs R. Morewood
Riverhill Rarity of Glenmist	B	BB	9	T	Carousel of Melvaig	Ch. Riverhill Rare Gold	Misses P. M. & F. M. Rogers	F. Mitchell
Riverhill Riddle	D	CHE	24	S	Heatherisle Hilarity	Riverhill Rock Rose	Misses P. M. & F. M. Rogers	Breeders
Scalloway, Rita of	B	BB	6	S	Ch. Shantung of Shelert	Merry Minx of Scalloway	Mrs Y. Bayne	Breeder
Shelert, Sigurd of	D	BB	5	S	Ch. Sweet Sultan of Shelert	Sigrid of Shelert	Misses B. & J. Herbert	Breeders
Shelert, Slipper Satin of	B	BB	24	S	Ch. Spark of Shelert	Shot Silk of Shelert	Misses B. & J. Herbert	Breeders
1962								
Dilhorne Blue Puffin	B	BB	8	BM	Ch. Graygill Nectar	Treales Blue Pigeon	Mrs C. Charlesworth	Breeder
Dilhorne Festivity	B	BB	8	T	Carousel of Melvaig	Dilhorne Damask	Mrs C. Charlesworth	Breeder

Name	Sex	Line	Family	Colour	Sire	Dam	Breeder	Owner
Duncryne Sealgair	D	BB	13	S	Hjatland Dee Don of Firholme	Firholme Gentle Lady	Mr J. Spence	Miss N. S. McLackian
Exford, Philander of	D	CHE	2	T	Ch. Lothario of Exford	Founder of Exford C.D. ex	Mr Dickinson	Mrs F. P. B. Sangster
Exford, Startler of	D	CHE	8	BM	Surprise Packet of Exford	Miss Muffet of Exford	Mrs F. P. B. Sangster	Breeder
Francehill Dry Ginger	B	BB	9	S	Ch. Kendoral Ulysses	Francehill Canada Dry	Miss M. Bagot	Breeder
Francehill Glamour Girl	B	CHE	9	BM	Marble of Exford	Ch. Francehill Glamorous	Miss M. Bagot	Breeder
Glenmist, Gypsy Star of	B	CHE	9	T	Ch. Popgun of Exford	Ch. Riverhill Rarity of Glenmist	F. Mitchell	Breeder
Kendoral Gay Gordon	D	BB	1	S	Kendoral Ensign of Tooneytown	Francehill Carioca	Miss M. Bagot	Mrs D. A. Baxendale
Kinreen Kirk	D	BB	9	S	Ch. Sweet Sultan of Shelert	Kinreen Kirsten	Mrs M. Wilson	J. P. Curtis
Tooneytown, Christie of	B	BB	24	S	Ch. Heatherdale Rufus	Clarinda of Lochland	Mrs M. Guest	Breeder
Una Jane	B	BB	4	S	Luna of Callart	Renamore	S. H. Spicer	Breeder
Upperslaughter, Duffus of	D	BB	16	T	Speeding Shadow of Callart	Luna Rose of Upperslaughter	Miss E. B. Bushby	Breeder
Whytelaw, Skye of	D	BB	8	S	Nutshell of Whytelaw	Gay of Whytelaw	Miss M. Heatley	Breeder
1963								
Antoc Sealodge Spotlight	D	BB	6	S	Riverhill Rolling Home	Sealodge Single	Miss J. Armstrong	Mrs A. Speding
Callart, Honeyboy of	D	BB	9	S	Ch. Miel of Callart	Tanera of Callart	Miss O. Gwynne-Jones	Breeder

Name	Sex	Line	Family	Colour	Sire	Dam	Breeder	Owner
Exford, Joy of	B	CHE	9	BM	Ch. Lothario of Exford	Joy of Exford	Mrs F. P. B. Sangster	Breeder
Hildane Twilight of Callart	D	CHE	16	BM	Ch. Dilhorne Blackcap	Sylphide of Callart	Miss O. Gwynne-Jones	Mrs H. Goodwin
Janetstown Jacqualine	B	BB	13	S	Helensdale Braw Lad	Janetstown Lousea Seton	Miss J. Goodrich	Mrs J. Durose
Kinreen Blue Kestrel	D	CHE	9	BM	Ch. Riverhill Rogue	Riverhill Rare Bird	Misses P. M. & F. M. Rogers	Mrs Horton
Penvose Cherry Brandy	D	BB	3	S	Ch. Penvose Brandy Snap	Penvose Daisy Belle	C. V. Smale	Breeder
Riverhill Rather Nice	B	BB	9	S	Ch. Riverhill Ratafia	Ch. Riverhill Rather Rich	Misses P. M. & F. M. Rogers	Breeders
Riverhill Runaway Match	B	BB	9	S	Ch. Shantung of Shelert	Riverhill Rare Romance	Misses P. M. & F. M. Rogers	Breeders
Scylla, Black Swan of	B	CHE	16	T	Ch. Dilhorne Blackcap	Scylla Swan Princess of Callart	Mrs M. Marriage	Breeder
Sheldawyn, Anchor of	D	BB	13	S	Brinkburn Amaranth	Moonbeam of Sheldawyn	Miss P. A. Todd	Breeder
Shelert, Sea Urchin of	D	BB	5	S	Sylvanius of Shelert	Sea Breeze of Shelert	Misses B. & J. Herbert	Breeders
Shiel, Swagman from	D	BB	5	S	Riverhill Ranger	Riverhill Rugosa	Miss M. Osborne	Breeder
1964								
Dilhorne Bluecap	B	CHE	8	BM	Ch. Dilhorne Blackcap	Ch. Dilhorne Blue Puffin	Mrs C. Charlesworth	Breeder
Durnovaria, Joyful of	B	BB	13	S	Lonesome of Nutbush	April Love of Greglinde	Mrs E. Day	Mrs J. Pallister
Ellendale Prim of Plovern	B	BB	13	S	Helensdale Frolic	Kinklebridge Foam	Mrs J. Turner	M. Baker
Francehill Light Fantastic	B	BB	1	S	Ch. Hightown Majestic Lad	Francehill Polka	Mr & Mrs R. Searle	J. Wayte

Name	Sex	Line	Family	Colour	Sire	Dam	Breeder	Owner
Riverhill Rather Dark	B	BB	9	S	Riverhill Ranger	Ch. Riverhill Rather Nice	Misses P. M. & F. M. Rogers	Breeders
Rockaround Blue Gamble	D	CHE	4	BM	Surprise Packet of Exford	Francehill Rollicking	Mrs J. Cann	Breeder
Starbonnie	B	BB	8	S	Fanfare of Tooneytown	Greenscrees Highland Girl	R. Walker	R. Howetson
Sumburgh Sirius	D	BB	13	S	Helensdale Frolic	Ch. Helensdale Vanessa	Mrs R. Morewood	Breeder
Tyneford Tarsus	D	BB	13	S	Helensdale Frolic	Echo of Northisle	Mrs L. Craven	Breeder
Wellswood Amberrae	B	BB	3	S	Wellswood Wizard	What-a-gem of Nutbush	Mrs J. Rae	Mr & Mrs Pering
Wytchfields, Bramble of	B	CHE	9	T	Ch. Dilhorne Blackcap	Buttonbush of Wytchfields	Mrs M. Nicholls	Breeder
1965								
Callart, Star Princess of	B	BB	16	S	Ch. Sumburgh Sirius	Crown Princess of Callart	Miss O. Gwynne-Jones	Mrs P. Barker
Exford, Blue Bird of	B	CHE	9	BM	Ch. Dilhorne Blackcap	Ch. Joyful of Exford	Mr & Mrs F. P. B. Sangster	Breeders
Francehill Silversmith	D	CHE	9	BM	Ch. Dilhorne Blackcap	Ch. Francehill Glamorous	Mr & Mrs R. Searle	Breeders
Greenscrees Osmart Statesman	D	CHE	1	S	Ch. Greenscrees Swordsman	Osmart Dandy Lass	Mr & Mrs N. Osborne	Messrs W. B. & N. Henry
Riverhill Raider	D	BB	9	S	Riverhill Ranger	Ch. Riverhill Rather Nice	Misses P. M. & F. M. Rogers	Breeders
Riverhill Rapparee	D	BB	9	S	Ch. Swagman from Shiel	Riverhill Rich Fare	Misses P. M. & F. M. Rogers	Breeders
Shelert, Samantha of	B	BB	5	T	Ch. Antoc Sea-lodge Spotlight	Sequin of Shelert	Misses B. & J. Herbert	Breeders
Tooneytown, Happy Song of	B	BB	24	S	Fanfare of	Chortle of	Mrs J. Steward	Mrs M. Guest

Name	Sex	Line	Family	Colour	Sire	Dam	Breeder	Owner
1966								
Blairside Dream Girl	B	BB	16	S	Penvose Russet Gold	Honeychile of Callart	J. Muir	Breeder
Bystars Wee Laddie	D	CHE	14	T	Ch. Philander of Exford	Plovern Piccaninny	Mr & Mrs R. Parker	Breeders
Dilhorne Blue Midnight	D	BB	8	BM	Strikin' Midnight at Shelert	Dilhorne Blue Dame	Mr G. Charlesworth	Mrs C. Charlesworth
Durnovaria Double-O-Seven	D	BB	13	S	Ch. Riverhill Ratafia	Durnovaria Delightful	Mrs J. Pallister	Breeder
Ellington Endless Folly	B	CHE	24	S	Ellington Elliston	Skippol Queen	Mrs J. Cartmell	Mrs C. Fishpool
Francehill Painted Lady	B	CHE	9	BM	Ch. Dilhorne Blackcap	Ch. Francehill Glamorous	Mr & Mrs R. Searle	Mrs A. Potter
Loughrigg Dragonfly	D	BB	24	T	Ch. Antoc Sealodge Spotlight	Faraway of Tooneytown	Mrs A. Britten	Breeder
Lysebourne, Loughrigg Day Festivity of	B	BB	24	T	Ch. Antoc Sealodge Spotlight	Faraway of Tooneytown	Mrs A. Britten	Mrs V. Rolls
Monkswood, Deloraine Dilys of	B	BB	6	S	Riverhill Rolling Home	Shencolne Darling Dorrity	Mrs F. Chapman	Miss M. Davis
Shelert, Skirl of	D	BB	5	S	Skol of Shelert	Sweet Harmony of Shelert	Misses B. & J. Herbert	Breeders
Shelert, Special Edition of	D	BB	24	S	Strikin' Midnight at Shelert	Summer Lightning at Shelert	Misses B. & J. Herbert	Breeders
Shelert, Strict Tempo of	D	BB	5	S	Spartan of Shelert	Sweet Harmony	Misses B. & J. Herbert	Breeders
1967								
Durnovaria Double Agent	D	BB	13	S	Ch. Riverhill Rapparee	Durnovaria Delightful	Mrs J. Pallister	Breeder

Name	Sex	Line	Family	Colour	Sire	Dam	Breeder	Owner
Greenscrees Glamour Girl	B	CHE	8	S	Ch. Greenscrees Swordsman	Greenscrees Shelley Girl	B. Lowry	W. B. & N. Henry
Greenscrees Nobleman	D	CHE	8	S	Ch. Greenscrees Swordsman	Greenscrees Shelley Girl	B. Lowry	W. B. & N. Henry
Jefsfire Freelancer	D	BB	1	S	Glenmist Golden Falcon	Ch. Heathlow Luciana	Mr & Mrs A. T. Jeffries	Breeders
Monkswood, Tumblebays Topaz of	B	BB	9	S	Riverhill Rolling Home	Tumblebays Black Diamond	Mrs S. Evans	Miss M. Davis
Rhinog Waltzing Matilda	B	BB	9	S	Ch. Swagman from Shiel	Rhinog Fiona	Miss D. Blount	Breeder
Rodhill Burnt Sugar	D	BB	9	S	Ch. Riverhill Ratafia	Rodhill What-a-Gem of Nutbush	Mrs J. Rae	Breeder
Sharval Burlesque	B	CHE	2	BM	Ch. Rockaround Blue Gamble	Blue Girl of Exford	A. Wight	Breeder
Shelert, Silken Sari of	B	BB	24	S	Siegfried of Shelert	Ch. Slipper Satin of Shelert	Misses B. & J. Herbert	Breeders
Sumburgh Little Hercules	D	BB	13	S	Ch. Sumburgh Sirius	Sumburgh Wild Honey	Mrs R. Morewood	Breeder
1968								
Dilhorne Blue Nobleman	D	BB	8	BM	Strikin' Midnight at Shelert	Dilhorne Blue Dame	Mr. G. Charlesworth	Mrs G. Charlesworth
Dilhorne Jester	D	BB	8	T	Strikin' Midnight at Shelert	Dilhorne Blue Folly	Mrs C. Charlesworth	Breeder
Exford, Black Lace of	B	CHE	9	T	Ch. Philander of Exford	Ch. Blue Bird of Exford	Mrs F. P. B. Sangster	Breeder
Helengowan Herda of Hardwick	B	CHE	8	S	Greenscrees Jacqman	Hardwick Hazel	Mrs M. Gardiner	Mr & Mrs A. McAdam

Name	Sex	Line	Family	Colour	Sire	Dam	Breeder	Owner
Hildlane Minstrel Knight	D	BB	24	T	Strikin' Midnight at Shelert	Hildlane Cloudy Sky	Mrs H. Goodwin	Breeder
Joywil, Winston of	D	BB	5	S	Warwick Lad of Joywil	Jewel of Joywil	Mrs J. Atherton	Breeder
Midnitesun Fourleaf Clover	B	BB	9	S	Ch. Trumpeter of Tooneytown	Kyleburn Mignonette	Mrs R. Wilbraham	Breeder
Pitempton, Brownie of	B	BB	8	S	Fiddler of Pitempton	Falcon of Flockfields	R. Davidson	Breeder
Riverhill Rampion	D	BB	9	S	Stalisfield Samphire	Ch. Riverhill Rather Nice	Misses P. M. & F. M. Rogers	Breeders
Riverhill Rash Promise	B	BB	9	S	Crown Jewel of Callart	Ch. Riverhill Runaway Match	Misses P. M. & F. M. Rogers	Breeders
Riverhill Richman	D	BB	9	S	Stormane Sir Stanley	Ch. Riverhill Rather Rich	Misses P. M. & F. M. Rogers	Breeders
Shelert, Shahreen of	B	BB	24	S	Strikin' Midnight at Shelert	Sundance of Shelert	Misses B. & J. Herbert	Breeders
Shelert, Signature Tune of	D	BB	5	S	Ch. Strict Tempo of Shelert	Syncopation of Shelert	Misses B. & J. Herbert	Breeders
Tumblebays Amethyst	B	BB	9	S	Riverhill Rolling Home	Tumblebays Black Diamond	Mrs G. Evans	Breeder
Whytelaw, Daisy of	B	CHE	1	S	Clyde of Whytelaw	Shetboro' Glenlynden	P. Howlett	Miss M. Heatley
1969								
Danvis Rhapsody	B	BB	9	S	Sumburgh Octavius	Seavall Snowdrop	T. Purvis	Breeder
Dilhorne Blue Mirth	B	BB	8	BM	Ch. Dilhorne Jester	Dilhorne Blue Cap	Mrs C. Charlesworth	Breeder

Name	Sex	Line	Family	Colour	Sire	Dam	Breeder	Owner
Drumcauchlie Amethyst	B	BB	9	BM	Riverhill Ranger	Drumcauchlie Blue Opal	Miss S. Sangster	Breeder
Exford Pipestyle Mystic Star	B	BB	9	T	Stargazer of Wytchfields	Pipestyle Ladykey Rebecca	Mrs E. Walters	Mrs F. P. B. Sangster
Monkswood Moss Trooper	D	BB	6	S	Ch. Riverhill Raider	Ch. Deloraine Dilys of Monkswood	Miss M. Davis & Mrs E. Knight	Miss M. Davis
Parrocks Nohow	B	CHE	5	BM	Francehill Tweedledee	So Real from Shiel	Mrs A. Glaiyser	Breeder
Sharval The Delinquent	D	BB	2	T	Carousel of Melvaig	Sharval Cilla Black	A. Wight	Breeder
Shelert, So Time Flies of	B	BB	24	S	Ch. Strict Tempo of Shelert	Sinderella of Shelert	Misses B. & J. Herbert	Breeders
Shelert, Streak Lightning at	D	BB	5	BM	Strikin' Midnight at Shelert	Summer Lightning of Shelert	Misses B. & J. Herbert	Breeders
Shelert, Such a Spree at	D	BB	5	BM	Strikin' Midnight at Shelert	Such a Lark at Shelert	Misses B. & J. Herbert	Breeders
1970 Bezzibruk Courtelle	B	BB	24	S	Bezzibruk Out-of-Step	Silken Whisper of Shelert	Mrs H. Liptrott	Breeder
Drannoc Susiley Space Girl	B	BB	9	S	Ch. Jefsfire Freelancer	Chevinsdale Shining Star	Mrs Pugh	Miss M. C. Hall
Ellendale Listo Luella	B	CHE	I	S	Ch. Greenscrees Swordsman	Gentle Adventure	Mrs Stokes	Mr M. Baker
Hildlane Winter's Night	D	BB	24	T	Ch. Hildane Minstrel Knight	Hildlane Misty Dawn	Mrs H. Goodwin	Miss D. Tate

Name	Sex	Line	Family	Colour	Sire	Dam	Breeder	Owner
Janetstown Journalist	D	BB	5	S	Janetstown Willum	Janetstown Jelsfire Sophia	Mrs J. Moody	Breeder
Melcette, Gorjess Waltz of	B	BB	1	S	Francehill Lisronagh Rumba	Candy Moss	Mrs. F. Griffin	Mrs. J. Harris
Rhinhog Honky Dory	D	BB	9	S	Ch. Riverhill Raider	Ch. Rhinuog Waltzing Matilda	Miss D. Blount	Breeder
Scylla Vaguely Blue	D	BB	16	BM	Strikin' Midnight at Shelert	Blue Swan of Scylla	Mrs M. Marriage	Breeder
Sumburgh Tesoro Zhivago	D	BB	9	S	Ch. Jelsfire Freelancer	Sumburgh Petunia	Miss Allan	Mrs R. Morewood
1971								
Cheluth Blackberry	B	BB	3	T	Ch. Cheluth Twinkleberry	Cheluth Serenade	Mrs R. Matthews	Breeder
Delamere Lady Miss Cherrie	B	BB	3	S	Jaylea Chestnut Ripple	Delamere Tina	Mr & Mrs Wilde	Breeders
Greenscrees Lynda Girl	B	CHE	9	S	Ch. Greenscrees Swordsman	Sumburgh Dolly	W. B. & N. Henry	Breeders
Heathlow Ermintrude	B	BB	1	S	Heathlow Linus	Heathlow Emelia	Mrs H. Lowe	Breeder
Monkreddan, Mirabell of	B	BB	1	S	Pedlar of Monkreddan	Miss Muffet of Monkreddan	Mrs M. Caldwell	Breeder
Scarabrae Sinjon	D	BB	13	S	Ch. Jelsfire Freelancer	Scarabrae Shani	Mr. P. Taylor	Breeder
Shelert, Such a Beano at	D	BB	5	T	Strikin' Midnight at Shelert	Such a Lark at Shelert	Misses B. & J. Herbert	Breeders
Sunbower, Shauntrae's Jamie of	D	CHE	13	S	Argegno Savoria Victor	Shauntrae's Maria	Mr & Mrs Coleman	Mrs Gillespie

Name	Sex	Line	Family	Colour	Sire	Dam	Breeder	Owner
Tynereoch, Day Dawning of	B	BB	3	S	Ruchie of Tynereoch	Ranna of Tynereoch	Mr R. Anthony	Mrs Haxton
1972								
Bystars Blakeney	D	BB	8	S	Ch. Skirl of Shelert	Bystars Bewitched	Mr & Mrs R. Parker	Breeders
Francehill Fling Low	B	BB	9	S	Francehill Lisronagh Rumba	Francehill Pasadena	Mr & Mrs R. Searle	Mrs Simpson
Francehill Hildlane Blue Cavalier	D	BB	24	BM	Francehill Solomon	Hildane Cloudy Sky	Mrs H. Goodwin	Mr & Mrs R. Searle
Glenmist Gaylord of Jaylea	D	BB	9	S	Glenmist Golden Falcon	Highstar of Glenmist	Mr & Mrs Sandford	Mr & Mrs F. Mitchell
Kyleburn Golden Eagle	D	BB	9	S	Loughrigg Harbour Pilot	Kyleburn Chiff Chaff	Mrs M. Eaves	Breeder
Lysebourne Sea Nymph of Mistmere	B	BB	24	S	Ch. Riverhill Raider	Amanda of Lysebourne	Mrs V. J. Rolls	Mrs P. Byrne
Monkswood Made of Money C.D. Ex	B	BB	9	S	Ch. Riverhill Richman	Monkswood Mischief Maker	Miss M. Davis	Miss A. Reuss
Parrock Possibility	B	BB	9	BM	Ch. Scylla Vaguely Blue	Parrock Rattle	Mrs Green	Mrs A. Glaisyer
Rance, Gypsy of	B	CHE	2	T	Gunner of Exford	Nutmeg of Rance	Miss D. Homfray	Mr Perry
Riverhill Ring the Bell	B	BB	9	S	Riverhill Rolling Home	Riverhill Ring The Moon	Mrs P. Pierce	Misses P. M. & F. M. Rogers
Rodhill Clouded Yellow	B	BB	9	S	Durnovaria Dangerman	Stormane Sweet Rebecca	Mrs J. Rae	Breeder
Sharval Small Dark 'N Handsome	D	BB	2	T	Riverhill Rolling Home	Sharval Cilla Black	Mr A. Wight	Breeder

Name	Sex	Line	Family	Colour	Sire	Dam	Breeder	Owner
Sheldawyn, Moonshadow of	B	BB	13	S	Brinkburn Amaranth	Moonbeam of Sheldawyn	Miss P. A. Todd	Breeder
1973								
Browgate Warpaint	D	BB	9	BM	Ch. Dilhorne Blue Nobleman	Browgate Black Magic	N. Hodgson	Mr & Mrs S. Collinge
Gay Choice	B	BB	5	S	Monkswood Moonrock	Gay Lass of Norton	G. Chatterton	Breeder
Janlynn's Candy Kisses	B	BB	24	BM	Cotsbelle Rover's Refrain	Blue Moss of Wychfields	Miss M. Hope & M. Davis	Mr & Mrs H. Phipps
Lyngold Blue Zinnia	B	BB	9	BM	Ch. Selskars Cloudberry of Greensands	Monkswood Maid in Waiting	Mrs E. Knight	Mrs E. Knight & Miss M. Davis
Lythwood Brandy Snap	D	BB	8	S	Jefsfire Allanvail Gold Spark	Lythwood Bonnie	Mr D. Rigby	Breeder
Mistmere Marching Orders	D	BB	24	S	Ch. Monkswood Moss Trooper	Mistmere Lysebourne Kursaal	Mrs S. E. Byrne	Breeder
Monkreddan, Gold Charm of	B	BB	1	S	Ch. Jefsfire Freelancer	Miss Muffet of Monkreddan	Mrs M. Caldwell	Breeder
Rhinog The Black Watch	D	BB	3	T	Ch. Rhinog Hunky Dory	Rhinog Mhairi	Miss D. A. Blount	Breeder
Selskars Cloudberry of Greensands	D	BB	3	BM	Ch. Loughrigg Dragon Fly	Selskars Myosotis	Mrs J. Hill	Mrs J. Edwards
Shelert, Sail Ho At	D	BB	24	S	Ch. Special Edition of Shelert	Sailor Suit of Shelert	Misses B. & J. Herbert	Breeders
Shelert, Such a Frolic at	B	BB	5	BM	Ch. Such a Spree at Shelert	Scarcely Fancy of Shelert	Misses B. & J. Herbert	Breeders

Name	Sex	Line	Family	Colour	Sire	Dam	Breeder	Owner
Shelert, Such a Gay Time at	B	BB	24	S	Ch. Such a Beano at Shelert	So Time Slips By at Shelert	Misses B. & J. Herbert	Breeders
Stalisfield Moonflower	B	BB	9	S	Stalisfield Sirocco	Monkswood Moonstone	Mrs R. Attlee	Miss C. Cormack
Shelfrect Sunlit Suzanne	B	BB	9	S	Shelfrect Sunspark	Shelfrect Suhali	Mr & Mr P. N. Fletcher	Breeders
1974 Francehill Pin Up	B	BB	8	S	Ch. Monkswood Moss Trooper	Francehill Realgar Rising Star	Mr & Mrs R. Searle	Breeders
Jefsfire Rich Reward	B	BB	1	S	Ch. Jefsfire Freelancer	Lathmere Zoe	Mr & Mrs A. T. Jeffries	Breeders
Loughrigg Kings Minstrel	D	BB	24	T	Loughrigg Concert Master	Loughrigg Joyous Idyll	Mrs A. Britten	Breeder
Monkswood, Gangster's Moll of Greensands	B	BB	6	T	Monkswood Marauder	Greensands Gretchen	Mrs J. Edwards	Miss M. Davis
Pruneparks Jason Junior	D	CHE	6	S	Ch. Greenscrees Swordsman	April of Scalloway	Mr & Mrs K. Barraclough	Breeders
Riverhill Ricotta	D	BB	9	S	Ch. Rodhill Burnt Sugar	Riverhill Rash Chatter	Misses P. M. & F. M. Rogers	Mr A. Cox
Scarabrae Statesman	D	BB	13	S	Ch. Jefsfire Freelancer	Scarabrae Shani	Mr P. Taylor	Breeder
Shelert, She's My Fancy at	B	BB	24	BM	Ch. Such a Spree at Shelert	Scarcely Fancy of Shelert	Misses B. & J. Herbert	Breeders
Sumburgh Tiger Jane	B	BB	9	S	Ch. Sumburgh Tesoro Zhivago	Sumburgh Petaline	Mrs R. Morewood	Breeder
Westaglow Nijinski	D	CHE	8	S	Hornet of Exford	Westaglow Kastonet	Mrs D. Chambers	Breeder

Name	Sex	Line	Family	Colour	Sire	Dam	Breeder	Owner
1975								
Felthorn Beachcomber	D	BB	9	S	Troubleshooter of Shemaur	Felthorn April Dancer	Mr & Mrs R. D. Thornley	Breeders
Francehill Beachboy	D	BB	9	S	Ch. Felthorn Beachcomber	Francehill Eidelweiss	Mr & Mrs R. Searle	Breeders
Midnitesun Justin Time	D	BB	9	S	Midnitesun Good News	Midnitesun Party Piece	Mrs R. M. Wilbraham	Breeder
Riverhill Ringmaster	D	BB	9	T	Ch. Riverhill Richman	Riverhill Ring Money	Misses P. M. & F. M. Rogers	Miss F. M. Rogers
Stevelyns Carousel	D	BB	9	S	Kyleburn Golden Eagle	Kyleburn Carolyn	Mr & Mrs D. Stott	Breeders
1976								
Cregagh Student Prince	D	BB	24	S	Ir. Ch. Hyunda Dancing Years	Cregagh Sea Breeze	Mr & Mrs J. Kirk	Breeder
Fairona Rockafella	D	BB	8	S	Beneagles of Flakfields	Fairona Valetta	Mr J. Shand	Breeder
Francehill Persimon	D	BB	8	S	Ch. Jefsfire Freelancer	Ch. Francehill Pin-up	Mr & Mrs R. Searle	Breeder
Imp of Lynray	D	BB	5	S	Jefsfire Allanvail Gold Spark	Shelfrect Samantha	Mrs J. Hindley	Breeder
Kyleburn Athena	B	BB	9	S	Ch. Loughrigg Kings Minstrel	Kyleburn Psyche	Mrs M. Eaves	Breeder
Parrock Red Dragoon	D	BB	9	S	Ch. Monkwood Moss Trooper	So Real from Shiel	Mrs A. Glaiyser	Miss C. Cormack
Scylla Snow Violet	B	BB	9	BM	Ch. Scylla Vaguely Blue	Parrock Truly Blue	Mrs M. Marriage	Breeder
Skerrywood Sandstorm	B	BB	3	S	Lyngold Maestro of Monkswood	Skerrywood High Noon of Heranmine	Mrs M. Karp	Mr & Mrs R. Murphy

Name	Sex	Line	Family	Colour	Sire	Dam	Breeder	Owner
1977								
Dunbrae Gold N'Bianco	B	BB	9	S	Lythwood Sloopy of Dunbrae	Sumburgh Fiona	Mrs Shovelton	Mr & Mrs R. Allen
Drumcauchlie Bumbleboy	D	CHE	9	T	Drumcauchlie Humorist	Drumcauchlie Bumble Bee	Miss S. Sangster	Breeder
Ellendale, Marksman of	D	BB	13	S	Ch. Scarabrae Statesman	Plovern Pearl	Mrs L. Coverdale	Mr M. Baker
Exford, Roaming of	B	CHE	1	BM	Crossbow of Exford	Gayshelty Gloaming	Mrs Shanks	Mrs F. P. B. Sangster
Francehill, Macintosh of	D	BB	9	S	Ch. Rhinog the Black Watch	Francehill Solo	Miss Moulds	Mr & Mrs R. Searle
Kyleburn Star Sound	B	BB	13	S	Ch. Kyleburn Golden Eagle	Kyleburn Breakfast Special	Mrs M. Eaves	Miss P. Ure & Mrs M. Eaves
Lirren Evening Shadow at Ramtin	D	BB	9	S	Ramtin Gypsy Moth	Perrietown Black Magic	Mrs L. I. French	Mrs J. Martin
Mistmere Marking Time at Stornaway	D	BB a	24	S	Riverhill Roux	Mistmere Lysebourne Kursaal	Mrs S. Byrne	Mrs B Gibbens
Monkswood Girl Friday of Greensands	B	BB	6	T	Ch. Riverhill Richman	Ch. Greensand Gangster's Moll of Monkswood	Miss M. Davis	Breeder
Rhinog the Gay Lancer	D	BB	9	S	Ch. Sharval the Delinquent	Ch. Rhinog Waltzing Matilda	Miss D. Blount	Breeder
Sharval, Sandpiper of	D	BB	3	S	Ch. Sharval the Delinquent	Charnwood Gay Girl	Mr & Mrs Young	Mr A. Wight
Shelert's Such a Gambol	D	BB	5	S	Ch. Such a Spree at Shelert	Shining Crystal of Shelert	Misses B. & J. Herbert	Breeders

Name	Sex	Line	Family	Colour	Sire	Dam	Breeder	Owner
Shetlo Sheraleigh	B	BB	5	S	Moonraker from Mistmere	Exbury Larkspur	Mrs D. H. Moore	Breeder
Snabswood Slainthe	D	CHE	8	S	Ch. Greenscrees Nobleman	Snabswood Sally Anne	Mr R. G. Fitzsimons	Breeder
Stormane Shining Light	B	BB	9	S	Ch. Rhinog the Gay Lancer	Stormane Sunshine	Mr & Mrs W. H. Tingley	Breeders
Waindale Minette	B	BB	6	S	Scarabrae Sun God	Charnwood Gay Girl	Mrs C. Wainwright	Breeder
1978								
Bridgedale Playboy	D	BB	13	S	Ch. Riverhill Richman	Bridgedale Band of Gold	Mr J. B. Bispham	Breeder
Cowellkot Crown Prince of	D	BB	16	S	Stormane Stormy	Syston Princess Sevena	Mrs B. H. Taylor	Mr & Mrs W. H. Tingley
Heathlow, Blue Opal of	B	BB	1	BM	Heathlow Cedar	Heathlow Pearl Beige	Mrs B. Hodgetts	Mrs H. Lowe
Kyleburn Wild Thyme	B	BB	9	S	Stevelyns Carousel	Peggy of Kyleburn	Mrs M. Eaves	Breeder
Myriehewe Spanish Romance	B	BB	9	S	Ferdinando of Myriehewe	Rodhill Elgin Moor	Miss G. Beaden	Breeder
Nitelife Rogue Star	D	BB	9	T	Riverhill Ringsider	Exford Solar Star	Mrs G. Hussey	Breeder
Salroyd's Buzzer	D	CHE	8	T	Drumcauchlie Bumble Boy	Salroyd's Lavender Blue	Mr & Mrs H. de Vine	Mrs C. Charlesworth
Shelverne Spun Gold	B	BB	1	S	Shelverne Sunbeam	Hillyacres Gold Locket	Mrs M. McConnell	Breeder

APPENDIX 2

DIET SHEETS

At 8 *Weeks of age*

7. 0 a.m.   Cereals or wholemeal bread with milk (about ½ teacup when mixed) plus ½ teaspoonful cod liver oil and ½ teaspoonful calcium phosphate.

11. 0 a.m.   2–3 oz. raw chopped meat.
2. 0 p.m.   Drink of milk with rusk or Lactol biscuit to chew.
5. 0 p.m.   As 11 a.m.
9.30 p.m.   Bowl of puppy meal (wholemeal) soaked with stock, gravy or milk, about 6 oz. total volume.

At 12 *Weeks*

7. 0 a.m.   As above, but increase quantity a little.
11. 0 a.m.   4–6 oz. raw meat.
5. 0 p.m.   As 11 a.m.
9.30 p.m.   As at 8 weeks but increase quantity.

At 6 *Months*

7. 0 a.m.   As before, but increase quantity, but do not increase quantity of cod liver oil or calcium.
5. 0 p.m.   8 oz. raw meat.
9.30 p.m.   As before.

Continue this diet while the puppy will take three meals; at 8 months discontinue calcium but continue cod liver oil, and in winter increase this to 1 teaspoonful.

Adult Diet

Breakfast cereals or wholemeal bread with milk or stock. 1 teaspoonful cod liver oil. Main meal, 8–12 oz. raw meat or other substitute. *See* Chapter 12.

APPENDIX 3

BREEDING TERMS AGREEMENT

AGREEMENT BETWEEN..

AND..

Date...

Mr.., having today taken
over the Shetland Sheepdog bitch...
from Mr.., on part-breeding
terms, agrees to return to Mr...
first and third pick* of the first litter, the bitch having been served,
at no cost to Mr..., by one of
Mr..'s dogs. In the event of an
outside stud-dog having been used both parties to this agreement
to share the cost equally. Mr...
agrees to take every possible care of the bitch during the terms of
this agreement, but he will not be held responsible for her death
unless this is caused by his negligence. When the puppies have been
returned to Mr...the transfer
form for the bitch will be handed over and she will become the
unconditional property of Mr...

Signed...

Signed...

* Here can be inserted any terms one wishes; it need not be
only two puppies, it can be more or fewer or it can be spread over
two litters or more.

FEES FOR REGISTRATION OF DOGS WITH THE KENNEL CLUB

Litter Recording	£3·00
If one or more puppies in litter are registered at the time of recording the litter	No fee
Puppy Registration by Name	£3·00
Registration in Obedience Record	£3·00
Registration Name Unchangeable (additional fee)	£2·00
Re-Registration	£3·00
Transfer (in Basic or Active Register)	£3·00
Export Pedigree	£10·00

APPENDIX 5

LIST OF BREED CLUBS IN GREAT BRITAIN

ENGLISH SHETLAND SHEEPDOG CLUB.—Mrs W. K. Thatcher, Hartfield, Soberton, Southampton.

SCOTTISH SHETLAND SHEEPDOG CLUB.—Mrs I. Elder, South Cottage, Coaltown of Balgonie, Fife

MID-WESTERN SHETLAND SHEEPDOG CLUB.—Mrs M. M. Dobson, Tavistock, Clifton Village, Nr Preston, Lancs.

NORTHERN COUNTIES SHETLAND SHEEPDOG CLUB.—Miss M. Gatheral, Sockburn Hall, Neasham, Darlington, Co. Durham.

SHETLAND SHEEPDOG CLUB OF NORTHERN IRELAND.—Mr J. Kirk, Robin Hill, Bresagh, Boardmills, Lisburn, N.I.

SHETLAND SHEEPDOG CLUB OF WALES.—Mr. P D. Wilbraham, Brynleg, Kereys Commander, Usk, Mon.

COMPARATIVE FIGURES
OF REGISTRATIONS
AT THE KENNEL CLUB

1946	..	453	1961	.. 3790
1947	..	584	1962	.. 4335
1948	..	576	1963	.. 4246
1949	..	706	1964	.. 4678
1950	..	745	1965	.. 5076
1951	..	788	1966	.. 4799
1952	..	753	1967	.. 5149
1953	..	908	1968	.. 5715
1954	..	1148	1969	.. 5872
1955	..	1288	1970	.. 5970
1956	..	1529	1971	.. 5160
1957	..	1967	1972	.. 5705
1958	..	2335	1973	.. 5328
1959	..	2727	1974	.. 5331
1960	..	3072	1975	.. 4282

In April 1976 the Kennel Club changed its system of registrations, thus preventing the continuation of the previous method of listing actual registration totals.

INDEX